D0572315

THE MENSCH CHEF

ALSO BY MITCHELL DAVIS

*Cook Something: Simple Recipes and Sound Advice
to Bring Good Food into Your Fabulous Lifestyle*

Foie Gras: A Passion

the mensch chef

or why delicious Jewish food isn't an oxymoron

MITCHELL DAVIS

Clarkson Potter / Publishers
New York

Copyright © 2002 by Mitchell Davis

All rights reserved. No part of this book may be reproduced or transmitted in any form or by any means, electronic or mechanical, including photocopying, recording, or by any information storage and retrieval system, without permission in writing from the publisher.

Published by Clarkson Potter/Publishers, New York, New York.
Member of the Crown Publishing Group, a division of Random House, Inc.

CLARKSON N. POTTER is a trademark and POTTER and colophon are registered trademarks of Random House, Inc.

Printed in the United States of America

Design by Maggie Hinders

Library of Congress Cataloging-in-Publication Data
Davis, Mitchell
    The mensch chef / Mitchell Davis
        p.   cm.
    Includes index.
    1. Cookery, Jewish.   I. Title.
TX724 .D382   2001
641.5'676—dc21   2001021326

ISBN 0-609-80781-1

10   9   8   7   6   5   4   3   2   1

First Edition

For my sisters, Leslie and Carrie,

whose love and inspiration taste better and are better for me

than all the chicken soup in the world.

And in loving memory

of our mother, Sondra Davis, whose spirit

lingers like the scent of a freshly baked

Russian Sour Cream Cake.

Contents

Introduction

You put in good, you get out good.

—Great-Grandma Eva Knaster, as quoted incessantly by my mother whenever she's in the kitchen

BEFORE I TELL YOU what this book is, let me tell you what it's not. It's not a comprehensive Jewish cookbook with a year's worth of recipes and menus for family and friends. It's not an impressive collection of never-before-eaten Jewish recipes from around the country or around the world. There are no dishes from lost tribes living in Africa and nothing that requires margarine. It's not a reference book about the laws of kashrut filled with helpful hints about how you can make kosher food taste like haute French cuisine (or Italian, or Chinese). It's certainly not light (or worse, "lite"), and it's not dinner-in-sixty-seconds, either.

There are already a lot of great books out there that cover these topics about Jewish cooking and more (for a list of some of my favorites, see pages 279–280). But what's harder to find is a basic book about Jewish cooking—a primer, if you will—that tells you how to make the iconic Jewish foods you dream of: foods of your childhood, presuming your childhood was spent, like mine, in a North American Jewish enclave surrounded by Ashkenazim.

I like to think of this book as an Ashkenazi ABCs, a book of good, solid recipes with plenty of explanations for traditional Jewish dishes, the ones you would recognize on the menus of good delicatessens in New York—which by the way, are getting fewer and farther between. It's a book for my friends, all of whom love food, but whose parents either didn't cook or didn't show them how. It's a book for the first time you have to host a Passover seder and you don't know what to serve. It's a book that will help you satisfy your craving for a steaming-hot bowl of sweet-and-sour cabbage borscht when it's cold outside and you're hungry for more than just food. There is something in here for everyone, whether you are a novice cook who's never made a tuna salad (see page 28) or a seasoned homemaker who trades recipes with your friends in Hadassah.

Somewhere between the Exodus from Egypt and the migration to New York City's Upper West Side, Jewish food got a bad rap. Perceived as old-fashioned, greasy, and overcooked beyond recognition, Jewish food has suffered from an unjustified s(ch)mear campaign begun by Borscht Belt comedians and perpetuated by guilt-stricken *bubbes* with heavy hands in the kitchen. Although I'm not sure Jewish food isn't always fattening—I must have gained twenty pounds testing the recipes for this book—it doesn't have to be heavy and greasy. Ironic though it sounds, using schmaltz is one of the ways to achieve that lightness. Schmaltz provides a finer texture and better taste than most oils, and its flavor can't be beat. By schmaltz, I mean of course rendered chicken fat, but I don't discriminate: duck fat and beef fat are equally delicious. As you flip through the book, you'll see that I recommend using schmaltz in just about everything, even pastry!

The only thing I like better than cooking with schmaltz is cooking with butter. If schmaltz makes food taste lighter than oil does, butter makes food that floats off the plate. My mother, who is an excellent Jewish cook, uses butter for just about everything. And when she's cooking things like mashed potatoes or sautéed mushrooms and onions, she uses enough butter to make a French chef blush. The thought of margarine sickens her almost as much as the thought of a glass of milk with a corned beef sandwich, paradoxical though it sounds. This is a (gag) reflex that she passed on to her children—all of us good cooks, I might add. Of course, cooking with butter poses a problem if you keep kosher. I have suggested alternatives where appropriate, but my preference is almost always for something other than oil.

Before you say, "*Oy vey,* how can I buy a *traif* Jewish cookbook?" let me point out that there is a long history in this country of just such books. According to a colleague of mine at New York University, Barbara Kirshenblatt-Gimblett—a Judaica scholar with a serious interest in food—up until World War II, Jewish cookbooks were filled with unkosher recipes. Pork, shellfish, even meat dishes with cream sauces were included in 19th-century Jewish community cookbooks, partly as an attempt to assimilate the habits of the surrounding gentile society, but also partly because the strict adherence to kashrut doctrine just wasn't that important. For those of you who know about such things, consider this book to come out of the tradition of *haskalah,* not *halakhah,* and you'll have a better idea where I'm coming from. For those of you who don't, Professor Kirshenblatt-Gimblett has a saying: "Jewish is as Jewish does." And that's an adage that serves well to describe what I've set out to do with this book.

Jewish food has become a cultural phenomenon, perhaps at the expense of its religious significance. Nevertheless, many people buying bagels, cream cheese, and lox at those national bagel chains aren't even aware of the iconic status this combination holds in the Jewish community. Even Jews themselves are increasingly more concerned about having the right foods at their holiday celebrations than knowing the religious significance of the occasions. What else would explain the recent proliferation of low-fat *baked* potato latke recipes, which subverts the whole point of the latke in the first place—the symbolic oil it's fried in! Professor Kirshen-blatt-Gimblett refers to this new zeitgeist as "Kitchen Judaism." And if my family believed in anything, I would have to say it was that God was in my sister Carrie's Passover Sponge Cake (page 168).

Jewish Spice Mix and Notes about Seasoning

A (Jewish) restaurant critic recently pointed out to me that the problem with people who have been raised kosher is that they have nothing to compare the taste of their food to, no point of reference. While this may be a serious (even offensive) overstatement, as a polemic argument it posits an interesting dilemma for the cookbook author trying to make tasty re-creations of traditional foods. Because of the nature of food, recipes are inexact. Every apple, every piece of meat, even every can of tomato paste has a different flavor that must be accounted for by the cook. A recipe can be made or broken on the phrase "season to taste." Luckily, Ashkenazi Jewish cooking has a limited spice palate. In fact, my siblings and I once joked about getting in on the trend of chefs marketing gourmet spice mixes and rubs by packaging Jewish Spice Mix: a pre-sifted blend of salt, black pepper, garlic powder, and paprika.

The flavor of Jewish food begins and ends with salt. You need enough of it to bring out the natural flavors of food—and then a little more to make your diners reach for the seltzer. My mother's favorite recipe direction is, "Salt it like you're salting the road." I have given measurements for salt that may seem excessive to some cooks. First, note that I recommend kosher salt, which is coarser and less salty (tablespoon for tablespoon) than ordinary iodized table salt. Kosher salt is purer than iodized table salt and sprinkles more easily. And I also happen to like the flavor better, even though some experts claim there is no difference. If you are using regular salt, you should reduce my salt measurements by a third. I've come to these measurements by making each of the recipes a couple of times, salting them to my taste, and then reducing the salt a little to accommodate for variances in ingredients. Salt is easier to add than it is to take away, so pulling back at the outset is always advised. But don't stop before you add enough. Obviously, "enough" is subjective. But as a rule, you should know the salt is there without being able to taste it. Of course, if you are making things like sauerkraut and pickles, the flavor of salt is what you're after.

As I've already said, the other seasonings are pretty limited. Choose the best peppercorns you can find and grind them as you need them. I like them from Tellicherry or Sarawak, but as long as they are fresh, you can't really go wrong. The same holds true for paprika, which should contribute more than just color. As a rule, Hungarian is sweet and Spanish is hot, but it really just depends on how it's processed. For garlic, I actually prefer a combination of dried (granulated) and fresh—they aren't substitutes, but each contributes its own flavor. The only thing to remember about other spices is to use the best you can afford and make sure they are fresh. Although you may think you can buy spices in bulk and keep them over the stove for twenty years, they actually deteriorate quickly, even more so in warm places. (For sources, see page 273.)

"Putting in Good" and What That Means

If you use the best ingredients you can find, you are ahead of the game in the kitchen. Be aware that the best ingredients are not necessarily the most expensive or even the prettiest. It's all about taste and—not to get too touchy-feely—wholesomeness. Shop wisely.

MEATS

I love meat. For me, nothing is as satisfying as sinking my teeth into a charred rib steak or a juicy piece of chicken. That's not to say I eat meat at every meal or that I don't love tofu, which I do. But like millions of Jews before me, when I think of a holiday celebration it always contains a lot of meat—and more often than not, a selection of two or three kinds.

Because of its elevated status, meat is often the most expensive part of the meal. And if you keep kosher (more about that later), the cost is even greater. So you don't want to mess around with unreliable sources. It pays to find a good butcher, someone who knows his (rarely her) way around a carcass. If you develop a relationship with him, you can expect some special services—chicken fat for rendering schmaltz, chicken feet when they are available, a perfectly trimmed and tied rib roast, a couple of marrow bones, whatever you need. The overall cost of the meat from such a butcher may be higher, but the trade-off—in terms of time spent in the kitchen or running around to track down your ingredients—is worth it.

PRODUCE

As a nation, we have an aversion to ripe produce. It doesn't ship well, it looks blemished, and it doesn't keep. But there is no comparison between a sweet, ripe, locally grown tomato and a hard, pale one shipped from overseas, whether or not the vine is still attached. The same holds true for fruit. Americans also seem to want our produce really big—like our cars. But if you'll allow me to make a gross generalization—I assure you it won't be the last one in this book—in most cases, smaller is better. Little, crunchy Kirby cucumbers make the best pickles, just as minuscule wild blueberries pack a powerful flavor punch.

The fresher, more locally grown produce you use—organically grown if you can find it—the better your finished dishes will be. And the better the planet will be for it.

CANNED GOODS

Processed foods are ingredients too, and you should use the same care in selecting them as you do vegetables and meat. Throughout the book I specify brands for canned foods and other commercial ingredients when I think it matters, not because I get promotional kickbacks from the companies that produce them, but because I think the dish is best made with one product over another.

FAT

I've already expressed my preference for schmaltz and butter over just about any other fat, and my distaste for margarine. But I should also say a few words about oil. Oil is really the only pareve fat, so if you are keeping kosher, your choice of oil will be tantamount to culinary success. When only oil will do—for deep-frying, coating, and the occasional baked good—I use peanut oil almost exclusively. Although I didn't know it until I started recording my mother's stories for this book, her grandmother used only peanut oil, too. Peanut oil has a rich, buttery flavor that I think enhances food without making it heavy and greasy. Although peanut oil tends to be more expensive than other types of oil, if you live near a Chinatown or an Asian market, you can usually find it at a good price.

A couple of times throughout the book I have recommended using Crisco vegetable oil. This is my mother's brand of preference because it is light in texture and neutral in flavor. It is 100 percent soybean oil. (Note that the vegetable oil is distinct from other Crisco oils.) These days it's hard to find any oil that doesn't contain canola. And although I was raised in Canada and they may take away my passport for saying so, I don't like the taste or texture of canola oil one bit. (In case that

Canadian comment flew over your head: canola oil was invented and heavily marketed by Canadian producers.) Olive oil is excellent, too, but its distinct flavor just wasn't part of the Jewish food of my childhood.

The Kosher Conundrum

The Jewish dietary laws (kashrut) are based on the Torah, and they have been discussed and debated by rabbis for millennia. The rules cover topics such as what can and cannot be eaten and in what combination; how food is raised, harvested or slaughtered, and prepared; and many esoteric and some dated topics. There are no recipes. If you ask most modern American Jews, they will say that the rules of kosher are grounded in ideas of hygiene and health. Apparently there is no solid historical or even anecdotal evidence to verify this claim. The reality is that the laws have evolved as a result of changing customs, technology, and social imperatives, and they were likely created in the same fluid environment. It may be interesting for some to know that chicken was at one time not considered "meat," and at least one Talmudic rabbi was known to eat it with milk. The point of keeping "kosher" (adhering to the Jewish dietary laws) is not what the laws are or what the rationale is behind them—it is an expression of faith.

Nevertheless, there are rules today that govern what certain groups of Jews consider kosher. None of these rules has anything to do with how I cook or eat Jewish food. And if detailed information about how to keep a kosher household is what you are after, you should buy another book. Granted, the Jewish recipes I have included in this book come out of a kosher tradition, but the Jewish food I grew up on was not kosher. That's not to say that you cannot use my recipes to prepare kosher meals. Where I believe the quality of the end result is not diminished, I have recommended substitutions that will make the recipes kosher. Usually the problem is butter. And as I note several times throughout the book, in my family butter was considered closer to pareve (neutral) than anything else. My mother cooked just about everything with it, whether milk or meat.

"Keeping kosher" requires separate dishes and utensils for milk (milchig) and meat (fleishig). Strictly speaking, it requires separate refrigerators, too. It also means you must examine whatever prepared food you buy for special symbols (the letter *u* in a circle is the most common) that show the production process has met the standards established by some certifying body (in the case of the *u*, the Union of Orthodox Jewish Congregations). Only certain animals killed in a certain way and butchered according to special ritualized specifications can be considered kosher. Pork and shellfish are out, as is anything from the back half of the cow (i.e., from the loin section on down). (Interestingly, if the cow is cleaned in a certain time-consuming way, the entire animal can be kosher.) Kosher meat is also salted in a special way to draw out any residual blood.

Keeping kosher for Passover requires an even greater level of scrutiny. Another two sets of dishes are required for the duration of the holiday, and all foods must be specially koshered for Passover. No bread or anything with leavening can be consumed (enter matzo and its derivatives). You also have to give your entire house a thorough cleaning and burn any crumbs you find.

I am no expert on keeping kosher, but I have consulted several in my research for this book. As the interpretation of the rules varies from community to community, I would say you are best off checking with some sort of rabbinical authority. Many have websites that outline the general and specific rules. Among the most helpful I have found is the one run by the Union of Orthodox Jewish Congregations of America, specifically their kosher primer located at www.ou.org/kosher/primer.html. The OU, as it is called, is the largest kosher certifying body in the nation.

Whatzits and Whaddaya Means

Although I admit to having an unhealthy addiction to buying expensive kitchen equipment, I have cooked very respectable meals on a camping stove with nothing more than a pocketknife at my disposal. As you flip through this book looking for something to make, I don't want to hear you whine about not having the right equipment. A bad cook blames his tools. In the instances when I have said that a particular dish requires a certain piece of equipment, it is almost always for convenience's sake. My mother used the same flimsy, dull serrated knife to chop onions for years. My great grandmother didn't have a food processor or a microwave at her disposal and it didn't stop her for a second. There was no electricity and nobody had a rolling pin in the desert, but our ancestors managed to make matzo anyway.

That said, having good tools does make life easier. I think the two most important things to splurge on are pots and knives. Many Jewish dishes have to cook for a long time, and cheap, thin pots will burn every time. The effort you expend trying to slice all of those mushrooms with a butter knife could be conserved for doing something more productive—like shopping for kitchen equipment. I also like to have a good, sharp vegetable peeler, and plenty of cutting boards. An instant-read thermometer—the kind you just stick into a roast or a loaf of bread to take its temperature—is invaluable if you are like most people and don't know when anything is done. If you are going to be cooking for a crowd, which will probably be the case if you cook only at holiday times, then I think a food processor is also essential. If you bake a lot, buy a KitchenAid mixer. Like the rest of your top-quality kitchen utensils, you will have it for a lifetime.

As for techniques, I have tried to be as explicit as space would allow in the methodology section of each recipe. I've also included an advice section for each recipe that I hope will answer any questions that arise while you are cooking. Think of me as your mother or your *bubbe* standing there next to you in the kitchen (but don't give me any grief). If you have a preferred way of doing something, feel free to use it. Jewish cooking is not really different from other types of cooking—except we probably use more onions.

On the Menu

If you are going to work Jewish food into your life the way most of my friends do, then you are probably just going to be making it two or three times a year, at the holidays. Admittedly, one of the reasons I can be so cavalier with schmaltz and butter in my Jewish cooking is that I don't eat Jewish food all the time. Anything in moderation is good for you, even chicken fat. The irregularity with which I eat this type of food makes menu planning easy. Every holiday meal at my mother's place or my sister Carrie's apartment (Leslie and Sheldon usually don't host) or in my home is pretty much the same, because when we gather we want to have the foods we get to eat only occasionally. It looks something like this:

CHALLAH

CHOPPED LIVER

GEFILTE FISH WITH HORSERADISH

CHICKEN SOUP WITH MATZO BALLS

BRISKET

ROAST CHICKEN

FARFEL

KASHA VARNISHKES

RUSSIAN SOUR CREAM CAKE

MANDEL BREAD

You will note a lack of vegetables. That comes from my mother, who historically didn't like any vegetables other than green beans and broccoli (she eats a wider variety now). Sometimes there will be a salad, but it usually just sits on the sideboard until the end of the meal, when everyone is too full to eat it. There may be roasted or mashed potatoes, maybe even tzimmes—no vegetables, but plenty of starch. Sometimes I make cabbage rolls. On occasion there's a standing rib roast or a stuffed shoulder of veal. My sister Carrie is actually more adventurous with her holiday menus than my mother or I; she usually has plenty of vegetables. The desserts vary from meal to meal, depending on the season and Carrie's mood (she does most of the baking). At Passover there will be my homemade matzos, matzo farfel, Carrie's sponge cake, and macaroons, and obviously no farfel or kasha. One thing is for sure: there is always too much food.

When you are planning your menus, think about the mix of food—there should be good variety—and also how much refrigerator and stove space you have. Vary temperatures (hot, cold, lukewarm), textures (soft, crunchy, mushy, firm), flavors (salty, sour, sweet, spicy), and colors. Remember that if you are having ten people, you don't need ten full portions of everything—the more dishes you have, the less of each dish you need. Anything you can cook ahead is a great help, and fortunately, most Jewish food gets better with age. Have some things that you can serve at room temperature (e.g., lokshen kugel) and some that you can serve chilled (e.g., pickled cucumbers). Be sure the hot dishes are a mixture of those that can be kept warm on top of the stove and those that can go in the oven. Also be sure to have a lot of plastic bags on hand so that you can give people leftovers to take home.

One Last Word (As If I Could Ever Shut Up!)

At this point you are probably wondering what a mensch is. Well, if it isn't clear already, it's a guy like me; you know, nice, funny, good-hearted, smart, handsome (hey, it's my book!). It's someone who is able to state a strong opinion but still willing to listen to yours. A mensch chef invites you to dinner, prepares too much delicious food, and then has a stack of containers so you can take leftovers home.

The other important thing about the word *mensch,* at least as it pertains to the title of this book, is that it rhymes with the word French. Thus, *The Mensch Chef* pays homage to one of my favorite cooking shows, *The French Chef,* by my first culinary hero, Julia Child.

There are many ways to judge the success of a cookbook—besides the author's reclining on a yacht somewhere. If I get two or three good recipes out of a book, I think it was worth the price. My hope is that you will find more than that here, that you will not just add a recipe to your repertoire, but also laugh and learn something beyond how to render chicken fat. Jewish food is food that binds (and I'm not just talking about your arteries!). It brings people together. My family shares more laughs around the table than you can imagine. And the food is always superb. Whether or not you are Jewish, I hope you will walk away with a fresh perspective on and appreciation of good, old-fashioned Jewish cooking. And I would really *kvell* if I was able to start a food tradition in your family or among your friends.

THE MENSCH CHEF

Dinner Starts at Five

chapter **1**

appetizers and salads

What is it
about Jews as they age and their need to eat dinner increasingly early? When I lived in Paris, friends of mine lived with an elderly couple who sat down to dinner every night around 11:00 P.M. Madame didn't even start cooking until after seven o'clock. But American Jews, my mother included, like to eat dinner as close to lunch as possible. Don't believe me? Just go to the Rascal House restaurant in North Miami around 4:30 in the afternoon; the place is a madhouse.

I CAN THINK OF SEVERAL THEORIES to explain the tendency of Jews to eat dinner closer to lunch, none of them backed by scientific fact. If you consider the prototypical Jewish meal, the Passover Seder, then you have to start early. If you sit down at the dining room table late, by the time you work your way through the Haggadah everyone will be either starving or fast asleep. On the sociological level, an early dinner means your mother gets to see you sooner. Another theory is that the food is so heavy that you need all the time you can get afterward to digest it. The explanation that pertains to this chapter, however, is that there are usually so many appetizers before the main meal—gefilte fish, chopped liver, cabbage rolls—that you have to start early to get it all in.

JUST WHAT CONSTITUTES AN APPETIZER? In this deconstructed, postmodern world it's really hard to say. Appetizers can be cold or hot—as a menu-planning rule, serve cold things first. In delicatessens, as in this book, appetizers are usually lumped together with things like scoops of tuna and other salads that are usually served on leaves of iceberg lettuce to make them "fancy." Many hot dishes that Jews consider appetizers, such as pierogi, cabbage rolls, kishke, and the like, other cultures would consider heavy enough to be main courses. In fact, if you serve just a small portion of anything, you can call it an appetizer. Although we've grouped a bunch of things together in this section, throughout the book there are other dishes that you might want to serve at the start of the meal (latkes and blintzes among them). In a cuisine that allows for sweet kugels and compotes and other dessertlike things to be served with brisket, there are no rules.

gefilte fish

I HAVE A DISTINCT MEMORY that must evoke the same sickening feeling in every young kid who grew up in a Jewish neighborhood. A day or two before any feast-worthy holiday, our entire block reeked of gefilte fish cooking. In the aggregate, the smell of those balls of fish simmering in fish broth produced a pungent, acrid smell. It was so off-putting that I couldn't bring myself to even taste gefilte fish until I was well into adulthood.

That's just about the time my mother started making her own gefilte fish. And it was she who realized that if you didn't use bones to make the stock, the gefilte fish didn't give off an unpleasant odor as it cooked. My mother also decided that she would bag the tradition of using carp or a combination of carp and pike and perch, and just use whitefish instead. Her delicate, snow-white gefilte fish has convinced its share of Jewish culinary conservatives that tradition isn't always the best way.

The truth is that the kind of gefilte fish you like seems to have a lot to do with the kind you grew up on. Some prefer salty, others sweet. Some like only carp, while others find the muddy taste of carp unpalatable. Some even prefer Rokeach gefilte fish out of a can. If you live in an area with a large concentration of Jews, such as my mother's neighborhood in north Toronto, then around holiday time fishmongers will likely sell freshly ground fish by the pound. This is usually some mix of freshwater fish that tends toward the mild side. If not, it takes a day or two's notice to special-order a fish and have your purveyor grind it for you. (If you want the bones, be sure to ask for them.) You will need twice as much fish whole as you want ground.

Either way, I think using bones is optional. If you are a fan of the jelly that coagulates around the cooked fish, then bones are a must. And truth be told, a rich, flavorful stock makes for a more flavorful gefilte fish. But if you'd rather just make a quick gefilte fish without the hassle (and the odor) of making stock, then omit the bones. Still figure on making the fish a day or two in advance, so it can chill and your house can air out.

a bissel advice

How much fish? I usually figure a 50 percent yield of ground fish from whole. This means a whole 4-pound whitefish will produce about 2 pounds of ground fish and 1 pound of bones (minus the head). If you have too much, you can store the cooked fish for up to one week.

Yuck, what's with the sugar? My understanding is that Polish Jews prefer their gefilte fish sweet and Russians prefer it salty. The offspring of mixed marriages probably like it somewhere in between. You can play with the amounts of salt, pepper, and sugar in both the cooking liquid and the fish mixture to suit your taste.

the whole meshpucha
You can adjust the ingredients in this recipe in proportion to the amount of fish you have on hand, figuring 1 egg per pound of ground fish. You will likely need less salt.

kosher status PAREVE

In the wide stockpot, combine the fish bones (if using), with 3 quarts (12 cups) cold water, the onions, celery, chunked carrots, salt, sugar, and peppercorns, and set over high heat. Bring to a boil, reduce the heat to low, cover, and simmer for about 1 hour. Remove the solids and discard. Keep the liquid simmering, covered.

Meanwhile, in a large mixing bowl, combine the fish with the eggs, grated carrot, grated onion, ½ cup cold water, matzo meal, sugar, salt, and pepper. Mix well to be sure the ingredients are evenly distributed. To test the seasoning, take a scant tablespoon or so of the fish mixture, shape it into a patty, and fry it in a small sauté pan. Adjust the seasoning, remembering that when chilled the seasoning will be less pronounced.

Once the mixture is to your taste, you are ready to shape and cook the gefilte fish. Wet your hands with cold water. Use about ⅓ cup (4 ounces) of the fish mixture and shape it in the palm of your hand into an oblong puck (somewhere between an egg and a sphere). Let the gefilte fish roll off your hand into the simmering cooking liquid. Repeat with the remaining mixture, wetting your hands regularly to keep the fish mixture from sticking. You should get about 12 gefilte fish and they should be totally submerged in the cooking liquid. Add the sliced carrots to the pot, and bring to a gentle boil. Turn down the heat to a simmer, cover, and let cook for about 50 minutes, until the gefilte fish is white and firm, and the carrots are tender. Turn off the heat and let cool to room temperature in the cooking liquid.

Using a slotted spoon, transfer the fish, one piece at a time, and the carrot slices to a storage container. Strain the cooking liquid over top to cover, and chill until you are ready to serve.

FOR THE COOKING LIQUID

1 pound bones from fresh-water fish, without the heads *(optional)*

2 large yellow onions (1 pound), sliced

2 celery stalks, with leaves (¼ pound), cut into chunks

3 large carrots (½ pound), washed but unpeeled, cut into chunks

1 tablespoon kosher salt

2 tablespoons sugar

1 teaspoon whole black peppercorns

FOR THE GEFILTE FISH

2 pounds ground fresh-water fish, whitefish, carp, pike, perch, or a combination (see headnote)

2 large eggs

3 large carrots (½ pound), 1 grated, 2 thinly sliced

1 medium yellow onion (6 ounces), grated

¼ cup matzo meal

2 tablespoons sugar

1 tablespoon kosher salt

½ teaspoon freshly ground black pepper

SPECIAL EQUIPMENT

Wide, heavy-gauge 8- to 10-quart stockpot

MENTAL NOSH

Gefilte is Yiddish for "stuffed," and traditionally this ground fish mixture would be stuffed back into a fish skin and cooked whole or in small packets. In fact, a friend of mine wanted to give me an old Ukrainian recipe for gefilte fish that required you to do just that. His recipe began, "Place a live carp in a bathtub filled with water for two days." Even though I have included recipes in this book for making your own sauerkraut, corned beef, and other old-fashioned, time-consuming dishes, I thought that asking you to keep live fish in your bathroom was pushing it too far.

chopped liver

EVERY TIME MY FRIEND LONNI eats my chopped liver, which is two or three times a year, she tells me it is the best I have ever made. In fact, I make exactly the same recipe every time. But I have to admit it is good. And although it wasn't included in the recent chopped liver wars that were fought between a columnist at the *New York Observer* and a former restaurant critic for *New York* magazine, I have every confidence I would have been a contender if I had been called into the ring.

My secret—actually, my mother's secret—is to grate fresh onion into the chopped liver a few hours before serving. I add this extra jolt in addition to onion that is sautéed in chicken fat (something my mother doesn't do but my friend Barbara does). The raw onion adds a sharpness that helps cut through the fat. The only problem with this technique is that after a day or two the raw onion turns bitter. Therefore, in order to be able to make the chopped liver in advance, I prepare the liver up to the point that I add the raw onion. Then a couple of hours before I intend to serve it, I grate in some raw onion. My friend Adam's mother, Maxine, gives her chopped liver a kick by adding a couple of heaping tablespoonfuls of horseradish and a little dry mustard to the mix (note: sauté all of the onion). This variation can be fully prepared in advance, and believe me, it's delicious.

I think I gain another edge with my chopped liver by using a wooden chopping bowl and a metal chopping blade to chop and mix it, just like my mother and her grandmother did. This technique gives the liver a better texture than if everything is just pureed to a mush in the food processor. If you do not have a chopping bowl and chopper and you intend to start cooking a lot of Jewish food, consider investing in one. Otherwise, try chopping the cooked liver by hand on a cutting board with a very sharp knife, then stirring everything together in a mixing bowl with a fork. Similarly, I chop the hardboiled eggs by slicing them with an egg slicer and then chopping the slices finely by hand. I like to have pieces of egg visible in the finished chopped liver.

a bissel advice

You want more fat? Add ¼ cup finely chopped Gribenes (page 237) to the liver.

Only chicken liver? There are people who believe that using liver other than chicken improves the flavor of chopped liver. I wholeheartedly disagree. To my taste, beef and calf livers give chopped liver an acrid, bitter flavor. For obvious reasons, pork liver isn't an option.

MAKES **3** CUPS

the whole meshpucha
You can increase this recipe by keeping the same proportions of liver to onion to egg. But you probably won't need as much chicken fat or salt.

kosher status FLEISHIG

1½ pounds chicken livers

6 to 8 tablespoons Chicken Schmaltz
    (page 236)

3 medium yellow onions (about 1 pound), 1
    peeled but left whole with the root end
    intact, the rest finely chopped

2½ teaspoons kosher salt

1 teaspoon freshly ground black pepper

3 large hard-boiled eggs, chopped
    (see page 27 for the cooking and
    chopping technique)

SPECIAL EQUIPMENT

Wooden chopping bowl

Handheld metal chopping blade

Handheld box grater

begin by cleaning the livers. Rinse each under cold running water. With a sharp paring knife, separate the two lobes. Cut away any visible fat, membrane, or green patches on the livers. Place in a strainer to drain.

Meanwhile, heat the schmaltz in a large, 10- or 12-inch heavy frying pan (I prefer cast iron). Add the chopped onions and sauté, over medium-high heat, until soft and translucent, 7 to 8 minutes. Add the cleaned, drained livers and sauté until cooked through, 15 to 20 minutes. Add the salt and black pepper. Allow any liquid that the livers release to evaporate as they cook. Remove from the heat and cool.

If using a wooden chopping bowl, transfer the cooked livers and onions to it. Using a metal chopping blade, chop the cooked livers into small dice. Some of the livers will break up to mush, others will hold their shape. The goal is to attain a spreadable combination of small pieces and paste. If not using a chopping bowl, chop each liver by hand on a cutting board using a very sharp knife, and transfer to a mixing bowl. Add the chopped eggs, mix well, and adjust the seasoning with additional salt and pepper if necessary. Adding more schmaltz will smooth out the flavor of the liver and the texture. Use your judgment. The chopped liver can be made up to two days in advance and refrigerated at this point.

On the day of serving, remove the liver from the refrigerator. Using a handheld box grater, grate the remaining onion into the liver, holding on to the root end for leverage. Mix well, taste, and adjust the seasoning, which will have changed after sitting and chilling.

MENTAL NOSH

Would you believe that the predecessor to modern-day chopped liver may very well be the French delicacy foie gras? Historians believe that it was medieval Jewish goose farmers who fattened geese for schmaltz who carried on and spread the tradition of foie gras production in Europe. Recipes for special fattened goose livers appear in Jewish cookbooks dating from the 15th and 16th centuries. Sometimes, just for historical accuracy, I make both chopped liver and foie gras (see page 10) as appetizers at large holiday gatherings.

mock chopped liver
(a.k.a. jewish guacamole)

BELIEVE IT OR NOT, there is s a longstanding tradition of "mock" Jewish dishes—mock kishka (stuffed derma), mock gefilte fish, and mock chopped liver among them. I'm not sure whether all of this faux feasting is the result of prescribed meat and dairy distinctions or whether it is an attempt to lighten up Jewish meals a little by lessening

the cholesterol load of other traditional dishes. (In fact, ancient Roman gastronomes were always making ingredients appear like things they were not.) None of the mock variants tastes anything like the originals, but there is something pleasing (if not humorous) about trying. The whole notion reminds me of the fake soy "meats" you see in Asian Buddhist restaurants. Why bother? On the other hand, why not? There are several versions of

mock chopped liver floating around—some use lentils, others green vegetables—but I happen to like the fresh taste of this one, built on a combination of string beans and peas. Really nothing like chopped liver at all, it is a vegetable spread whose bright green color prompted one of my friends to coin it Jewish Guacamole.

Although I have seen recipes that tell you to puree everything together in the food processor, I like to carry the illusion a little further by preparing it as though I were making chopped liver, leaving some of the onions and eggs visible by chopping them by hand. I also happen to think the dish tastes a lot better if you fry the onions in chicken schmaltz instead of butter or oil, but there goes the rationale for making something lighter or vegetarian. Your call.

a bissel advice

That doesn't taste anything like chopped liver. **I know, I know. But it makes a nice alternative for people who hate liver. The mock chopped liver is best if it is allowed to sit for a day before serving, enabling the flavors to blend and mature. If you plan to serve it chilled (as I do), taste it again before serving, as the flavor of seasonings tends to lessen at lower temperatures.**

But you said there were plenty of variations? **Substitute 2½ cups of cooked green lentils instead of the green beans and peas. To prepare the lentils, sift through 1 cup of dry lentils to remove any stones. Place in a small saucepan with 4 cups water. Bring to a boil, turn down the heat, and simmer for 40 to 45 minutes until tender. Drain and proceed with the recipe.**

kosher status MILCHIG, with butter
FLEISHIG, with schmaltz
PAREVE, with peanut oil

³⁄₄ pound fresh string beans, ends trimmed

2 cups frozen peas (one 10-ounce package), defrosted

4 tablespoons Chicken Schmaltz (page 236), unsalted butter, or peanut oil, depending on your reasoning for making this dish in the first place

3 medium yellow onions (1¼ pounds), chopped

20 TamTams, saltines, or other crackers, or 1 matzo

3 large hard-boiled eggs, finely chopped (see page 27 for a cooking and chopping technique)

2 to 3 teaspoons kosher salt, depending on the saltiness of the crackers

¾ teaspoon freshly ground black pepper

SPECIAL EQUIPMENT
Food processor

place the green beans in a saucepan with about 1 inch of water on the bottom. Set over high heat, cover, and bring to a boil. Cook until tender, 7 or 8 minutes. Add the frozen peas, cover, and bring back to a boil. Turn off the heat, uncover, and cool.

Meanwhile, heat the fat in a large sauté pan set over medium-high heat. Add the onions and sauté until tender and light golden brown, about 20 minutes. Stir regularly to prevent burning. Cool.

Place the TamTams or crackers in the bowl of a food processor fitted with the metal chopping blade. Pulse until ground to fine crumbs, about 20 pulses in total. Remove the crumbs from the processor to a mixing bowl; you should have about ½ cup. Without cleaning it, reassemble the processor bowl with the metal chopping blade. Place the cooked, drained string beans and peas in the bowl and pulse until the vegetables are ground or roughly pureed, 20 to 25 pulses in total. Scrape down the sides if necessary to ensure even processing.

Transfer the vegetable mixture to the bowl of crumbs. Add the cooked onions along with the fat they were cooked in, the chopped eggs, salt, and pepper. Stir well. Adjust the seasoning, cover, and refrigerate until serving.

MENTAL NOSH

The ancient Roman tradition of making food resemble something it isn't derives from the value that that society placed on manipulating the natural environment. By contrast, the Chinese tradition of soy "meats" is partially rooted in the difficulty of obtaining protein in poor economic conditions. These faux meats were later adopted by Chinese Buddhists, who were prohibited from consuming living creatures.

whole-roasted foie gras with apple and caramelized onion

ONE OF THE MOST INTERESTING things I learned while working on my last cookbook, *Foie Gras: A Passion,* is that much of the European—and especially French—tradition of raising geese, fattening them, and cooking with the fat and the fattened liver comes from Ashkenazi culture. Jewish women in medieval Europe would raise and fatten geese as a source of income. The rendered fat, *gense schmaltz* in Yiddish, would be used to cook just about everything, sweet and savory, almost as a substitute for lard. And the prized liver would be reserved for special occasions, such as the Passover seder. I take great pleasure in knowing that the historical antecedent of modern-day chopped liver was actually foie gras.

This recipe actually has its roots in old Jewish cooking. It is similar to a classic recipe for "Goose Liver, Old Jewish Law" that appeared in the 1901 German cookbook *Ausfuhrliches Kochbuch,* and that had been made for a long time before that.

You will need a beautiful duck foie gras and some extra duck fat. (Although goose foie gras and goose fat would be more historically accurate, it is not produced in this country.) Sources for both are recommended in the back of the book (page 273).

Don't be nervous about cooking foie gras; nothing could be simpler than this dish. Although the original recipe called for cooking the apples with the liver. You can add them to the hot fat at the end of the cooking process, which keeps them tart and crisp so they are better suited to cut through the richness of the liver. Serve this with a large loaf of challah or peasant bread, and encourage your guests to spread the liver on the bread along with the onions, apples, and fat. Though not quite a substitute for chopped liver, this dish is nevertheless a welcome addition to any holiday feast.

a bissel advice

So much fat? **Well, first let me say that the people of Gascony, France's foie gras region, who consume more saturated fat than any population on the planet—and in the form of fattened duck liver, no less—also happen to have among the longest life expectancies. That's the French paradox. Shut up, pour yourself a glass of red wine, and enjoy.**

Can I make a smaller amount? **You can really only make one liver's worth of this dish because once you start cutting into the liver, it loses its fat more readily and tends to disintegrate when it is baked. Besides, this is a dish for special occasions only.**

1¼ pounds (about 2 cups) rendered
    duck fat
3 large yellow onions (1½ pounds), thinly
    sliced
6 medium garlic cloves, minced
1 whole grade-A foie gras (about
    1½ pounds), cleaned of any visible
    surface imperfections
2 teaspoons kosher salt
Freshly ground black pepper
2 large, sweet eating apples (1 pound), such
    as Golden Delicious, Mutsu, or Gala

SPECIAL EQUIPMENT
Deep 10-inch baking dish, preferably ceramic

p reheat the oven to 300°F.

In a large sauté pan set over medium-high heat, melt the duck fat. Add the sliced onions and cook until lightly golden brown, about 10 minutes. Add the garlic and continue cooking an additional 2 or 3 minutes, until soft. Transfer this mixture to a deep 10-inch ceramic baking dish.

Meanwhile, season the whole foie gras with the salt and pepper. Bury the foie gras, smooth side up, in the onion and fat mixture so that it is more than halfway covered with the fat. Set in the middle of the preheated oven and bake for about 1 hour and 10 minutes, or until the liver feels firm. It will have released some of its fat and shrunk somewhat, but it will still be more or less intact.

While the liver is baking, peel, quarter, and core the apples. Cut the quarters into ⅛-inch slices. As soon as you remove the foie gras from the oven, place the apple slices in the hot fat surrounding the liver. Cool to room temperature in the baking dish on a wire rack. The foie gras should be served at room temperature or slightly warmed in the baking dish with plenty of challah. Guests should just dig in with a knife to get some liver, and spread it onto the bread with some of the apple, onion, and duck fat from the pan. Yum.

MENTAL NOSH

Foie gras is considered one of the most luxurious culinary indulgences. And throughout history, because it was produced by Jewish butchers, the question of its kosher status has been seriously scrutinized. It just so happens that Israel is one of the world's largest producers of foie gras today, and some of it is kosher. The ducks are scrupulously observed to make sure they are not injured in the process of making the liver. And then the liver is koshered like any other liver.

hummus

I KNOW THIS UBIQUITOUS CHICK-PEA spread is not exactly Ashkenazi cuisine, but I love it, and it makes a nice appetizer. For me, the thing that often makes homemade hummus less desirable than store-bought is the texture: homemade versions are usually lumpy. But the smooth, creamy texture of commercially made hummus can be achieved at home if you have a food processor and if you can strike the right balance between liquid and fat to make an emulsion. What's more, the flavors of homemade hummus are stronger, fresher tasting, and more appealing than anything I've been able to buy.

I am a fan of cumin, but I know as a seasoning cumin has many detractors. You can leave it out if you prefer. In one of my limited attempts at fusion cuisine, I use a Vietnamese-style chili-garlic sauce to give my hummus a little heat; you can use any spicy condiment you like. The hummus is best made a day in advance so that the flavors have a chance to meld.

a bissel advice

Canned chick-peas? Don't bother starting with dried chick-peas for this recipe. Although there may be subtle nuances in flavor, the thing you gain most from using dried chick-peas is texture. But because you are pureeing the chick-peas in this instance, you would want to cook them until they are soft and mushy, anyway. Be aware, though, that the amount of salt varies from can to can (some organic chick-pea producers don't use any). Adjust the seasoning after the hummus has sat for a day.

2 medium garlic cloves
2 (15½-ounce) cans chick-peas, rinsed and
　　drained (3 cups)
Juice of 2 or 3 lemons (½ cup)
1¼ teaspoons ground cumin
1 teaspoon hot sauce or Asian chili paste, or
　　a pinch of ground cayenne
3 tablespoons tahini
Pinch of kosher salt
Freshly ground black pepper to taste
¼ cup extra-virgin olive oil

SPECIAL EQUIPMENT
Food processor

MAKES 3 CUPS

kosher status PAREVE

place the garlic, chick-peas, 5 tablespoons of water, lemon juice, cumin, hot sauce, tahini, salt, and pepper in the bowl of a food processor fitted with the metal chopping blade or blender. Process using on/off pulses until the mixture is pureed. Then turn on the machine and let it run for a steady 2 or 3 minutes, until the hummus is smooth. With the machine running, pour the olive oil in in a slow, steady stream through the feed tube to make an emulsion. Adjust the seasoning.

fava bean chips

THOUGH NOT EXACTLY A STAPLE while I was growing up—I had them for the first time only a few years ago at a fancy New York City restaurant—these salty, spicy bar snacks are a nice apéritif to serve at the start of a holiday meal. Try some Chopped Liver on a piece of challah with a couple of these chips on top.

MAKES **3** CUPS

kosher status PAREVE

½ pound (1¼ cups) dried, shelled fava beans

2 cups vegetable oil

2 tablespoons kosher salt

½ teaspoon cayenne pepper

2 teaspoons sugar

Pick through the beans to remove any stones or shriveled-up or discolored beans. Place the beans in a container and cover with cold water at least 2 inches above the level of the beans. Let soak at room temperature for 12 hours or overnight. Drain.

Line a cookie sheet with paper towels. Heat the oil in a large, deep frying pan (I use cast iron) over medium-high heat; you should have about 1 inch of oil. To test if the oil is hot enough, put one of the soaked beans in it. It should sizzle immediately. Place about ¾ cup of the soaked beans in the frying pan. Use a fork to move the beans around so that they cook evenly. They will bubble and sizzle vigorously at first, but then as they start to brown, the sizzling will subside after about 3 or 4 minutes. As soon as it does, pay close attention. The beans should turn lightly golden brown, but no more, or they will have a strong, almost burned flavor and the texture of rocks. Using a slotted spoon, remove the beans, drain well, and place on the paper-towel-lined cookie sheet. Repeat with the remaining beans, frying them in small enough batches so that the oil doesn't take long to get hot again once they are put in.

Meanwhile, in a small bowl, combine the salt, cayenne pepper, and sugar, and mix well. Using more paper towels, roll the fried favas around to remove some of the excess oil. Sprinkle with the salt mixture to taste. Once completely cool, the fava bean chips can be stored in an airtight container or resealable plastic bag for up to 1 week.

a bissel advice

Seems like a lot, nu? It is, but as I said, everyone loves them and they make a healthful snack. You can make these chips in any quantity you like. I just wanted to give you a guideline.

Can I use any other beans? The only other one I have used is chick-peas, and they are also delicious. But because of their starchiness, fried chick-peas sort of stick in your throat when you eat them.

cabbage rolls

THERE IS SOMETHING ABOUT the flavor of sweet-and-sour cabbage rolls (sometimes called stuffed cabbage, or *holishkes*) that sends me. Basically a meatball wrapped in cabbage and cooked in tomato soup, the combination produces a rich, satisfying dish that can be served as either an appetizer or an entree. The problem is,

no matter what you do, making cabbage rolls is kind of a production. But unlike some other productions, this one is worth it. There are a couple of things to be aware of. The cabbage rolls have to cook slowly for a long time, about 2 hours. This requires a good, heavy pot and a burner that can be accurately regulated at the lower ranges. Otherwise the cabbage will

burn. If you don't have both of these things, you should probably bake the cabbage rolls in the oven just to be safe. After all this work, it would be a shame to have to throw them away.

a bissel advice

What's with the gingersnaps? I use them instead of ordinary bread crumbs or matzo meal because I think they give the meat a rich, sweet flavor. If you can find imported European ginger-snaps, which tend to be less sweet than American varieties, use them.

Can't I cheat to make the process easier? **There is one shortcut if, unlike me, you have extra room in your freezer. Two days before you plan to make the stuffed cabbage, remove the core of the cabbage and wrap the cabbage in plastic wrap. Place it in the freezer for at least 24 hours. Remove the cabbage from the freezer, place it in a strainer or colander in the sink, and let it defrost. The leaves will fall apart, wilted and ready to use without boiling. This is easier, but clearly not quicker.**

What if my cabbage rolls burn? **It happens to the best of us. Depending on how badly burned they are, you can lift off and save the rolls on the top of the pot. Remove them gently so as not to disturb or kick up any of the really burned stuff on the bottom. You will find that even these cabbage rolls on top have a slightly burned taste, but part of it is psychological. I have served these salvaged cabbage rolls and thought they were so burned tasting I would die of embarrassment, but people loved them anyway and didn't even know what I was talking about.**

FOR THE CABBAGE ROLLS

1 large head green cabbage (about
    3½ pounds), the less densely packed the
    better

20 small gingersnaps (7 ounces)

2 pounds ground chuck or other ground beef
    that isn't too lean

3 large eggs

1 medium yellow onion (6 ounces), grated

⅓ cup raisins

¼ cup uncooked white rice

1 tablespoon kosher salt

½ teaspoon freshly ground black pepper

FOR THE COOKING LIQUID

1 (28-ounce) can crushed tomatoes

1 (28-ounce) can whole tomatoes with their
    juice, cut up into chunks

1 (6-ounce) can tomato paste

Juice of 8 to 10 lemons (1¼ cups)

½ cup sugar

2 teaspoons kosher salt

½ teaspoon freshly ground black pepper

¼ cup raisins

¼ cup uncooked white rice

SPECIAL EQUIPMENT

Wide, heavy-gauge 8- to 12-quart pot
    with lid

Food processor *(optional)*

the first task is to separate and wilt the leaves of the cabbage. Bring a large pot of salted water to a boil. With a small, sharp knife, remove the core of the cabbage by cutting deeply around it in a conical shape. Place the whole cabbage in the boiling water. Roll it around in the boiling water for several minutes until the outer leaves begin to wilt and loosen, 3 to 5 minutes, depending on how fresh or dense your cabbage is. Carefully remove the outer leaves without tearing them, keeping the rest of the cabbage in the water. Continue peeling off leaves as soon as they are soft enough to loosen. By the time you are finished you should have about 16 nice, big leaves that are pretty much intact and a few smaller leaves that you will also be able to patch together in order to stuff. Reserve the rest of the cabbage, too.

To prepare the filling, first grind the gingersnaps to fine crumbs either in a food processor fitted with a metal chopping blade or in a resealable plastic bag with a rolling pin. In a mixing bowl, combine the gingersnap crumbs, ground beef, eggs, grated onion, raisins, rice, salt, and pepper, and mix until blended. To stuff the cabbage, lay the first leaf on the counter so that it curls upwards. Toward the end that was closest to the core (the thicker, firmer side), place about 3 tablespoons of the meat filling. Roll up, folding the sides of the leaf in toward the center to form a tight package. Repeat with the remaining leaves. If the leaves are too small or they are ripped, you can patch two pieces of cabbage together by overlapping them and treating them as one. If you have any leftover filling, shape it into meatballs.

Roughly shred or chop any cabbage that hasn't been used to form the rolls. Arrange this cabbage on the bottom of the large, wide, heavy pot. Arrange a layer of cabbage rolls, seam side down, on top of the shredded cabbage. Pour over the crushed tomatoes, tomato chunks with their juice, tomato paste, lemon juice, sugar, salt, and pepper. Arrange the remaining cabbage rolls and any meatballs in the liquid. Add enough water so that everything is just covered. Sprinkle in the raisins and white rice.

Set the cabbage over low heat and bring to a simmer. Turn down the heat to very low, cover, and continue simmering for about 1½ hours, or until

recipe continues →

cabbage rolls

(continued)

MENTAL NOSH

Holishkes, *which are thought to have originated in Russia, are traditionally eaten on Succoth, a week-long harvest festival that usually falls in mid-October. Stuffed things are thought to symbolize abundance, and that's exactly what you want at harvest time. Since at harvest time there are presumably plenty of vegetables around, I find the tradition of eating cabbage—a winter vegetable—counterintuitive. But what do I know? Don't limit yourself. Eat cabbage rolls all year long!*

the cabbage is tender, the rice has swelled, and the meat is cooked through. If the liquid ever falls below the surface of the cabbage, add some more water to the pot, but avoid making the cooking liquid too watery. Remove from the heat and cool in the cooking liquid to room temperature.

Alternatively, you can bake the cabbage rolls covered in a preheated 325°F. oven for 1½ hours. Then raise the temperature to 350°F., remove the cover, and continue baking for an additional 30 minutes or until the cabbage is fully cooked and the meat is done. Remove from the oven and allow to cool to room temperature in the cooking liquid.

Store the cabbage rolls in the refrigerator for up to 1 week or in the freezer for up to 2 months. Reheat in some of the cooking liquid in a 300°F. oven or in a microwave until the filling is warm.

pierogi

THESE POLISH POCKETS (*varenikehs* in Yiddish, *vareniki* in Russian) are among my favorite foods. You used to be able to get decent pierogi at the all-night Ukrainian restaurants in Manhattan's East Village neighborhood. But these days the pierogi they serve are tough and doughy. (The Communist Party sympathizers are gone, too.) To make

matters worse, now instead of pan-frying their pierogi, most restaurants deep-fry them, and the result is greasy and unappetizing. You can still get decent pierogi in Brooklyn's Greenpoint neighborhood, where there is so much Polish spoken you could mistake it for Warsaw. But even my Polish-born roommate had to concede that this recipe produced some of the best pierogi she's ever tasted. She made me an honorary Polish citizen, though I'm not sure about her authority to do that.

a bissel advice

What if I always order the assorted plate? **Make a double batch of dough and a couple of different fillings.**

Does size matter? **You can make pierogi any size you like. Small ones make nice hors d'oeuvre but they require more futzing.**

Because my original recipe uses a milchig combination of canned evaporated milk and butter, I set out to produce an equally delicious pareve version. I settled on a combination of soy milk and peanut oil, and the result was pretty good. The only problem arises when you want to smother the pareve pierogi in lots of onions that have been caramelized in butter. But to each his or her own religion.

Just about anything can be stuffed inside a pierog, from potatoes and cheese to sauerkraut and meat to sour cherries. Use any of the fillings on pages 220 to 233. If you're using a sweet filling, it's probably a good idea to omit the onion.

recipe continues →

pierogi

(continued)

2½ cups unbleached all-purpose flour

¾ teaspoon kosher salt

1 tablespoon unsalted butter, melted and
    cooled, or peanut oil

½ cup canned evaporated milk or unflavored
    soy milk

5 tablespoons potato cooking water
    (from making the potatoes for the
    filling), or plain water

2 to 2½ cups filling, chilled (pages 220–235)

Additional 1 or 2 tablespoons peanut oil, for
    coating

Additional 4 tablespoons unsalted butter, for
    frying

1 large yellow onion (½ pound), thinly sliced
    (optional)

Sour cream and/or applesauce (page 212),
    for garnish

SPECIAL EQUIPMENT

Round cutter, 3½ inches in diameter
Large frying pan with tight-fitting cover

MENTAL NOSH

Just in case you were wondering, pierogi *is a Polish plural.*
Pierogis *is grammatically incorrect. One is simply called a*
pierog.

MAKES **30** PIEROGI

the whole meshpucha
As long as you're cooking, make a lot and keep them in the freezer. But don't crowd
the pan when you cook the pierogi or they won't get nicely browned.

kosher status Pay attention to your doughs and fillings. As I said in the headnote, the
combination of soy milk and peanut oil makes a good dough. For fleishig or pareve
pierogi, fry them in peanut oil or, better yet, chicken schmaltz. For traif pierogi,
use the evaporated-milk dough and stuff them with brisket.

In a large mixing bowl combine the flour and salt. Make a well in the center
and add the butter or oil, milk, and 4 tablespoons of the potato water. Stir
with a wooden spoon to form a dough. If you cannot incorporate all of the
flour, or the dough seems crumbly, add an additional tablespoon (or more) of
water. Turn the dough out onto a floured surface and knead with your hands
for about 5 minutes, until the dough becomes smooth and soft to the touch.
It should be soft but not sticky. Wrap in plastic and let sit at room temperature
for a couple of hours before shaping.

Divide the dough in half, keeping the half you aren't working with
wrapped in plastic to prevent drying. With a rolling pin, roll out the dough as
thin as possible. (Modern-day pierogi makers use Italian pasta machines for
this task.) Using a sharp, round cutter about 3½ inches in diameter, cut out
circles of dough. Stretch the dough slightly with your
fingertips and set it in the palm of your left hand (or
right hand if you are a lefty). Spoon about a tablespoon of filling into the center of the dough.
(Depending on the type of filling, each pierog will
hold more or less—for instance, I can get more
sauerkraut in than I can potato.) Fold the dough in half to form a semicircle
and pinch the edges to seal. If the dough won't hold, moisten the edges with
cold water. Set the pierog on the counter, and, using the tines of a fork
dipped in flour, flute the edge to further seal and decorate. Be careful not to
pierce the dough with the tines. Place the pierog on a cookie sheet, cover

with a clean dish towel, and repeat until all of the dough is used up. Reroll the dough scraps only once; they get too difficult to handle after that.

In a large pot, bring 5 quarts of water to a boil with 1½ tablespoons kosher salt. Drop about half of the pierogi in the boiling water and cook (blanch) for about 3 minutes. The pierogi will sink to the bottom and then rise to the surface while cooking. With a slotted spoon, remove the pierogi from the water and set on another clean dish towel to drain. Meanwhile, blanch the remaining pierogi and drain the same way. To refrigerate for up to a week, place the 1 or 2 tablespoons of peanut oil in a large, shallow container and toss the drained pierogi to coat with the oil (in order to prevent them from sticking to each other). To freeze for up to 2 months, lay the blanched pierogi in a single layer on a cookie sheet, wrap with aluminum foil, and set in the freezer. Once frozen solid, transfer to a resealable plastic bag. Defrost the pierogi overnight in the refrigerator. Alternately, you can defrost them on low in a microwave for 5 to 7 minutes, checking frequently to make sure they haven't begun to cook.

To serve, heat 2 or 3 tablespoons of butter in a large frying pan set over medium-high heat. Add the sliced onion, if using, and sauté until soft, 8 to 10 minutes. Remove the onion from the pan and set aside. Add another tablespoon or so of butter to the pan. Add the pierogi, no more than 10 or so at a time, and toss once or twice to coat with the butter. Let cook for about 5 minutes. Add about 2 tablespoons of water to the pan and cover tightly. Let the pierogi steam like this for an additional 7 to 10 minutes, until they are golden brown on the bottom and heated through. Add the sautéed onion back to the pan, toss once or twice to heat, and serve immediately with sour cream and/or applesauce.

duck prosciutto

MANY OF THE WORLD'S CUISINES RELY on pork and pork products for flavor and fat (one and the same thing, really). Without them, where would French cuisine be? In my quest for some ingredient that would give Jewish food a little of the richness and flavor that pork products afford, I thought about using duck prosciutto. Duck prosciutto is a cured cold cut made from magret—the large, fatty breast of a foie gras duck—that is easy to make at home. It is delicious sliced thin and served like prosciutto on sandwiches or in salads. And finely diced and sautéed along with onions and other vegetables, it is a terrific addition to soups, stews, and many other savory dishes. It's even good fried for breakfast. Experiment with different seasonings until you find the combination you like best. Because duck prosciutto is cured, it can keep for months in the refrigerator. Don't get caught without it.

a bissel advice

Now what am I supposed to do with this stuff? **You can eat it, as is, in sandwiches or on salads. It's best sliced paper thin—an electric slicer helps—but treat the slices gently so that the fat remains attached (that's the best part). A wonderful appetizer is made from draping thin slices of duck prosciutto over fresh figs. If you are going to use the prosciutto to cook with, just cut the meat and fat into tiny cubes and add it to whatever you are sautéing.**

1½ cups dark brown sugar

1½ cups kosher salt

3 juniper berries

1 bay leaf, crumbled

1 teaspoon black peppercorns

1 teaspoon coriander seeds

2 duck magrets (1¾ pounds total), rinsed
and patted dry

SPECIAL EQUIPMENT

**Glass loaf pan or other deep, nonreactive
dish of similar size**

In a small bowl, combine the brown sugar, salt, juniper berries, bay leaf, peppercorns, and coriander seeds. Mix well. Place about one-third of this mixture in the bottom of the loaf pan. Lay one magret, fat side up, on the salt and sugar mixture. Cover with another third of the mixture and lay the second magret on top of that. Top with the remaining salt and sugar mixture, being sure that the duck breasts are well coated. Cover with plastic wrap and refrigerate for 6 to 8 days, until the meat is cured. The prosciutto is done when the duck breasts are firm to the touch, with the stiff texture and dark color of cooked meat. The fat should be a creamy, off-white color. Completely wipe off the seasoning and wrap in plastic. Store in the refrigerator until ready to use.

MENTAL NOSH

Magret is a French term that refers specifically to the breast of a duck that produced foie gras. These ducks are older and have more fat on them than regular roasting ducks, so the breasts are larger and more fatty, too. You can make duck prosciutto from regular duck breasts, but the meat won't be as flavorful. (Reduce the curing time by 1 or 2 days.) You can find magret in gourmet stores and fine butcher shops, or you can order it directly from the source (see page 273) and have it shipped to you overnight.

knishes

WITH ITS OWN NEAT LITTLE PACKAGE, I think a knish is the ultimate street food. My friend Oliver recently told a funny story about his arrival in New York City from Southern California. He was still adjusting to the change in climate and pace when a colleague invited him to the beach at Coney Island. He went, thinking that spending time on a beach might make him feel a little more at home. Of course, Coney Island is not exactly a welcoming place, and the beach feels nothing like California. In the height of summer, it's a zoo. The craziness was only emphasized by an elderly woman who was dragging a basket through the sand calling out in a high-pitched voice, "Delicious knishes. Get your delicious knishes." Oliver had never heard of a knish before. And he wouldn't know what they were for some time because when he finally figured out that she was selling something you could eat, there were none left.

Although my knish dough simulates the wrap you find on gargantuan knishes in delis and on street carts around New York, I like to make my knishes a little smaller and more manageable. For party hors d'oeuvre, I sometimes make miniature knishes. The dough can be mixed in a bowl with a fork in a matter of minutes. While it sits, you can prepare the filling (any of the savory filling recipes on pages 220 to 225 will work well). If I don't feel like making the dough from scratch, I sometimes use frozen puff pastry—a delicious substitute, if a little recherché.

Knishes aren't exactly a side dish—more like a snack—but I think they are the rightful accompaniment to any deli-style sandwich. Just the other day I saw someone order a potato knish "special" from a cart on Washington Square. The vendor split it in half, squirted deli mustard inside, and filled it with sauerkraut and sautéed onions. How can you argue with that?

a bissel advice

Such a production? **Really, it isn't. After you make knishes one time you will be a master. The measuring cup trick works (believe me, I've tried a lot of tricks). If you still think it's too much of a hassle, you can substitute frozen puff pastry for the dough with delicious results.**

2 large eggs

½ teaspoon kosher salt

3 tablespoons plus ¼ teaspoon Chicken Schmaltz (page 236) or butter, melted and cooled, or peanut oil

1 teaspoon baking powder

1⅓ cups plus 1 tablespoon unbleached all-purpose flour

About 2 cups savory filling, chilled (see pages 220 to 225)

1 egg yolk beaten with 1 teaspoon water

2 teaspoons poppy or sesame seeds (optional)

SPECIAL EQUIPMENT

5-inch and 2½-inch round cutters (for large knishes), or 4-inch round cutter (for miniature knishes)

kosher status Depends on the filling. Note that if you use a dairy filling in the hopes of making a kosher knish, be sure not to use schmaltz in the dough. Likewise with meat knishes and butter. You're safely pareve with peanut oil.

In a small bowl, beat together the eggs and salt with a fork. Beat in 3 tablespoons of the fat. Add the baking powder and all of the flour, and stir to form a dough. Turn out onto a lightly floured work surface and knead for 3 or 4 minutes, until the dough is smooth and elastic. Shape into a ball. Place the remaining ¼ teaspoon of fat in a small, clean bowl and place the ball of dough in the bowl, turning it once or twice to coat with the fat. Cover with plastic wrap and let sit at room temperature for about 1 hour while you prepare your filling.

Grease a cookie sheet or line with parchment paper. Divide the dough in half; keep covered the piece that you are not working with to prevent drying.

To make large knishes: Roll out the dough as thin as possible—it should be almost transparent. Cut out four 5-inch circles and four 2½-inch circles. Then roll out the scraps and cut out another one of each. (You can reroll the scraps only once; after that, the dough gets too tough to handle.) Place one of the large circles of dough into a ½-cup measuring cup or a container of similar size and shape, gently stretching the dough if necessary to create a ¼-inch overhang. Spoon about 3 tablespoons of filling into the center of the cup and gently pack down to fill out the cup shape. Lay one of the smaller circles of dough on top of the filling. Wet your finger by dipping it into a bowl of cold water and moisten the circumference of the smaller disk of dough. Fold the overhang of dough toward the center disk and seal to form a complete package. Invert the cup onto the cookie sheet, being sure the dough remains sealed. Tuck under any edges of dough that flare out. Repeat with the remaining dough. Cover with plastic wrap and refrigerate about 2 hours before baking.

To make miniature knishes: Roll out the dough as thin as possible. Cut into as many 4-inch circles as possible. Then roll out the scraps and cut out however many more you can. You should have about 2 dozen. (You can

recipe continues →

knishes

(continued)

reroll the scraps only once; after that, the dough gets too tough to handle.) Place a circle in the palm of your hand. Spoon about 1 tablespoon of filling into the center of the circle. Using a fingertip, dab a tiny bit of cold water around the edge of the circle. Pinch the dough together to envelope the filling and seal. Invert onto the cookie sheet to produce a plump, round cushion with the pinched seam tucked underneath. Very gently tap the top of the knish down to flatten slightly, and if necessary coax the sides into a nice round shape. Repeat with the remaining circles of dough, and then roll out the remaining portions of dough until everything is used up. Depending on how efficiently you cut your circles, you should have between 20 and 24 miniature knishes arranged evenly on the cookie sheet. Cover with plastic wrap and refrigerate about 2 hours before baking.

If you are making the knishes in advance, you can prepare them to this point and freeze them on the cookie sheet. Once frozen solid, transfer them to a resealable bag and bake as needed. You do not need to defrost them before baking but they will require more time in the oven.

To bake, preheat the oven to 400°F. Brush the knishes with the beaten egg yolk and sprinkle with the seeds, if using. Poke a small hole in the top of each knish to allow the steam to escape. Bake in the preheated oven for about 15 minutes, until the knishes brown, puff up, and are heated through. An instant-read thermometer inserted into the center of a knish should reach 180°F. degrees when finished. Don't be alarmed if some of the filling has seeped out (I find potato has a tendency to escape); the finished knishes are no less delicious.

Remove from the oven and cool slightly before transferring to a rack. Knishes are best eaten fresh. If necessary, store refrigerated in an airtight container and reheat in a 300°F. oven for 10 minutes before serving.

chicken salad

AS FAR AS I'M CONCERNED, THIS IS THE best (some would say the only) use for soup chicken, the stringy texture of which makes it unappetizing unless it's cut up into little pieces. You can also use leftover roasted or stewed chicken. This is just a basic recipe, but you can use it as a springboard for creativity. I add pickled green tomatoes and chopped scallions if I have them. Play around with different pickles: Kosher Dills (page 204), Bread-and-Butter Pickles (page 206), gherkins (from the grocery store). You can add dried fruit and nuts, hard-boiled eggs, sun-dried tomatoes, jalapeños—you name it. My tastes tend toward simplicity, however, so usually I just leave well enough alone.

a bissel advice
What if I don't have any soup chicken? Any cooked, leftover chicken will work fine.

MAKES **6** CUPS, ABOUT **10** SERVINGS

kosher status FLEISHIG

In a mixing bowl, combine the chicken, celery, onion, mayonnaise, pickles, parsley, salt, and pepper, and mix well. Don't overmix the salad or the chicken will completely fall apart. Cover and chill a couple of hours or overnight before serving so that the flavors have a chance to blend.

1½ to 1¾ pounds cooked chicken, diced (about 5 cups) and chilled

2 large celery stalks, finely chopped (about ¾ cup)

½ large red onion (about 4 ounces), finely chopped (about ⅔ cup)

¾ to 1 cup Hellmann's (or Best Foods) mayonnaise, or to taste

2 large dill pickles (about 7 ounces), finely chopped

2 tablespoons chopped fresh Italian parsley

1 teaspoon kosher salt

½ teaspoon freshly ground black pepper

egg salad

CALLED "CHOPPED EGG" IN THE Jewish dairy restaurants where I grew up, egg salad is one of those things that is easy to make good but difficult to make great. I think a great egg salad results from a combination of factors: properly cooked hard-boiled eggs, actually chopping the eggs, Hellmann's mayonnaise, fresh parsley and chives, and plenty of salt. To properly cook the eggs means that they don't have any of that unsightly and unpleasant gray ring around the yolk. I use a boil-and-sit method to ensure they aren't overcooked. Chopping the eggs rather than pureeing them in a food processor or mashing them with a fork gives the finished salad a good, toothsome texture. (Chop your eggs by hand for chopped liver, too.) One of the great sandwiches at Eisenberg Sandwich Shop in Manhattan is the combination egg and tuna salad sandwich on toasted rye—which has enough filling for three ordinary sandwiches. Use this recipe as a starting block for your own great egg salad.

a bissel advice

What's in the egg salad at the Second Avenue Deli? **They sometimes make an egg salad with sautéed mushrooms and onions in it. To simulate it, use my recipe, omitting the celery, chives or shallots, and parsley and substituting instead ¾ cup chilled Mushrooms and Onions (page 244).**

8 large eggs

1 large celery stalk, finely chopped (½ cup)

10 to 12 chives, finely chopped, or 1 small
shallot, minced (2 to 3 tablespoons)

3 tablespoons chopped flat-leaf parsley

½ teaspoon kosher salt

Pinch of freshly ground black pepper

½ cup Hellmann's (or Best Foods)
mayonnaise

SPECIAL EQUIPMENT

Wooden chopping bowl with handheld metal
chopper or egg slicer

Place the eggs in a small saucepan and cover with cold water. Set over high heat and bring to a boil. As soon as the water boils, turn off the heat, cover the pan, and set a timer for 20 minutes. After exactly 20 minutes, place the pan under cold running water, and as soon as the eggs are cool enough to handle, peel.

To chop the eggs, I like to use one of two methods: I place the eggs in a wooden chopping bowl, and, using a handheld chopping blade, I chop them until the whites are in a uniform, tiny dice, but not mushy. Alternatively, I use an egg slicer to slice the eggs. Then I transfer half the sliced egg, yolk side down, to the cutting board. Using a sharp paring knife, I chop the egg like an onion, cutting thin strips first one way and then the other to produce a fine, uniform dice. The secret is to actually cut the white instead of mashing it (i.e., with a fork), and this holds true for any recipe that calls for chopped egg. I am not a fan of egg salad mousse, which I think is what you get when you overchop your eggs or use anything like a food processor to do the chopping for you. Once all of the eggs are uniformly chopped, add the celery, chives or shallot, parsley, salt, pepper, and mayonnaise. Stir with a fork to blend. Refrigerate until ready to serve. Egg salad will keep just under a week in the refrigerator.

tuna salad

IT SEEMS FUNNY TO TAKE UP SPACE in a Jewish cookbook with a recipe for tuna salad, but I get so many compliments on mine—and conversely I've been served so many poor renditions—that I thought I should include it. My mother still makes a tuna salad at least once a week. Every time tuna goes on sale she buys a dozen or so cans. At one time I was sure that if there was a nuclear holocaust, we could live on tuna until the half-life of uranium had expired.

You can't use just any tuna, either. My mother and my sister Carrie react to "light" tuna the way a gourmet might respond to a plate of worms. "It's cat food," Carrie will screech as she averts her nose from the offending smell and tries to stop herself from retching. Although it doesn't gross me out in the same way, for a few extra cents, splurging on white-meat tuna seems worth it.

Then there is the question of oil or water. I have read two studies that suggest that the actual difference in calories from fat in tuna packed in water versus tuna packed in oil is negligible in the finished tuna salad. This should be good news for anyone who finds him- or herself choking on tuna salad made from tuna packed in water. There is no question when it comes to the selection of mayonnaise: it's Hellmann's or nothing. Let me point out to you that Kraft Miracle Whip is not mayonnaise and should never darken the pantry of a serious (Jewish) cook.

There is the option of purchasing jars of exorbitantly priced tuna packed in olive oil imported from Italy or Spain. But this is usually so moist it should just be eaten plain on a salad niçoise or something like that; drowning it in Hellmann's just doesn't seem right.

As for garnishes, I've been known to stir some crazy things into my tuna salad. Celery and fresh lemon juice are musts, as far as my family and I are concerned, but onion or shallot and chopped egg are optional. Finely chopped dill pickles or green olives are tasty, too. A tablespoon or two of freshly chopped parsley is a nice touch. Experiment at your own risk.

a bissel advice

Chilled tuna straight from the can? My sister's trick for tuna salad in a jiffy (actually it's a trick from her friend André) is to keep a couple of cans of tuna in the fridge at all times. That way you are always ready to make tuna salad, and it's already chilled.

kosher status PAREVE

2 (6-ounce) cans white tuna, drained

1 or 2 celery stalks, finely chopped

5 to 6 tablespoons Hellmann's (or Best
    Foods) mayonnaise

Juice of 1 to 1½ lemon(s), about 4 or
    5 tablespoons

Pinch of kosher salt

Pinch of freshly ground black pepper

1 small dill pickle, finely chopped *(optional)*

¼ small onion or shallot, minced *(optional)*

1 hard-boiled egg, finely chopped *(optional)*

1 tablespoon freshly chopped parsley
    (optional)

place the drained tuna in a small mixing bowl. Using a fork, flake it so that no large chunks remain. Add the celery, 5 tablespoons of the mayonnaise, the lemon juice, salt, and pepper, as well as the chopped pickle, onion or shallot, egg, and parsley (if using). Stir with the fork to blend. Depending on how moist the tuna is and how much of the optional stuff you are or are not using, you may need to add an additional tablespoon of mayonnaise. If you have the time to let the tuna salad chill for a couple of hours, the flavors will have a chance to blend. But it can be eaten right away. Adjust the seasoning before serving. Tuna salad can be kept in the refrigerator for about 5 days.

whitefish salad

THE METALLIC GOLDEN-BRONZE SKIN of the whole smoked fish in the refrigerated counter of Jewish appetizing shops shines like a beacon for Sunday brunch. What can transform a dreary Sunday morning into a time of joyous celebration more effectively than the appearance of a smoked whitefish or some of its smaller cousins, ciscoes and chubs? (Okay, so hot bialies, strong coffee, and the *New York Times* can help, too, but haven't they fallen into the realm of the quotidian already?) I'd say the popularity of smoked whitefish salad in bagel shops around the country speaks to this delicacy's delicacy.

a bissel advice

How do I get the smell of smoked fish off my hands? That's a tough one. The only thing that seems to work is washing your hands with fresh lemon juice. Be sure you don't have any open cuts on your hands, or you'll hit the ceiling when the lemon juice comes into contact with them.

But this isn't like the whitefish salad at my bagel shop on the corner? Nope. For that type of whitefish salad, more like a spread, really, prepare the sardine spread on page 35 but substitute 6 ounces (1½ cups) of smoked whitefish meat for the sardines.

Oy, my arteries! For a lower fat version, substitute ⅔ cup nonfat buttermilk for the mayonnaise and omit the lemon juice. This produces a light, tangy whitefish salad that I think is almost as good as the full-fat version.

For fancy luncheons, my mother used to buy a large smoked whitefish. She'd remove the meat and bones while keeping the shell, the head, tail, and skin intact. Then she'd make a salad with the meat and stuff it back into the skin to serve like a gefilte (or "stuffed") fish true to its name. Place a sprig of curly parsley where the eye used to be and you have an elegant Jewish luncheon entree. My sister Carrie occasionally treats a whitefish in this way, too. Since I don't seem to host luncheons, I just make a big container of whitefish salad and keep it in the fridge to spread on my toasted bagel in the morning.

to begin, you must flake the whitefish. If you intend to serve the salad stuffed back in the skin, than you must very carefully remove the flesh and bones from the fish, paying attention not to tear the skin as you pull it back and keeping the head and tail intact. If you are planning to serve the salad in a platter or bowl, you can just peel off the skin indiscriminately. The flesh will vary in thickness and density in different areas of the fish, as will the concentration of bones. To flake the fish, I like to mush it between my fingertips, breaking it into small pieces and removing any bones I see or feel as I work. Some pieces don't break easily into flakes, and so these I chop finely with a knife. I get about 1 pound 2 ounces (2½ to 3 cups) of flaked meat from a 2-pound smoked fish.

Once the meat is flaked and the bones have been removed, add the celery, scallions or chives, parsley, lemon juice, mayonnaise, black pepper, and chopped eggs (if using). Stir to combine, and adjust the seasoning to taste. The salad is best after it sits for a couple of hours in the refrigerator so the flavors have time to meld.

To serve inside the fish shell, be sure the inside of the fish is cleaned of any stray bones. Lay the fish on its side on a bed of lettuce arranged on a serving platter. Spoon the salad into the cavity to approximate the original shape of the fish. If there is too much salad, it's fine to let it spill out of the belly. You can hide any tears in the skin with sprigs of parsley or fresh chives.

1 (2-pound) whole smoked whitefish, or a combination of whitefish, ciscoes, and chubs

2 celery stalks, finely chopped

2 scallions or a small handful of chives, finely chopped

8 to 10 sprigs parsley, stems removed, finely chopped

Juice of 2 lemons (about 3 tablespoons)

¾ cup Hellmann's (or Best Foods) mayonnaise

¼ teaspoon freshly ground black pepper

2 hard-boiled large eggs, finely chopped (optional)

herring in sour cream with potatoes and beans

THIS IS A VARIATION OF CLASSIC HERRING in sour cream with onions, a little more fancy because of the addition of beans, potatoes, dill, and Dijon mustard. The combination is totally flexible, and you can play around with whatever ingredients you like. Apple adds sweetness and crunch, but adding it decreases the shelf-life of the dish. A touch of horseradish adds zing. Be creative.

When I was in Amsterdam recently with my sister Leslie, we stumbled upon an outdoor market. At one end of the market was a stall around which twenty or so young schoolchildren were gathered. They were all rather impatiently waiting their turn to buy some snack that looked like a hot dog—at least it was handed to them on a hot dog bun. Never willing to pass up an interesting food opportunity, we got on line. What the snack turned out to be was herring on a hot dog bun. The idea of American schoolchildren lining up for a herring sandwich seemed quite funny to us.

a bissel advice

So many options? As I said, this is a salad, so you can put in whatever you want. I happen to think it is best with all of the ingredients I've listed, but you may disagree.

What if I want to use the apple but I want to keep the herring around for a while? Just add a little chopped apple to the herring salad when you eat it. Then you can store it for up to 8 days.

What type of herring? Jarred herring is made by many companies and comes in many varieties. Herring in wine sauce is pickled herring in a clear, mildly acidic sauce commercially prepared. Herring in sour cream is just what it sounds like. As far as I can tell, the only difference between the brands is the seasoning of the cure. Once you find one you like, use it for whatever herring dish you are making.

place the diced potato in a small saucepan, cover with water, and bring to a boil. Reduce the heat to a simmer and cook just until the potato is tender, but not to the point that it falls apart, about 15 minutes. Cool.

Meanwhile, in a large mixing bowl, combine the herring with the beans, onion, and pickle, as well as the chopped eggs, apple, and dill (if using). Add the cooked and cooled potato, the pinch of salt, and a couple of grinds of fresh pepper. Toss.

In a small bowl, stir together the sour cream, Dijon mustard, horseradish (if using), and lemon juice. Add the sour cream mixture to the herring mixture and stir to combine. If possible, let sit overnight so the flavors have a chance to meld.

Without the chopped apple, the herring can be stored in the refrigerator for about 1 week. With the chopped apple, it should be eaten within 2 days.

1 small Yukon Gold or Russet potato
   (6 ounces), peeled and diced
1 (1-pound) jar herring in wine sauce, drained
   and cut into bite-size pieces
½ cup cooked white beans, such as
   cannellini or northern beans (you can
   use the beans from the Bean Salad on
   page 136, or canned) (optional)
½ large yellow or white onion (¼ pound),
   finely chopped
1 dill pickle (about 2 ounces), finely chopped
2 hard-boiled eggs, chopped (optional)
½ large Golden Delicious or Gala apple,
   peeled and chopped (optional)
2 teaspoons chopped fresh dill (optional)
Pinch of kosher salt
Freshly ground black pepper to taste
¾ cup sour cream
2 tablespoons Dijon mustard
1 teaspoon white Horseradish (page 202)
   (optional)
Juice of ½ lemon (about 2 tablespoons)

MENTAL NOSH

Although herring is one of the most popular fishes in the world and was once the most plentiful, it is underappreciated in America. Many species of herring call the North Atlantic home, and they vary in size and shape. They are oily fish that are traditionally cured in a variety of ways, including smoking (kippers), salting (Swedish Süstromming), pickling (Bismarck and Rollmops), and many others. Herring are also eaten grilled or fried.

herring salad with apple, walnuts, and beets

HERE'S A PAREVE ALTERNATIVE to herring in sour cream that has a light oil-and-vinegar dressing. The pretty color and earthy flavor of the beets and the sweetness and crunch of the apple make for an excellent combination with the pickled fish. The salad is best if allowed to chill overnight, but it can also be eaten as soon as it is prepared.

a bissel advice

What rules apply? **The same as those given for the Herring in Sour Cream recipe on page 32.**

¼ cup white vinegar (5 percent acidity)

3 tablespoons sugar

¼ cup peanut or vegetable oil

Pinch of kosher salt

1 (1-pound) jar herring in wine sauce, drained

2 medium (¾ pound) cooked beets (see page 248), diced

½ red onion (¼ pound), thinly sliced

½ sweet, crisp apple (3 ounces), such as Golden Delicious, Cortland, or Empire, peeled and diced

½ teaspoon caraway seeds

¼ cup coarsely chopped fresh Italian parsley

3 tablespoons chopped walnuts

MAKES 4 TO 6 SERVINGS

kosher status PAREVE

In a small mixing bowl, combine the vinegar and sugar. Whisk for a minute or two, until the sugar has completely dissolved. Continue whisking and beat in the oil in a steady stream. Add a pinch of salt. Set aside.

In another bowl, combine the herring, beets, red onion, apple, caraway, and parsley. Toss to mix. Beat the dressing once or twice and pour over the salad. Toss to coat. If possible, let the salad sit, covered, in the refrigerator overnight.

Before serving, heat a small frying pan over medium-high heat. Put the chopped walnuts into the hot, dry pan and toast for 5 to 7 minutes, swirling the pan around from time to time, until you can smell a distinct toasted nut smell. Sprinkle the herring salad with the toasted walnuts.

sardine spread

THIS ONIONY CONCOCTION WAS A STAPLE for sandwiches and canapés in my house. My

mother was always using sardine spread in roly-poly pinwheel sandwiches for company. It is delicious on bagels.

If you substitute smoked whitefish for the sardines, you make something that approximates the whitefish "salad"

served at bagel shops throughout

New York City.

a bissel advice

**What if I hate sardines? The cream cheese and lemon really
take the edge off of the sardines, making this a sardine spread
for people who don't think they like sardines. If you still can't
stand them, use 6 ounces (1½ cups) of flaked smoked whitefish
instead.**

MAKES 1½ CUPS, **6** SERVINGS

kosher status MILCHIG

4 (6.5 ounce) cans skinless and boneless
    sardines packed in olive oil, drained
6 ounces cream cheese, at room temperature
1 small shallot or a small piece of onion,
    minced (about 3 tablespoons)
Juice of 1 lemon (3 tablespoons)

Place the drained sardines and cream cheese in a bowl and mix with a
wooden spoon until evenly combined. Add the shallot or onion and
lemon juice and continue mixing until blended. Chill before using.

chapter 2

soups

If It's Tuesday, It Must Be Cabbage Borscht

Although matzo is probably the most sacred Jewish

food, I wonder if second place doesn't go to soup. Can you have a Jewish holiday without chicken soup? What would a meal in a delicatessen be without a cup or a bowl of the soup du jour? When I was a kid I could tell you what day of the week it was based on what soup I smelled cooking at our local deli (Tuesday was cabbage borscht, Thursday, navy bean.) Soup holds a preeminent place in Jewish cuisine. It brings people together—quickly: "Come let's eat, right away before the soup gets cold." Soup gets the juices flowing. It makes you warm when it's cold outside. It's also a good way to use up stray vegetables, handfuls of beans, bones, and pieces of meat.

THERE ARE MYRIAD VARIETIES OF SOUP—whole books written about them, in fact. But the basic principle is almost always the same: Combine onions and other aromatic vegetables with some sort of meat, some starch such as beans or barley or potatoes, a few herbs or spices, and cover it all with cold water. Bring it to a boil and cook it a long time. If you can let the soup sit overnight before you serve it, you're almost guaranteed success.

THERE SEEMS TO BE A PROSCRIPTION IN JEWISH COOKING against serving anything as simple as a bowl of broth. Chicken soup gets matzo balls or kreplach or lokshen or at least some vegetables. Other soups are usually left chunky and thick. Nothing as recherché as pureeing a soup and passing it through a fine sieve, as is often done in French cuisine, feels appropriate.

THIS CHAPTER CONTAINS A FEW RECIPES for classic Jewish soups. Follow them to the letter or use them as inspiration to invent your own.

chicken soup

JEWISH PENICILLIN — THE CURE for whatever ails you. Since Jews eat so much chicken soup, it's surprising they are forever kvetching about their health. In the Jewish community and outside of it, chicken soup is iconic. A bowl of matzo ball soup is served at the start of just about every holiday meal. And the quality of it in some ways determines the spiritual openness of the participants in the event. I find nothing more comforting or satisfying or soothing than a steaming bowl of nature's medicine.

There are just about as many ways to prepare chicken soup as there are *bubbes*. Mimi Sheraton even wrote an entire award-winning book on the subject, *The Whole World Loves Chicken Soup,* which provides recipes and lore from around the world. I make a slightly different soup from my mother's because I add a different mix of vegetables to the pot. There are some things she does that are sacred, however. A good soup starts with a good chicken, and there is nothing like an old, tired stewing hen or pullet for soup. This is not some young, plump fryer hussy. It's an old bird that you probably wouldn't buy if you saw it on display in the grocery store. That's why you usually have to order them from a butcher. For added flavor I throw in a couple of chicken necks if I have them saved from roasting chickens. (Keep them in a bag in the freezer until you have to make a pot of soup.) And if I can get a couple of chicken feet from my butcher, which are high in collagen and give the soup a rich flavor and texture, I chop off the claws and add those, too.

The best soup — by which I mean the darkest, richest, most healthful and flavorful soup — requires a high proportion of chicken and vegetables to water. If you skimp, you end up with salty water. Although some recipes have you boil the chicken first and then add the vegetables, my mother just threw everything in the pot and let 'er rip. I find the results of this technique better than acceptable — they're delicious. I use the boiled chicken meat for Chicken Salad (page 25), but I

a bissel advice

But what to serve in it? In addition to the Vegetable Garnish (page 40), you should have some sort of starch. I like Egg Noodles (lokshen, page 240), Kreplach (Jewish wontons, page 46), Matzo Balls (knaidlach, page 41), Mandlen (soup puffs, page 260), Farfel (toasted egg noodles, page 110), cooked barley, rice — you name it.

What about all that chicken? I happen to love soup chicken but some people think it is mealy and tasteless. I sometimes cut up some of it to serve with the soup. More often I use it to make Chicken Salad (page 25). A 4½-pound soup chicken will give you 1½ to 1¾ pounds (5 cups) cooked chicken.

dump out the vegetables, spices, and herbs that are cooked to make the broth: they end up over-cooked and mushy, having given all of their soul to the broth. If I want to serve the soup with some vegetables in it as garnish, I cook those after the fact in some boiling broth. If I think I might want to set aside some of the soup for chicken stock, I don't put the dill in the soup until I reheat it to serve: the dill gives the soup a distinct flavor that might not work well in whatever I use the stock for.

When I have room in my refrigerator and enough storage containers lying around, I make the soup a day or two in advance. You can also freeze it for up to a month in advance. Either way, this helps make skimming easy because you can simply lift off the fat that congeals at the top once it is chilled.

MAKES 3½ TO 4 QUARTS SOUP, ABOUT 16 TO 20 SERVINGS

kosher status FLEISHIG

place the quartered chicken, necks or feet (if using), onions, celery, parsley root or parsley, carrots, turnip, parsnip, peppercorns, star anise, and salt in a 12-quart stockpot. Add 5 quarts (20 cups) of cold water and set over high heat to boil, about 30 minutes. Turn down the heat to a simmer, set the cover ajar on top of the pot, and allow to cook for 2 hours, using a large spoon to skim off any scum that rises to the surface. Add the dill and simmer an additional 45 minutes. Turn off the heat and allow to cool.

When cool enough to handle, ladle the soup through a fine sieve into storage containers. Chill overnight. To serve, remove any fat that has con-gealed on the top of the soup. Reheat to boiling. Adjust the seasoning with salt and pepper.

1 (4½ pound) soup chicken, stewing hen, or roasting chicken, cut into quarters and rinsed

2 or 3 chicken necks or chicken feet, claws removed *(optional)*

4 large yellow onions (2 pounds), roughly chopped

8 celery stalks (1 pound), with leaves, roughly chopped

1 parsley root (½ pound) with top, cleaned and roughly chopped, or about 10 sprigs flat-leaf parsley

7 to 8 carrots (1½ pounds), peeled and halved

1 medium turnip (½ pound), peeled and roughly chopped

1 medium parsnip (½ pound), peeled and roughly chopped

1 tablespoon whole black peppercorns

1 small point of a star anise

2 tablespoons kosher salt

6 sprigs fresh dill

SPECIAL EQUIPMENT
12-quart stockpot

vegetable garnish for chicken soup

Use any combinations of vegetables that you want to enhance the look and flavor of the soup. Below is the combination I usually prepare. When the vegetables are finished cooking, just dump everything—the cooking liquid and the cooked vegetables—back into the larger pot of soup and keep warm until you are ready to serve.

6 cups Chicken Soup (page 38)

3 medium carrots (½ pound), sliced ⅛ inch thick

1 medium turnip (½ pound), cut into ⅓-inch dice

2 celery stalks (¼ pound), cut crosswise into ¼-inch slices

5 sprigs fresh dill, chopped (1½ tablespoons)

MAKES ENOUGH GARNISH FOR **10** PORTIONS, WHICH WILL LEAVE SOME SOUP LEFT OVER TO COOK WITH

kosher status FLEISHIG

In a medium saucepan, bring the chicken soup to a boil. Add the sliced carrots and diced turnip, and cook for 30 minutes. Add the celery and cook about 15 more minutes, until all of the vegetables are tender. Add the dill. Return the soup and cooked vegetables to the larger pot of soup and keep warm until ready to serve.

matzo balls

ALTHOUGH MATZO BALLS OR *KNAIDLACH* (pronounced KNAYD-luhkh) bear a slight resemblance to gefilte fish, that's where the similarity ends. A matzo ball is really nothing more than a Passover-friendly variation of an Eastern European bread dumpling. In fact, matzo balls were originally made *only* during Passover, but they have become so popular that now it's hard to imagine a bowl of chicken soup at any time of year without them.

Up there with Brillat-Savarin's great tests of culinary discernment should be whether you prefer your matzo balls as "floaters" or "sinkers." Floaters are light and airy. They are held together with a gentle tension that gives way after you apply ever-so-little pressure with the edge of your spoon. Sinkers are heavy and dense. Their core is solid. Sometimes a knife is required. I am not making any judgments of merit—both have their place. (And one's preference usually stems from a famil-iarity with one's mother's or grandmother's version.) I prefer matzo balls the way my mother makes them, like puffy clouds. She, on the other hand, prefers them like cannon balls.

Although the ingredients are pretty much the same for both floaters and sinkers, my family has determined that the textural differences result from four factors: the ratio of egg to matzo meal, how long the mixture sits in the refrigerator, the way the matzo balls are handled once they are cooked, and divine inspiration. Whether you use schmaltz (rendered chicken fat) or oil as the fat also makes a difference—oil produces a heavier matzo ball, and the flavor isn't nearly as good. (Similarly, if you use water instead of chicken soup, you will forgo some of the nuance of the flavor.) Butter is permissible, but if you keep kosher you had better not put your buttered matzo balls in chicken soup.

I have stumbled across a couple of techniques that I think produce delicious matzo-ball results, each with its own merits. There is my mother's version, which I think of as "basic" because that is my

MENTAL NOSH

For the last three years, Ben's, a chain of kosher restaurants around New York City, has held an annual matzo-ball eating contest in the beginning of February. The contest is sanctioned by the International Federation of Competitive Eating, a regulatory body that requires contestants to sign a "no vomiting" clause. The record was set in 1999 by Bruce D. Stock, who ate 13 matzo balls in 5 minutes and 25 seconds. Funny thing is, I feel like I've had that many myself on occasion.

recipe continues →

matzo balls

(continued)

reference point. On good days, they are tender and light. I have also made one based on an old recipe for matzo kleis, or "dumplings," that starts with whole matzos. These are about the most flavorful matzo balls I've ever had, although they tend to be dense. Think of them as sinkers.

I should also note that even by following the directions for both of these variations to the letter, because of that fourth factor (referred to in Hebrew as *adonay*), your floaters may still turn out on the heavy side. Years ago, my sister and I tried to mimic my mother's technique, right down to using the same bowls and pots, with disappointing results. For a while we were sure she was forgetting to tell us a step or two. But then once we had made them several times—once we had the music in our bones, and we didn't have to concentrate on getting the notes right, so to speak—we were able to produce cloudlike puffs just like our mother's.

Common wisdom says that matzo balls are best made as close to service as possible. I'm not so sure. I kind of like the water-logged flavor and texture of matzo balls that have sat for a day in the soup. (My mother disagrees.) Either way, they should be transferred into simmering soup as soon as they are cooked. Whether or not you then serve them right away or wait a day is up to you. Leftover matzo balls are delicious drained, sliced, and fried in butter with onions as a breakfast side dish. To prepare the matzo balls more than a day or two in advance, remove them from the cooking liquid and let them drain on a cookie sheet. Freeze them on the sheet until they are firm, and then transfer them to a resealable plastic bag. Defrost them in simmering soup directly from the freezer.

a bissel advice

Can I make them in advance? Matzo balls can be made in advance and stored in a couple of ways. The easiest is to keep them refrigerated in the soup. (As I've said in the introductory notes, I prefer them this way.) They will get heavier than when they were first made, but they will remain flavorful. If you want to freeze the matzo balls, remove them from the cooking water after the full 35 to 40 minutes' cooking time, and lay them on a cookie sheet to cool. Freeze on the cookie sheet until firm, then transfer to a resealable plastic bag. To reheat, place the frozen matzo balls directly into the cold soup and bring to a gentle boil. Reduce the soup to a simmer and cook until heated through.

Why so small? Make them as big as you like, but remember the bigger they are the fewer you will get. If you make them the size they serve at the Carnegie Deli, this recipe makes only two or three matzo balls!

basic matzo balls

THIS IS AN APPROXIMATION of the matzo ball recipe my mother always uses. It is based on the one on the Manischewitz matzo meal box, but with a few important modifications to account for my mother's heavy hand with the schmaltz and her inexact measuring technique. Whatever you do, don't work too hard to shape them into balls—rolling the matzo balls around for too long in the palm of your hands toughens them up. Instead, coax them into a spherical shape, and don't be too anal about it. Also, be sure to have the chicken soup simmering when the matzo balls are ready, so you can put them straight into the hot soup.

MAKES **10** TO **12** MEDIUM-SIZE MATZO BALLS

kosher status FLEISHIG, if made with schmaltz and chicken soup
PAREVE, if made with oil and water
MILCHIG, if made with butter
PESADICH

the whole meshpucha
You can double or triple this recipe as needed. (You can halve it, too.) Just be careful not to crowd the pot you are cooking the matzo balls in or they will not cook properly.

5 large eggs

1 teaspoon kosher salt

3 tablespoons Chicken Schmaltz (page 236), butter, or peanut oil, at room temperature

4 tablespoons hot chicken soup or water

1 cup plus 2 tablespoons matzo meal

Combine the eggs, salt, schmaltz, and soup or water in a mixing bowl and whisk until blended. Whisk in the matzo meal and beat until smooth. Let set in the refrigerator for 30 minutes, up to 2 hours for sinkers.

Bring about 5 quarts of water to a boil with 1½ tablespoons of kosher salt. Remove the matzo ball mixture from the refrigerator. Wet your hands with cold water and shape a heaping tablespoonful of the mixture into a ball in the palm of your hands. Coax the matzo ball into a sphere. Rolling it too tightly will prevent it from achieving its puffiest. Drop into the boiling water and repeat with the remaining mixture, wetting your hands as necessary to keep the matzo balls from sticking. Bring the pot back to a boil, turn down the heat to a simmer, cover tightly, and cook for an additional 35 to 40 minutes, until the matzo balls have risen from the bottom of the pot and have blown up to about twice their original size. Occasionally, a matzo ball or two will stick on the bottom of the pot. Give it a nudge with a spoon to loosen. Using a slotted spoon, remove the matzo balls from the boiling water and place them directly into the simmering chicken soup.

matzo matzo balls

NO, THAT RECIPE TITLE ISN'T A TYPO. Unlike the Basic Matzo Balls on page 43, these matzo balls are made from whole matzos, with a little matzo meal to hold them together. For best results, use salted matzo, whether plain, egg, or egg and onion.

I like to cook these matzo balls just before they are served. They should be transferred from the cooking liquid directly into the simmering soup (you can keep them for a few hours this way). But if you have to make them in advance, you can shape the balls up to a day before you intend to serve them, cover them in plastic wrap, and refrigerate until you are ready to cook them.

6 matzos, broken in half

6 tablespoons Chicken Schmaltz (page 236),
    unsalted butter, or peanut oil

1 medium yellow onion (6 ounces), finely
    chopped

1½ teaspoons kosher salt

¼ teaspoon freshly ground black pepper

4 large eggs

7 to 8 tablespoons matzo meal

MAKES ABOUT **16** MATZO BALLS

kosher status FLEISHIG, if made with schmaltz and chicken soup
PAREVE, if made with oil and water
MILCHIG, if made with butter
PESADICH

place the matzos in a wide bowl and cover with cold water.

Heat the fat over medium-high heat in a large frying pan and sauté the chopped onion until translucent, about 8 minutes. Add the salt and pepper.

Meanwhile, drain the matzo in a sieve. Using your fingertips, press the matzo against the sides of the sieve to squeeze out water. This will also break the matzo up into tiny pieces. Add the squeezed matzo to the onions in the frying pan. Continue sautéing for 5 to 7 minutes to heat through. Remove from the heat and transfer to a bowl. Let cool 10 to 15 minutes. Stir in the eggs along with 6 tablespoons of the matzo meal. The mixture should be thick enough to hold its shape but not clump. Add more matzo meal if necessary. Refrigerate uncovered for about 1 hour.

Bring 5 quarts of water with 1½ tablespoons kosher salt to a boil. Wet your hands with cold water. Gently shape heaping tablespoonfuls of the matzo mixture into balls and drop into the boiling water. When the water comes back to a boil, turn down the heat to a simmer. Cover and let cook for 25 minutes, until the matzo balls double in size and are cooked through. Using a slotted spoon, remove from the liquid and place them in the soup.

lima bean and barley soup

THIS WAS A SOUP MY great-grandmother Eva used to make—soup was one of her specialties. My mother always marvels at how much her grandmother seemed to know about nutrition. For example, she would use the nutrient-rich water from cooking vegetables as the liquid for her soups. In the hopes of invoking her spirit for this book,

I've started saving my vegetable cooking water to do just that. The resulting soups have a deep flavor that is in many ways superior to soups made with plain water. I've also begun rendering the fat I trim off of brisket and other beef (see page 58). It makes for a pretty good soup, too.

As my mother remembers it, her grandmother used to make this soup with a dried black mushroom that gave it a haunting, earthy flavor. I'm guessing it was something like dried Chinese shiitake, but who knows.

MAKES JUST OVER **2** QUARTS, ABOUT **8** SERVINGS

kosher status FLEISHIG
TRAIF, if made with butter

heat the fat in the bottom of a small stockpot set over medium-high heat. Add the onion and sauté until translucent, about 7 minutes. Add the celery and continue cooking until tender, 3 or 4 minutes more. Add the carrots, barley, shiitakes, lima beans, beef shank, and marrow bones (if using), along with 2 quarts of vegetable cooking liquid or cold water. Add the salt, pepper, and bay leaf. Bring the soup to a boil and skim off any scum that rises to the top. Reduce the heat to a simmer, cover, and let cook for 2 hours, until the meat and the lima beans are just about tender. Add the green beans and continue cooking for another 15 minutes or so. Remove the bay leaf. The soup can be eaten right away, but it is better if allowed to sit overnight. If the soup is too thick, add some water to thin it before reheating.

4 tablespoons Beef Schmaltz (page 238), Chicken Schmaltz (page 236), butter, or peanut oil

1 large yellow onion (½ pound), chopped (1 cup)

2 celery stalks (¼ pound), with leaves, chopped (1 cup)

3 large carrots (½ pound), sliced ¼ inch thick

¾ cup pearl barley

5 dried shiitakes (¾ ounce), soaked in warm water until soft, about 30 minutes, drained and thinly sliced

1 cup dried lima beans

1¼ pounds beef shank

1 or 2 marrow bones *(optional)*

1 tablespoon kosher salt

½ teaspoon freshly ground black pepper

1 bay leaf

¼ pound green beans, cut into 1-inch pieces

kreplach

MAYBE THIS LITTLE MEAT-FILLED soup dumpling is the root of the Jewish affinity for Chinese food. After all, what are kreplach but wontons that speak Yiddish? Kreplach might also explain why we like Italian food so much. At a recent holiday dinner, my friend Andrew, who is a great chef at an exclusive restaurant in Manhattan, took one bite of my kreplach and asked, "What's in these ravioli?" The answer is leftovers—leftover brisket, a chicken liver or two from a roast chicken, whatever's lying around. If I'm making my kreplach from scratch, I use my Egg Noodle dough (page 110) and Beef Filling (page 222). Sometimes I cheat and buy wonton wrappers. What's important is to cook the kreplach in salted water, not in the soup, and then transfer them to the soup once they are done. This keeps the soup clear and the kreplach fresh tasting. I like to serve a couple of kreplach in a bowl of chicken soup along with matzo balls.

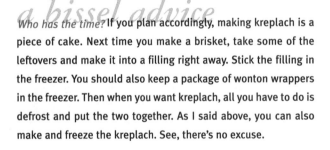

a bissel advice

Who has the time? **If you plan accordingly, making kreplach is a piece of cake. Next time you make a brisket, take some of the leftovers and make it into a filling right away. Stick the filling in the freezer. You should also keep a package of wonton wrappers in the freezer. Then when you want kreplach, all you have to do is defrost and put the two together. As I said above, you can also make and freeze the kreplach. See, there's no excuse.**

6 ounces Egg Noodle dough (½ batch using
    the proportions for 12 ounces lokshen,
    page 110) or 24 wonton wrappers
1 cup (½ batch) Beef Filling (page 222)
2 tablespoons all-purpose flour

SPECIAL EQUIPMENT
3-inch round cutter

If using fresh Egg Noodle dough, roll out as directed for making the noodles, to the thinnest setting on the pasta machine, or as thinly as possible by hand. If using wonton wrappers, lay them out on the work surface. Cut the dough into circles using a 3-inch round cutter. Place a scant teaspoonful of beef filling in the center of each circle. Dip your finger in water and moisten the circumference of the circle. Gather the edges of the circle together to form a small packet that envelopes the filling snugly. Pinch together to seal. Place on a cookie sheet, toss with a sprinkling of flour, and repeat until all of the kreplach are prepared. You can make the kreplach a few hours in advance and keep them in the refrigerator, covered to prevent drying, for about a day. To keep them longer, freeze them on a cookie sheet and then transfer to a resealable plastic bag.

To cook, bring a large pot of salted water (4 quarts water with 1½ tablespoons salt) to a boil. Have the soup warm. Drop the kreplach into the salted water and cook for about 2 minutes once the water comes back up to the boil. If your kreplach are frozen, don't defrost them. Drop them right into the boiling water and cook them about 5 minutes, or until soft. Lift out of the water with a slotted spoon and place in the warm soup.

beef barley soup

WHEN MY SIBLINGS AND I WERE kids (well, really just Leslie and I) we used to live on Campbell's Beef

Barley soup. Although the thought sickens me now, I used to eat it cold out of the can, undiluted! Anyway, the pursuit of

a beef barley soup that was as rich and beefy, but much less salty and canned-tasting, has occupied Leslie for the

better part of her adult life. (Did I mention she's a psychotherapist by trade?) And about two years or so ago, she perfected the recipe. Here it is, a beef barley soup in the style of Campbell's but much more delicious. Leslie likes to think of it in the same vein as real movies with actors playing cartoon characters. As with most soups, it's better if you can make it a day or two in advance.

a bissel advice

What's with removing the vegetables? **After cooking as long as it takes the meat to become tender, the vegetables get water-logged, soggy, and tasteless. That's why Leslie removes the first vegetables halfway through the cooking process and adds new ones for the second half. This is the same reason I have you cook the vegetable garnish for the chicken soup after the broth is made (see page 40).**

What does it mean to pick through the lentils? **Remove any stones or blemished beans. See page 55 for a good technique.**

So much soup? **You can halve the recipe if you'd like and still get great results.**

In a large, heavy-bottomed stockpot, place the onion, the 2 carrots cut into large chunks, the top of the celery, the bay leaf, barley, lentils, parsley, flanken, tomatoes, salt, and pepper. Add 10 cups of cold water and set over medium-high heat. Bring to a boil, skim off any scum that rises to the surface, turn down the heat, cover, and simmer for 2 hours.

After 2 hours, remove the carrots, celery, and parsley with a slotted spoon or tongs and discard. Add the remaining diced carrot, zucchini, green beans, peas, and sliced celery. Continue simmering 1 to 1½ hours, until the meat falls apart and the vegetables are tender. Adjust the seasoning with additional kosher salt and freshly ground black pepper.

If possible, chill the soup for a day or two before serving. Reheat in small portions as necessary. You may have to add a little water to thin it out, but don't do so until the soup is warm and you can actually assess how thick it is going to be. This soup will keep refrigerated for 10 days. It can also be frozen for up to 2 months.

1 large yellow onion (½ pound), diced

4 large carrots (¾ pound), 2 cut into large chunks, 2 diced

1 bunch celery, top half only, with leaves

1 bay leaf

1 cup pearl barley

1½ cups brown lentils, picked over to remove stones

⅓ bunch (12 sprigs) flat-leaf parsley

5 pounds flanken or beef short ribs, rinsed

1 (28-ounce) can tomatoes with juice, cut up into chunks

1½ tablespoons kosher salt

1 teaspoon freshly ground black pepper

1 medium zucchini (½ pound), diced

6 ounces green beans, cut into ½-inch pieces (about 1 cup)

1 cup frozen peas

1 additional celery stalk, sliced

SPECIAL EQUIPMENT

Heavy-gauge 10- to 12-quart stockpot

beefy beet borscht

THE INSPIRATION FOR THIS BORSCHT CAME from the many late-night bowls of crimson soup I've enjoyed at a 24-hour Ukrainian restaurant called Veselka in New York City's erstwhile-bohemian East Village neighborhood. My Polish-born friend Izabela and my Philly friend Barbara also had their hands in its inception. The two predominant flavors are beets and beef, but the other root vegetables add an earthy element that makes it a beet borscht for people who don't think they like beets. The recipe yields a generous (read huge) amount, but since it gets better as it sits in the refrigerator—it will keep about 10 days—and can be frozen, you shouldn't worry about having it around. In fact, for best results, plan to make the borscht a day or two before you intend to serve it.

a bissel advice

Too much soup? You can cut the recipe in half, but don't adjust the cooking time. You may have to add more water as the soup cooks to be sure there is enough liquid to cover the ingredients. Alternately, you can freeze the soup in small, airtight containers for up to two months.

Too heavy? You can lighten the soup by substituting a 4-pound stewing hen or soup chicken for the flanken and omitting the marrow bones. Reduce the cooking time by 45 minutes.

Too much time? Don't try to shorten the cooking time by substituting cooked or canned beets. The resulting soup will be flavorless and mushy, and the meat will be tough. The reason I gave you such a large recipe in the first place was because I figured as long as you are cooking, you may as well make enough to eat for a while.

Something different? You can experiment with a lot of different ingredients. Try adding chunks of potatoes (but remember they don't freeze well), diced Duck Prosciutto (page 20), or wild mushrooms. Stirring a scant teaspoonful of Horseradish (page 202) into the bowl at the table adds a little pizzazz.

5 or 6 pieces flanken or beef short ribs
   (about 4 pounds), with bones, rinsed

3 marrow bones (1 pound) *(optional)*

4 large yellow onions (1½ pounds), sliced

2 garlic cloves, smashed and roughly
   chopped

1 large turnip (½ pound), peeled and cubed

1 large parsnip (½ pound), peeled and cubed

3 medium carrots (½ pound), sliced

12 medium red beets (4 pounds without
   tops), peeled and cut into strips,
   approximately ½ by ½ by 2 inches (like
   French fries)

¼ cup tomato paste

Juice of 8 lemons (about 1¼ cups)

6 to 8 tablespoons sugar, or to taste

1 tablespoon caraway seeds

3 tablespoons kosher salt

2 teaspoons freshly ground black pepper

¼ cup chopped fresh dill (about 1 bunch,
   14 sprigs)

SPECIAL EQUIPMENT

Heavy-gauge 10- to 12-quart stockpot

lace the beef, marrow bones, onions, garlic, turnip, parsnip, carrots, beets, tomato paste, lemon juice, sugar, caraway, salt, and pepper in a 10- or 12-quart stockpot. Add about 4 quarts (16 cups) cold water. (Be sure to leave at least 1 inch of space between the level of the soup and the top of the pot, so the liquid doesn't boil over.) Place the stockpot over high heat and bring to a boil, about 35 minutes. Using a large spoon, skim off any froth that rises to the top. Lower the heat to a gentle simmer, set the lid ajar over the pot, and cook, stirring occasionally, for 3½ hours. Continue skimming off and discarding any scum that rises to the surface during the cooking process.

If you intend to serve the soup on a different day, cool completely, transfer to covered containers, and refrigerate. When ready to serve, remove any fat that has congealed on the surface. Also discard the bones, which should have separated from the meat, anyway. Reheat the soup to boiling over medium-high heat. Add the chopped fresh dill and adjust the seasoning with salt and pepper before serving.

MENTAL NOSH

Borscht *is the Russian word for an entire genre of beet soups (*borsht *in Yiddish,* bartcht *in Polish) that are thought to have originated in the Ukraine, where the widest variety of beets is cultivated. It has been said that no cuisine in the world offers as many varieties of soup as Russian. Borscht can be made with duck, various game, cabbage, mushrooms, or any number of ingredients. Depending on the variety, borscht is served either hot or cold. In my family we used borscht to refer to cabbage soup even though it didn't contain any beets at all (see Cabbage Borscht, page 52).*

cabbage borscht

MY FAMILY ALWAYS CALLED THIS sweet-and-sour soup cabbage borscht, but I learned a few months ago from a Russian friend that *borscht* implies beets. My mother doesn't like beets, so she never put any in her cabbage borscht. Never you mind. I can say categorically that I never make a soup that is better received. The flavor—not unlike that of Cabbage Rolls (page 14), but without as much futzing—is rich and satisfying, with just a hint of sweet, sour, and tomato that reaches back to the Old World and soothes the soul.

Because I dare not alter my mother's proportions, I make this soup only in a very large quantity—enough soup for a large family with plenty of leftovers. But if you remove the potatoes before you freeze it, the soup will keep perfectly well for a couple of months. You can also make a good vegetarian version without the flanken and marrow bones, but you will sacrifice some of the richness. As with most soups, cabbage borscht is best made a day or two in advance so the flavors can blend and you can skim it properly.

a bissel advice

So much soup? **Remove the potatoes, which turn to mealy mush when defrosted, and freeze in small containers. You can also cut the recipe in half, but don't cut the cooking time.**

kosher status FLEISHIG, with meat
MILCHIG, with butter, but without meat
PAREVE, without butter or meat

In a heavy 12-quart stockpot, combine the onions, beef, marrow bones (if using), cabbage, tomato paste and its rinsing water, lemon juice, sugar, salt, and pepper. Cover with 3½ quarts (14 cups) cold water. All of the cabbage may not fit into the pot, but as the soup cooks, the cabbage will shrink and you will be able to add the rest. Set over high heat and bring to a boil, which will take about 30 minutes. Turn down the heat to a simmer, set a cover askew on top of the pot, and continue cooking for 1 hour, skimming off any frothy scum that rises to the surface. Add the potatoes and continue cooking for an additional 1½ hours, until the potatoes are tender and the flanken falls off the bone. Remove from the heat and cool to room temperature. Transfer to smaller containers to chill, discarding the flanken bones that have fallen to the bottom of the pot.

Once chilled, remove any fat that has coagulated on the top. Reheat in small batches, adjusting the seasoning with more salt, pepper, lemon juice, and sugar, as desired.

2 large yellow onions (1 pound), thinly sliced

2¾ pounds flanken (about 6 strips) or beef short ribs

2 marrow bones (½ pound) (*optional*)

4 pounds green cabbage, thinly sliced into shreds

1 (12-ounce) can (a little less than 1¼ cups) tomato paste, plus 1 canful of water to rinse it out

Juice of 6 lemons (about 1 cup), or more to taste

¼ to ½ cup sugar, or to taste

3 tablespoons kosher salt

1½ teaspoons freshly ground black pepper

4 to 5 Yukon Gold or Red Bliss potatoes (2 pounds), peeled and cut into large chunks

SPECIAL EQUIPMENT
Heavy-gauge 12-quart stockpot

vegetarian cabbage borscht

You can use the same proportions as the original recipe, omitting the meat. I also like to add a little butter and modify the technique somewhat. Sauté the onions in the butter or peanut oil in the bottom of the stockpot until nicely browned, about 12 minutes. This replaces some of the body and flavor that the meat gives to the soup. Add the shredded cabbage, tomato paste, lemon juice, sugar, salt, and black pepper, along with 3 quarts (12 cups) of cold water, and bring to a boil. Cover, reduce the heat, and simmer for about 45 minutes. Add the potatoes and simmer for an additional hour, or until the potatoes are tender and the cabbage is soft. Adjust the seasoning as desired.

same ingredients as above except for the meat and bones

6 tablespoons unsalted butter or peanut oil

lentil soup

AS YOU CAN PROBABLY TELL by now, there isn't much variation from soup recipe to soup recipe. Onions, carrots, celery—the French call it *mirepoix,* the Jews call it cooking. But that doesn't mean that every soup tastes the same. The principal ingredients change, and that changes everything. This is a basic lentil soup that has a strong flavor of lentils, depending on which lentils you use and how fresh they are. I like small green lentils, but red, black, and even large lentils will work fine. The beauty of using lentils over other types of legumes is that because they are small and tender, you do not have to soak them overnight to soften up.

a bissel advice

When is a lentil done? I think it is better to err on the side of underdone when determining the finishing point of beans. (You can always cook them longer if need be.) Lentils should be buttery and tender, but they should retain their shape when they are properly cooked. If you have overcooked them, or if you prefer a smooth lentil soup, once it is cooked you can puree the whole thing in a food processor or blender and pass it through a sieve before finishing with the parsley and olive oil.

kosher status MILCHIG, with butter
FLEISHIG, with schmaltz
PAREVE, with peanut oil

1 cup dried lentils, green, red, or black

3 tablespoons butter, peanut oil, or Chicken Schmaltz (page 236)

1 large yellow onion (½ pound), finely chopped

1 large carrot (¼ pound), peeled and finely chopped

2 celery stalks (¼ pound), finely chopped

1 small garlic clove, minced

2½ teaspoons kosher salt

½ teaspoon freshly ground black pepper

2 tablespoons chopped fresh parsley

4 tablespoons top-quality extra-virgin olive oil *(optional)*

b efore cooking, you have to sift through the lentils to remove any small stones. I like to lay them out to one side of a cookie sheet and then pass them to the other side while I look for anything suspicious such as stones, black beans, what have you. Once you have sifted through all of the lentils, set aside.

Heat the fat in a 4-quart saucepan. Add the onion and sauté over medium-high heat about 5 minutes, until translucent. Add the lentils, carrot, celery, garlic, salt, pepper, and 6 cups of cold water, and bring to a boil, about 10 minutes. Place a cover askew over the pot, turn down the heat, and simmer about 45 minutes, until the lentils are soft but not mushy. You can prepare the soup up to this point a day or two in advance. Keep it covered and refrigerated until you plan to serve it.

To serve, heat the soup to just below boiling. Stir in the chopped parsley. Ladle into warm bowls and drizzle each bowl with about ½ tablespoon of the olive oil (if using).

chapter **3**

meats,

fish,

and other

main courses

meats,
fish, and
other
main
courses

Even with

the high number of today's youth becoming vegetarians for ethical or health reasons, it's hard to imagine a Jewish meal without a large piece of meat (or two). I don't think my mother was ever happier than when she was shopping at the butcher—the same one I would later work in—buying enough meat to keep a Chinese family well fed for a year, but my siblings and I dieting for a week. At holiday meals, a brisket was never enough. A roast chicken, a turkey, some chicken wings—"There has to be a choice."

DESPITE HIS SURROUNDINGS—OR MORE LIKELY because of them—my older brother Sheldon was a strict vegetarian for about 25 years. Although there were always plenty of side dishes (mostly starches) for him to make into a meal, the main course put a strain on my mother's repertoire. Once in a while Sheldon would bring his own nut loaf to family gatherings. Sometimes my mother would make extra sides just for him, in case he might starve. (The idea that anyone in my family would starve makes me chuckle to this day.) The psychological hurdle for her to get over wasn't about the total consumption of calories, clearly; it was just that without a piece of meat, he didn't have a real meal.

I AM OF THE SCHOOL THAT THE LESS done to meat or fish or chicken the better. Nothing compares to the taste of a roasted prime rib—a little salt and pepper and you have a meal fit for a king. Even with brisket, I think you should exercise restraint. Let the flavor of the different cuts of meat come through, and you shouldn't have a problem.

SOMETHING MUST BE SAID ABOUT DONENESS. There are as many jokes about well-done meat as there are Jewish comedians. My family is no different, although I personally walk on the rare side now. In my opinion, there's nothing wrong with overcooked meat if you can keep it moist and tender. By any contemporary food-science measure, my mother's chicken should be dry and stringy after the good two-plus hours she roasts it. But, in fact, her chicken falls off the bone into succulent, flavorful morsels. Even her fish, which she cooks far longer than is trendy, stays moist—no doubt because she fries it in so much butter.

basic brisket

THIS IS THE RECIPE FOR MY MOTHER'S brisket, a dependable, delicious rendition of the quintessential Jewish entree. Although she never really doctored it up with anything but plenty of onions, I sometimes add carrots and mushrooms to the mix. As is always the case, the better the meat you begin with, the better the finished dish will be.

Trim away any excess fat from the brisket before you cook it (there should still be a good layer of fat on top), and render that fat to make Beef Schmaltz for other dishes (see page 238).

It is easiest to slice the meat halfway into the cooking, before it is so cooked through that it falls apart into shreds. Then finish cooking the slices in the gravy, which makes them moist and tender.

a bissel advice

How does it keep? **Store the brisket in the gravy in the refrigerator for up to 5 days or freeze. Reheat the brisket covered in a 325°F. oven for 30 to 45 minutes, or until heated through.**

3 large onions (1½ pounds), coarsely chopped

2 large garlic cloves, smashed

2 large carrots (½ pound), diced *(optional)*

6 ounces mushrooms (button, portobello, or a combination), chopped *(optional)*

1 (5- to 7-pound) brisket, trimmed of excess fat

1 tablespoon kosher salt

1 teaspoon freshly ground black pepper

1 teaspoon granulated garlic

1 teaspoon Hungarian paprika

1 (6-ounce) can tomato paste

1 bay leaf

SPECIAL EQUIPMENT

Large roasting pan with a tight-fitting cover or aluminum foil

MAKES **10** TO **15** SERVINGS, WITH PLENTY OF LEFTOVERS

kosher status FLEISHIG

Preheat the oven to 350°F. Place the chopped onions, smashed garlic, carrots, and mushrooms (if using) in the bottom of the roasting pan. Place the brisket fat side down on top of the vegetables. Sprinkle half the salt, pepper, granulated garlic, and paprika on the brisket. Turn it over and sprinkle with the remaining half of the spices. Spread the tomato paste all over the top of the brisket. Fill the can with water and pour it into the pan. Add the bay leaf, cover, and set in the preheated oven.

After 2 hours of cooking, remove the brisket from the oven. Let it cool slightly, then transfer to a cutting board. Now you can trim away the fat. Slice the brisket less than ¼ inch thick on the diagonal across the grain (see page 60 for details). Return the slices to the cooking juice. Once all of the brisket is sliced, re-cover the roasting pan and return to the oven for another 1½ to 2 hours, or until the meat is easily cut with a fork. Remove from the oven and cool to room temperature in the gravy.

the-secret-is-pears brisket

THIS IS A RECIPE FROM MY EDITOR, CHRIS PAVONE (who happens to be Jewish even with a name like that, sort of). It is similar to my basic brisket, but with wine instead of tomato paste and pears (!) instead of mushrooms. (Okay, so it's pretty different. I lied. Sue me.) Although I've said several times throughout the book that I am not a fan of meat cooked with overly sweet ingredients, for some reason in this instance the flavors work. But not until the point that you actually puree the cooking juices to make the gravy. So if you are planning to skip that step, skip this brisket.

MAKES 10 TO 15 SERVINGS, WITH PLENTY OF LEFTOVERS

kosher status FLEISHIG

Preheat the oven to 275°F. Mix the flour with 2 tablespoons kosher salt, 1 teaspoon freshly ground black pepper, and the thyme. Dredge the brisket in this mixture until it is evenly coated. Heat the peanut oil in a large Dutch oven with a tight-fitting lid. Brown the flour-coated brisket for 8 to 10 minutes per side. Remove to a plate. In the same pan, sauté the chopped onions, chopped carrots, and chopped pears until soft, about 10 minutes. Add the stock, red wine, and honey (if using). Bring to a boil and place the brisket back in the pan. It should be completely submerged in liquid. If not, add more stock and wine in the proportion of 2 to 1. Add the rest of the kosher salt and pepper. Cover the pan and set in the oven to braise for 3 hours. Then place the large chunks of carrot and peeled potato on top of the brisket, re-cover it, and cook for an additional 1½ to 2 hours, or until the chunks of vegetables are tender. Remove from the oven and lift out the large chunks of potato and carrot; set aside. Place the brisket on a cutting board and slice it thinly across the grain (see page 60). Ladle the cooking liquid into a blender or food processor and puree in batches until smooth. Adjust the seasoning of this gravy with additional salt and pepper, and pour it over the meat to serve.

1 cup all-purpose flour

3 tablespoons kosher salt

1½ teaspoons freshly ground black pepper

1 teaspoon dried tyme

1 (5- to 7-pound) brisket, trimmed of excess fat

½ cup peanut oil

3 large (1½ pounds) onions, chopped

8 large (1½ pounds) carrots, 4 chopped, 4 cut into large chunks

2 large (1 pound) Anjou or Bosc pears, peeled, cored, and chopped

4 cups beef or veal stock

2 cups dry red wine

½ cup mild-flavored honey (optional)

2 pounds potatoes, peeled and cut into chunks

SPECIAL EQUIPMENT

Large Dutch oven with tight-fitting lid that can go on top of the stove and in the oven.

spicy beef brisket

THIS IS A BRISKET RECIPE from my friend Adam's mother, Maxine. As Adam told me to expect, the first time

I made it, everybody loved it—even my mother, whose own brisket has been known to garner a rave or two (see her

recipe on page 58). The gravy is flavored with a combination of spices and ingredients that approximates barbecue

sauce. And that sauce is delicious on everything from mashed potatoes and Egg Noodles (page 240) to Spätzle (page 124) and Kasha (page 116).

As with any brisket, I find it easier to handle if I stop the cooking at the halfway point, slice it, and put it back in the juice to finish cooking. Maxine suggests refrigerating or freezing the sauce and the meat separately, but reheating them together.

Save the fat trimmings to render for cooking (see page 236), as my great-grandmother did. By the way, Mr. Smarty Pants, she lived to be ninety-two years old.

a bissel advice

What's the "grain"? The grain is the term used to refer to the striations of muscle in meat. The grain of most briskets usually runs lengthwise, diagonally, along the whole piece of meat. If you cut the brisket—or any other meat, for that matter—*with* the grain, it ends up stringy and tough. Cutting it *across* the grain produces tender slices. Sometimes you have to angle your knife slightly to be sure you get it perpendicular to the striations of the meat. If you aren't sure, you can ask your butcher to score the meat in the direction you should cut it once it's cooked.

So much meat? An entire brisket is actually more like 10 or 12 pounds. It has two different sections: the single, or first-cut brisket, which comprises the thin, flat tip; and the double, or second-cut brisket, which is thicker because of a layer of fat in between the muscle. When you see a brisket of 5 pounds or less, it is usually a single brisket. I find that without the extra layer of fat, this cut has a tendency to be dry. I prefer to make a whole brisket and use the extra meat for sandwiches, Pierogi (page 17), Knishes (page 22), or what have you. Cooked brisket also freezes very well.

How do I slice a double brisket? Slice off the double (top) part of the brisket and cut away any fat or gristle from between the top and bottom layers. Slice each section across the grain as indicated above.

5 tablespoons peanut oil

1 (5- to 7-pound) brisket, trimmed of excess fat

2 teaspoons kosher salt

1 teaspoon freshly ground black pepper

2 large onions (1 pound), coarsely chopped

2 large garlic cloves, minced

2 tablespoons dark brown sugar

2 tablespoons Worcestershire sauce

1 tablespoon dry mustard

1 tablespoon white vinegar

1 teaspoon chili powder

½ teaspoon paprika

1 (14-ounce) bottle Heinz ketchup

2 large bay leaves

SPECIAL EQUIPMENT

12-inch frying pan

Large roasting pan with a tight-fitting lid or aluminum foil

Preheat the oven to 350°F.

Place the oil in a large, 10- or 12-inch sauté pan over high heat. Place the trimmed brisket in the hot oil, fat side down, and cook until browned, 5 to 7 minutes. Season the brisket with ½ teaspoon of the salt and ¼ teaspoon of the ground pepper. Turn over the brisket and brown the other side. Season this side with the same amount of salt and pepper. If the brisket is too large to fit in the pan, you may have to cut off the tip and brown it separately.

Meanwhile, in a large mixing bowl, combine the onions, garlic, brown sugar, Worcestershire sauce, mustard, vinegar, chili powder, paprika, remaining salt and pepper, the ketchup, and 1¼ cups water. Use some of the water to rinse out the ketchup bottle. Stir until well blended.

Transfer the browned and seasoned brisket to a roasting pan or Dutch oven just big enough to hold the meat with about an inch of space around it. Place the 2 bay leaves on top of the meat and pour the ketchup mixture over. Cover the roasting pan (use aluminum foil if the pan doesn't have a cover), and set in the preheated oven. Roast for 2 hours.

MENTAL NOSH
Where does a moyl keep his tools? *In a briss-kit. (I'll keep my day job.)*

Remove from the oven and uncover. When the brisket is cool enough to handle, transfer it to a cutting board. Slice the brisket on an angle across the grain (see "advice," page 60). The slices should be less than ¼ inch thick. As you slice the meat, transfer the slices back to the cooking liquid. When all of the meat is sliced, pour any juice on the cutting board back into the roasting pan, re-cover it, and return it to the oven for 1½ to 2 hours, or until the meat is tender enough to cut with a fork. Remove from the oven and cool.

To store, lift the meat out of the gravy and store separately. To reheat, layer the meat with some of the gravy, cover, and bake in a 325°F. oven for 30 to 45 minutes, or until warm.

standing rib roast

THE KING OF ROASTS. A PRIME rib in the refrigerator while I was growing up was the sign we were having company. To this day, my family prefers roast beef made from this colossal cut of meat to just about any other. While snobs tend to gravitate toward the more pricey filet, its soft, wimpy texture and delicate flavor can't hold a candle to the rib's juicy, rich beefiness. As a bonus, a rib roast is just about the easiest thing you can make. You literally just put it in a roasting pan, turn on the oven, and away it goes. Served with mashed potatoes and steamed broccoli, you have a simple meal that is fit for royalty. As is almost always the case in the kitchen, simplicity in the preparation requires a commitment to quality from the cook. Here are a few pointers:

1. Buy your roast from a good butcher or reputable purveyor. He or she can trim it, crack the bones, tie the roast, and make it oven-ready, so all you have to do is cook it. Plus, for all that money you want to ensure you have the best quality meat. A good rib roast has nice, bright red flesh that is well marbled with fat — meaning that the fat is not just around the outside, but distributed within the meat, too.

2. Rib roasts are usually ordered by the number of ribs. For instance, "I want a 3-rib standing rib roast." A 3-rib roast will weigh anywhere from 6½ to 8½ pounds. The size and quality of the ribs changes as you move along the body of the animal. As a rule, the smaller ribs, which come from the middle of the animal toward the loin, are more desirable than the larger ribs, which come from the front of the animal toward the shoulder. Although you will sometimes hear people order the "first 4 ribs," they actually mean they want the *last* 4 ribs, or the 4 ribs from the smaller loin end. To avoid confusion, order your ribs by number and add "from the loin end." You can tell they are from the loin end because the ribs are smaller, the central muscle of meat (the "eye") is compact and uniform, and there isn't a thick layer of tough meat and fat (the "cap") on the top.

3. Although you may not want so much meat, I think you are better off with a roast of 3 or 4 ribs than one of 2. (A 1-rib roast is a rib steak!) A larger roast cooks more evenly, browns better, and to my taste has better flavor. You can reheat the leftovers for another meal, or use them cold for roast-beef sandwiches; you can also use the meat in fillings for Knishes (page 22) or Kreplach (page 46). Besides, since like my mother you are probably going to be making a standing rib roast for company, you don't want to seem like a cheapskate.

4. Get yourself an instant-read thermometer. Since you don't want to ruin your roast by overcooking it—unless like my family you like it well done—the only way to be sure it is cooked to your liking is to insert a thermometer in the center of it. The $10 or so for the thermometer is a lot less than the cost of the roast.

a bissel advice

When is it done? **Use an instant-read thermometer inserted in the center of the main muscle of the roast and this chart as a guideline:**

DONENESS	INTERNAL TEMPERATURE
Rare	125°F. to 130°F.
Medium-rare	132°F. to 138°F.
Medium	140°F. to 150°F.
Medium-well	155°F.
Well	160°F.
Dead	170°F.

Why don't you sear the meat first in a hot oven? **Although this was a popular technique at one time, supposedly to sear in the juices of the meat, it has been scientifically proven that no such effect occurs. Searing meat does affect flavor, however. But I find that a large roast browns perfectly well when it is cooked at an even temperature. If you have a small roast, and you just cannot resist the flavor of crispy fat, you can start the roast in a pre-heated 450°F. oven for 20 minutes or so and then turn down the heat to finish roasting as directed. It will take a little less roasting time to reach the final internal temperature.**

Just pepper? Are you nuts? **That was the response my sister Carrie gave me when she read this recipe. When she makes a standing rib roast she makes a mixture of chopped garlic, Dijon mustard, and tons of black pepper that she schmears on the roast the day before she cooks it. I must confess, her rib roast is delicious, too.**

5. I don't salt a rib roast until it is cooked, and even then I usually just have people salt it at the table. Although I know it has not been proven scientifically, some people believe salt draws out some of the juices and makes the roast dry. I'm no scientist, but my mother never salted it, so I never salt it. And besides, if you are using kosher meat, it will likely be salty enough already.

6. Rib roast is called "standing" because you actually cook it standing up on the bones. It has a sort of built-in roasting rack that allows the fat and other juices to run off into the pan while the meat cooks. The fat side should be facing up, and the cut ends should face out. Remove the roast from the refrigerator about an hour before you intend to cook it to remove the chill.

7. Figure about 16 minutes of roasting at 325°F. per pound for medium-rare beef (132°F. on an instant-read thermometer inserted into the center of the roast). Factor in at least half an hour to allow the roast to sit at room temperature once it is roasted and before it is carved, and another half hour just in case your roast cooks more slowly than mine. The roast actually continues to cook while it sits on the counter, and the juices retract back into the meat.

8. Don't let your sisters pick off all the crispy fat parts while the roast relaxes on the counter after it's cooked.

recipe continues →

standing rib roast

(continued)

1 (4-rib) standing rib roast, cut from the loin
    end, cap meat and chine bone removed,
    tied (about 9 to 11 pounds)
1 teaspoon freshly ground black pepper
Salt, to taste

SPECIAL EQUIPMENT

An open, shallow roasting pan large enough
    to hold the meat with at least an inch of
    clearance on all sides

MAKES **12** SERVINGS WITH LOTS OF LEFTOVERS

kosher status I'm not even going to answer that

take the roast out of the refrigerator about 1 hour before you intend to
cook it. Preheat the oven to 350°F.

Place the roast, resting on its bones, in the roasting pan. Season with
the pepper. Turn the oven down to 325°F. and set the roast in the middle of
the oven. Figure about 16 minutes per pound for medium-rare, 1 or 2 minutes
less for rare, and 2 to 5 minutes more for medium or well. After 2 hours and
15 minutes of roasting, begin to check the internal temperature with an
instant-read thermometer (see the chart on page 63). Once you are within
15 degrees of your desired internal temperature, start checking every
5 to 10 minutes or so. Remove the roast as soon as it reaches the desired
temperature. Then let it sit on the counter for ½ hour. After ½ hour, you can
season it with salt if you like.

To carve, place the roast bone side up on a cutting board. Using a long,
sharp knife and a big fork, cut between the bones and the main portion of
the roast to remove the entire rack of ribs. Separate the ribs by cutting
straight down between the bones, and serve these on the side (they will
make a dog very happy, too). Turn the main portion of the roast right side up
and cut straight down into slices, about ¼ inch thick.
The meat at the smaller loin end of the roast will be
more cooked than that at the larger, shoulder end.
Serve some from both sides to please your guests. If
some prefer their meat more well done, you can return
the slices to the oven to cook as much as they desire.

a bissel advice

What's the difference between a standing rib and prime rib? Nothing, but the nomenclature can be confusing. "Standing" refers to
the way the roast is cooked—literally standing on its ribs. Prime
rib is the technical name of the cut of beef, which comes from the
primal rib portion of the cow. The confusion arises, however,
because "prime" is also a grade of beef, like "choice" and "standard." The best rib roast money can buy is actually a prime prime
rib, but that just seems an awkward thing to say.

jewish meatballs

THIS IS A VARIATION OF THE *GEDEMPTE* (Yiddish for "potted" or "overcooked") meatballs that are a favorite of my niece, Helen. Whenever her grandmother (my mother) baby-sits, Helen wants them for dinner. My mother called them Jewish, but they could easily be Swedish or Latin American. For best results, don't use lean ground beef, and mix the ingredients in a wooden chopping bowl with a metal chopper. If you can, cook the meatballs a day in advance so the flavors have time to meld.

MAKES **14** TO **18** MEATBALLS, ABOUT **8** SERVINGS

kosher status FLEISHIG, duh

In a wide, heavy-gauge 8-quart pot, combine the onions, garlic, tomato paste, dry mustard, Worcestershire sauce, salt, pepper, and 5 cups cold water, and set over high heat. Cover and bring to a boil, then reduce the heat to a simmer.

Meanwhile, in a wooden chopping bowl or ordinary mixing bowl, combine the ground beef, grated onion, eggs, salt, pepper, matzo meal, and ½ cup cold water, using a metal chopper or a wooden spoon to mix well. Be sure that all of the ingredients are evenly mixed.

Remove the cover from the pot of cooking liquid. The liquid should not simmer for more than 30 minutes. If you want to make the meatball mixture in advance and keep it in the refrigerator for a couple of hours before you actually cook the meatballs, turn off the cooking liquid.

To shape the meatballs, wet your hands with cold water. Take a scant ⅓ cup of the meat mixture (about 4 ounces), and shape into a smooth ball about 1¾ inches in diameter. Place in the simmering liquid and repeat with the remaining meat. You should have 14 to 18 meatballs in total. Add the potatoes to the cooking liquid. Be sure all of the meatballs are submerged in the liquid. Bring to a simmer and cook, uncovered, for about 1 hour, or until the meatballs are cooked through and the potatoes are tender.

FOR THE COOKING BROTH

2 large yellow onions (1 pound), roughly chopped

2 large garlic cloves, smashed

¼ cup tomato paste

1 teaspoon dry mustard

2 teaspoons Worcestershire sauce

4 teaspoons kosher salt

1 teaspoon freshly ground black pepper

4 or 5 potatoes (about 2 pounds), peeled and cut into 2-inch chunks

FOR THE MEATBALLS

3 pounds ground chuck or medium-ground beef, no more than 85 percent lean

1 large yellow onion (½ pound), grated

3 large eggs

1 tablespoon kosher salt

½ teaspoon freshly ground black pepper

¼ cup matzo meal or unflavored bread crumbs

SPECIAL EQUIPMENT

Wide, heavy-gauge 8-quart pot

meatloaf with roasted potatoes

THOUGH OFTEN MALIGNED, meatloaf is one of America's great gifts to gastronomy. I often crave my mother's meatloaf and the potatoes she puts in the pan that get crispy in the juices as they roasted. The beauty of meatloaf is that it's good hot or cold, as an entree or in sandwiches. I am not a fan of meatloaves that are so overmixed or have so much bread in them that they have a soft, mealy texture. I like mine to have a toothsome, meaty texture, more like a hamburger log. Like anything my mother makes with ground meat, she always mixes her meatloaf in a wooden bowl with a metal chopper, and this is one of the things that gives hers the texture I'm talking about. A few years ago these bowls and handheld chopping blades became popular again, and they started appearing in gourmet stores across the country. I was happy to be able to find one. If you don't have one, you can use a mixing bowl and a wooden spoon, but never the food processor.

a bissel advice

Fusion meatloaf? I don't like getting fussy with my meatloaf, but that doesn't mean you can't. Sometimes for a little fun I grate the onion and mix it into the meat instead of scattering it around the roasting pan. But that's about as much fun as I like to have with meatloaf. You can try adding different combinations of seasonings, an herb or two, some cayenne, a hard-boiled egg in the center—whatever tickles your fancy. But with meatloaf, as in life, some restraint is advised.

How do I grate an onion? Because you need only one, I wouldn't drag out the food processor. Use a box grater. Cut off the top of the onion, leave the root end intact, and peel. Holding on to the root end, grate the onion on the large shredding side of the grater, directly into the meat. Discard any large pieces and the root end when you are finished.

Preheat the oven to 375°F.

In a large mixing bowl, combine the ground beef, eggs, mustard, salt, pepper, ketchup, Worcestershire sauce, garlic, matzo meal or bread crumbs, and 2 tablespoons of cold water. Mix with a metal chopping blade or wooden spoon until well blended and all of the ingredients are evenly distributed. Transfer this mixture to a roasting pan or baking dish and shape with your hands into a log, roughly 11 inches long and 3 inches wide. Scatter the onion and potatoes around the bottom of the roasting pan.

Place the meatloaf in the preheated oven and roast for about 1½ hours, until the meatloaf is nicely browned and it feels firm to the touch; an instant-read thermometer inserted in the center should register at least 165°F. As it bakes, some of the juices will ooze out onto the meatloaf, giving it an odd appearance. Don't worry, these will settle into the pan as the cooking continues. If you are not sure if the meatloaf is ready, you can slice it in half and take a look inside (you are going to slice it to serve it anyway). The meat should be pink, but cooked through. Remove from the oven and let cool for 10 minutes before you slice and serve it.

2½ pounds ground chuck or other ground beef that's no more than 85 percent lean

2 large eggs

1 tablespoon Dijon mustard

2 teaspoons kosher salt

¾ teaspoon freshly ground black pepper

¼ cup ketchup

2 teaspoons Worcestershire sauce

1 garlic clove, minced, or ½ teaspoon granulated garlic powder

⅓ cup matzo meal or unflavored bread crumbs

1 large yellow onion (½ pound), roughly chopped

1½ pounds potatoes (about 3 large), peeled and cut into chunks

SPECIAL EQUIPMENT
Roasting pan or baking dish
Instant-read thermometer

potted flanken

POTTED OR *GEDEMPTE* (YIDDISH FOR "OVERCOOKED") flanken is a Jewish way of braising beef short ribs. Flanken are beef short ribs that are cut into strips across the rib bones. Each piece of flanken is usually about 1 to 1½ inches wide and 6 or 7 inches long, with four or five little pieces of bone, actually a cross-section of the rack or ribs. Where I come from, "Miami ribs" are the same as flanken, only they are cut about ¼ inch thick. English-style short ribs, on the other hand, are cut square, with longer pieces of rib bones or sometimes no bones at all. Korean short ribs, *kalbi,* are from the same part of the cow, but are cut altogether differently. You can use whichever cut of flanken you like.

Although some people find flanken too fatty and gristly, I think it has a delicious flavor and a succulent texture that is brought out by long, slow cooking. That's why I use flanken in soup, and why I like it potted. You can substitute chuck if you prefer. Or else, if the bones and the gristle are just too much for you, you can trim them away before you cook the meat, leaving you with thin strip of beef that will cook up very nicely, indeed.

a bissel advice

What if my meat is still tough? **Keep cooking it until it is tender. This will happen eventually. Trust me.**

What do I serve this with? **Mashed potatoes or noodles or spätzle or kasha or farfel. The options are endless.**

3 tablespoons peanut oil, Chicken Schmaltz
(page 236), or Beef Schmaltz (page 238)

4 pounds (about 6 pieces) flanken or
3 pounds chuck

1 tablespoon kosher salt

1 teaspoon freshly ground black pepper

1 large yellow onion (½ pound), thinly sliced

1 large garlic clove, minced

1 cup dry red wine or water or a combination

2 tablespoons tomato paste

1 bay leaf

¼ pound white mushrooms (about 5 large),
sliced (optional)

SPECIAL EQUIPMENT

Wide, deep frying pan with a tight-fitting lid

lace the fat in the large frying pan and set over high heat. Season the flanken with the salt and pepper and place in the hot pan to sear, 4 or 5 minutes per side; it should be nicely browned on all sides. Remove it from the pan. Add the onion to the pan and sauté until light golden brown, about 7 minutes. Add the garlic and continue cooking another minute or so. Arrange the meat back in the pan. Add the wine or water, tomato paste, and bay leaf. Cover, turn down the heat, and simmer for about 20 minutes. Turn over the meat and continue to simmer, covered, for another hour or so, until the flanken falls off the bone in tender chunks. About 30 minutes from when the meat will be done, add the sliced mushrooms (if using). Adjust the seasoning with salt and pepper to taste.

cholent

"THE FRENCH HAVE CASSOULET, WE HAVE CHOLENT," reads a sign at the entrance to New York City's living shrine to Ashkenazi Jewish food, the Second Avenue Deli. For years I was puzzled by it—the sign, I mean. I was familiar with the French dish from the Languedoc, a rich bean stew with preserved goose, sausage, lamb, and a flavorful crust. But of cholent I knew nothing. My family practiced gastronomic Judaism, not religious Judaism, and thus there was no need for a dish that cooked from Friday night to Saturday noon so you would have something warm to eat for lunch that didn't require you to turn on the stove and thereby disobey the proscription of doing any work on the Sabbath.

After years of frequenting the deli, I finally ordered my first bowl of cholent. What I got was a somewhat unappetizing-looking bowl of bean stew with tender meat and a pleasing, slow-cooked flavor and texture. I liked it immediately. I have since talked to many people about cholent. I have a former rabbi friend, Harold, who was raised Orthodox and whose mother, it turns out, made a different cholent every week of the year. (In fact, Harold wants to write a book with me called *A Year of Cholent,* or something to that effect.) He told me of a cholent society at Cambridge University and the raging debates about exactly what the ingredients should be.

In preparation for this book, I began doing some research on and experimentation with cholent. There is something appealing to me about a dish you can stick in the oven before you go to bed and have it be ready to eat the following morning, not unlike traditional Boston baked beans.

a bissel advice

But my mother put in . . . This recipe is just a guideline. You can add just about anything to the pot and create your own variation of cholent. Some things to keep in mind are that if you add more starch—such as additional beans, dumplings, sweet potatoes, or what have you—you will have to increase the amount of water proportionately. I sometimes add carrots and celery, but not always; root vegetables are delicious in winter months. Add a piece of kishka or sausage that's been seared until brown. Many people add sweet things, such as honey, prunes, or dates, treating the cholent like a tzimmes, but I find the combination of meat and sweet unappetizing. I do, however, like cholents rich with spices—more like curries, really. Treat it like the ultimate Crock-pot experiment and see what you come up with.

Fly me to the moon . . . Several compounds in beans cause gas. Because the most effective of them, the oligosaccharides, are water soluble, soaking beans helps make them more digestible, provided you toss out the soaking liquid. (By the way, the same compounds are also in cabbage and broccoli.) If cholent gives you bad gas, soak the beans overnight in cold water, at least 2 inches above the level of the beans. Dump the water and proceed with the recipe.

Truth be told, you can put just about anything in a cholent—also called *chamim* or *adafena,* depending on who's doing the cooking—that can withstand a long cooking time. Beans, barley, potatoes, and meat seem to be de rigueur, but dumplings, kishka (stuffed derma), meatballs, spices, and herbs in any combination are fine, too. It is also traditional to put whole eggs (in the shell) in the cholent. My friend Michael remembers these eggs fondly because he liked how the egg whites turned brown from cooking with the beans and meat, but the shells remained white. The eggs are either removed from the pot for breakfast, or peeled and eaten with the cholent for lunch after temple. Whether you like your cholent soupy or sludgy depends on personal taste; mine falls somewhere in between.

In fact, on my cholent-recipe quest I've been trying to get as close to cassoulet as I can without the use of pork. There are some who believe cholent may have originated from the Jews of southwest France, and those of us who believe, as far as food is concerned, we should think about going back. To that end, I usually use duck fat or Duck Prosciutto (page 20), and I add fresh thyme and a piece or two of duck confit (see page 274 for a source) to the mix. Sometimes I even add a piece of ham or pork sausage, as God is my witness. Experiment and have some fun.

One thing to note is that many of the recipes for cholent I have read tell you to soak the beans before cooking them. This step is not necessary to soften the beans—they will cook for more than 12 hours, anyway—but it may help if you find that cholent gives you bad gas. I omit soaking in my recipe, but you can do it if you prefer.

Because of the extended cooking time, you need to cook the cholent sometime when you won't be needing the oven for other purposes. Obviously, if you are an observant Jew and you are cooking cholent on the Sabbath, this doesn't pose a problem. But if you just want to make cholent for a party, and you have some other baking to do, be sure to plan accordingly.

recipe continues →

cholent

(continued)

2 pounds beef flanken, short ribs, chuck,
    stewing beef, or shank

2 tablespoons kosher salt

2 teaspoons freshly ground black pepper

4 ounces (¼ cup) Chicken Schmaltz
    (page 236), duck fat, peanut oil, or a
    combination

2 ounces regular or Duck Prosciutto (page
    20), finely chopped *(optional)*

3 large yellow onions (1½ pounds), thinly
    sliced

3 garlic cloves, peeled but left whole

2 marrow bones (½ pound) *(optional)*

2 legs duck confit *(optional)*

2 cups (½ pound) dried white beans, such as
    cannellini or great northern, picked over
    to remove stones or blemished beans

¾ cup pearl barley

4 potatoes (2 pounds), peeled and cut into
    large chunks

5 sprigs fresh thyme

1 bay leaf

6 to 8 eggs, in the shell *(optional)*

SPECIAL EQUIPMENT

An ovenproof 8-quart pot or Dutch oven with
    a tight-fitting cover that can also be used
    on top of the stove

MAKES 8 TO 10 SERVINGS

kosher status FLEISHIG
TRAIF, if you use pork

preheat the oven to anywhere between 225°F. and 250°F. (the lowest temperature of your oven depends on the make and model).

Season the beef with 1 tablespoon of the salt and 1 teaspoon of the pepper. Place the ovenproof pot on top of the stove over high heat and add the fat. Add the beef and cook until nicely browned on all sides, 5 to 7 minutes per side. Remove the meat from the pan and set aside. Add the chopped prosciutto (if using), and sauté for a minute to release some fat. Add the sliced onions and garlic and sauté until translucent, 5 to 7 minutes. Spread the onions out evenly across the bottom of the pan and remove from the heat. Return the meat to the pan. Add the marrow bones and duck confit (if using), the beans, barley, potatoes, thyme, bay leaf, and whole eggs. Sprinkle with the remaining 1 tablespoon of salt and 1 teaspoon of pepper. Add 8 cups of cold water and cover.

Place the covered pot into the preheated oven and cook for a minimum of 8 hours and a maximum of 12. Remove from the oven and let cool slightly. You can serve the cholent right away, as is the custom, or let it cool to store. Remove the eggs and as soon as they are cool enough to handle, peel them and return them to the pot whole. Reheat the cholent on top of the stove over very low heat, stirring occasionally to prevent burning, or in a 250°F. oven.

MENTAL NOSH

The link between cholent and cassoulet has an etymological basis, too. Some linguistic scholars believe cholent is a contraction of two French words, chaud, *meaning "hot," and* lent, *meaning "slow."*

broiled skirt steak
with mushrooms and onions

THIS IS NOT ROCKET SCIENCE. You buy a skirt steak, season it, slice it, and serve it with sautéed mushrooms and onions. Still, it is a dish from my youth. And skirt steak, the Jewish man's flank steak, is a lean, flavorful piece of meat, also called hanger steak (*onglet* in French), that has found its way onto bistro menus across the country.

Skirt steaks come from the diaphragm area of the cow and are butchered into long, narrow strips no more than ½ inch thick. I worked in a kosher-style butcher shop during high school that used to sell skirt steaks rolled up into pinwheels called "Delmonico Steaks." Although the reference to New York City's great dining dynasty was clearly intentional, to this day I can't figure out what relationship they could have had to the lowly skirt steak. Given that we were charging kosher meat prices for meat that wasn't kosher, there was probably none.

a bissel advice

What if I can't find skirt steak? **Look for hanger steaks (also called "butcher's tenders"). If you aren't keeping kosher, you can use flank steak. Because they are thicker, flank steaks will take longer to cook.**

MAKES 4 SERVINGS

kosher status FLEISHIG, if your mushrooms and onions are made with oil or schmaltz
TRAIF, if they are made with butter or you use flank steak

1½ pounds skirt steak
2 teaspoons kosher salt
½ teaspoon freshly ground black pepper
1 batch (2 cups) Mushrooms and Onions
   (page 244)

SPECIAL EQUIPMENT
Broiler pan or hot barbecue

Preheat the broiler or fire up the barbecue. The hotter the cooking device, the better the steak. Lay out the skirt steak on the broiler pan or a sheet pan and sprinkle with the salt and pepper. Cook the skirt steaks for just 4 or 5 minutes per side, depending on how you like your beef done. My mother used to cook it until it was charred—about 15 minutes per side. Remove the steak from the heat and let it sit for about 10 minutes on the cutting board. Slice the steak on an angle across the grain (perpendicular to the direction of the striated muscle fibers). Angle your knife blade toward the cutting board to produce wide, thin slices. Heat the mushrooms and onions until boiling and spoon them over the steak slices to serve.

pepper steak

SOMEWHERE IN THE LATE 1950S this dish was adopted into the Jewish culinary vernacular. Pepper steak is even on the menu at the Second Avenue Deli. More Chinese or Latin American than Eastern European, it is nevertheless delicious. We ate it regularly when we were growing up, and recently my sister Carrie called to say she had made it for the first time in years and she had forgotten how delicious it could be. According to Carrie, there are two secrets: the first is to cook the meat for a long time before you add the peppers; the second is to use a lot of cubanelle peppers— the long, light green sweet cooking peppers available in most grocery stores. Serve pepper steak with steamed rice, mashed potatoes, or any other starchy accompaniment.

a bissel advice

Shouldn't this be cooked quickly like stir-fry? **Well, the truth is that shoulder steak is a tough but flavorful cut of meat. And in order for it to become tender enough to be palatable, it needs to cook awhile. I also happen to like the texture of the slow-cooked beef in this dish.**

What's wrong with bell peppers? **Nothing really. They are delicious to eat. But for cooking, especially slow cooking, I think cubanelles work better. Cubanelles have less water, and although they aren't very good raw, their flavor is very pronounced when cooked. If all you can find is green or red bell pepper, however, you can substitute them. I have done it before, myself.**

4 tablespoons peanut oil

1½ pounds shoulder steak (3 thin steaks)

1 teaspoon kosher salt

½ teaspoon freshly ground black pepper

1 large yellow onion (½ pound), roughly chopped

2 pounds cubanelle peppers (a.k.a. cubanel, cubanella, or cubanello), seeded and cut into ½-inch wide strips

2 teaspoons Worcestershire sauce

SPECIAL EQUIPMENT

1 large nonstick skillet with a tight-fitting lid

heat the oil in a large nonstick skillet set over high heat. Season the steak with the salt and pepper and place in the hot oil to brown, about 4 minutes. Flip and brown the second side. Transfer the steak to a cutting board and slice crosswise on the diagonal into ¾-inch strips. Catch any juice that runs off. Meanwhile, return the pan to the heat. Add the chopped onion and sauté until soft and translucent, 3 or 4 minutes. Add the sliced steak and stir to mix. Turn down the heat to low, add 2 or 3 tablespoons of water to the pan, cover, and cook for about 45 minutes. Stir the meat regularly, scraping the bottom of the pan, and adding more water, a tablespoon or two at a time, if the liquid has completely evaporated and/or the meat has begun to stick or burn. You do want the meat and onions to get nicely browned, however.

After about 45 minutes of slow, steady cooking, remove the cover and add the strips of pepper. Stir to distribute and cover. Cook, covered, continuing to stir, for an additional 20 minutes or so, until the peppers have wilted and browned. Stir in the Worcestershire sauce and adjust the seasoning with salt and pepper.

The pepper steak can be made several hours or up to a day or two in advance. To reheat, add 2 or 3 tablespoons of water and reheat in a frying pan.

corned beef

DON'T ASK ME WHY, BUT the first thing I did when I found out I was going to be writing a Jewish cookbook was to make a corned beef brisket from scratch. Actually, I made many. I guess I was just looking for an excuse to experiment with different techniques to see if I could come up with anything at home that approximated the delicious

hand-sliced corned beef served at Katz's delicatessen on the Lower East Side. Because I live in New York and have easy access to excellent corned beef, the whole endeavor was a little *mashugana*. I tried wet cures and dry cures and various combinations of spices. I corned some beef with nitrate—a preservative that keeps the meat rosy pink and fresh looking—and some without. Now, I don't think you should turn your kitchen into a delicatessen. But if you happen to live in a no-corned-beef zone—people in or near Montreal can console themselves with Montreal Smoked Meat—or the exorbitant price of deli-made corned beef gets you

down, I wanted to give you the option of making it yourself.

As long as you are corning beef, choose a nice big brisket with a lot of fat—remember, fat equals flavor. I settled on a dry cure because it takes up less room in the refrigerator than a vat of salt water big enough to hold a large piece of meat. And although I liked the look of the corned beef made with nitrates better than that made without, the flavor was the same and I wouldn't want to contribute to anyone's potential for developing cancer (a heart attack is a different story). So here is a good recipe that I think you will find produces a very acceptable corned beef. It is a combination of many recipes and many experiments, but it is based on a technique I first saw in a book by Julia Child. It takes about two weeks, but most of that time the meat is just sitting in the refrigerator.

a bissel advice

Make my own corned beef, are you crazy? Yes. But I think that there is something to be said for trying new things. Besides, if not for some nice sandwiches, why not for St. Patrick's Day? *Should I be worried if some of the liquid oozes out of the bag?* Only because it will make a mess in your fridge (that's why I had you put it in a roasting pan). I have given you enough salt in the cure to be sure that the meat will be fine. Anything lost to a small leak in the bag will be nominal.

kosher status FLEISHIG, but if you put it in a Rueben sandwich
with Swiss cheese, it will become TRAIF

1½ cups kosher salt

4 bay leaves, crumbled

1 tablespoon coriander seeds, cracked by
whacking them with a hammer, a meat
tenderizer, or the bottom of a frying pan

1 tablespoon black peppercorns, cracked
(see technique above)

1 tablespoon yellow mustard seeds

1 dried hot pepper, broken into ½-inch pieces

5 garlic cloves, smashed but not peeled

1 (8- to 10-pound) beef brisket

SPECIAL EQUIPMENT

2 sturdy plastic bags large enough to hold
the brisket

Large roasting pan

lace one plastic bag inside of the other and roll down the top to form a collar that will keep the bag open. Inside the bag, combine the salt, crumbled bay leaves, cracked coriander seeds, cracked peppercorns, mustard seeds, hot pepper, and smashed garlic; mix around to distribute the spices evenly. Rinse off the brisket, trim away any blue USDA markings, and place it in the bag of salt and spices. Seal the inner and outer bags very tightly. Roll the bag around to be sure the meat is coated with the spice mixture. Place the bag in a roasting pan and set it in the bottom of the refrigerator. I like to put it at the bottom of one of my drawers and then put whatever was in the drawer back on top of it to weigh down the meat.

By the second day, the salt should have drawn out some blood from the meat. Turn the meat over while still in the bag, and massage it to make sure the salt and spices are penetrating evenly. Continue to let it sit in the refrigerator for 12 to 14 days, turning it over once every day or so after the third day. When the meat is finished curing, it will have a flat, gray color and the firm texture of cooked meat. Once fully cured, it can keep for months in the refrigerator. You can cut off small portions of the meat and cook as you want.

Before you cook the meat, though, you must first remove most of the salt. Rinse off the salt cure and set the meat in a tub or basin filled with cold water. Allow the meat to soak overnight and up to 1 day, changing the water every 8 hours or so, until the brisket has the texture of fresh meat again. Note that at this point the corned beef must be cooked within a day or two. To cook, I find that steaming best approximates deli-style corned beef. Unfortunately, if you don't have a large steamer, you will have to cook the corned beef in small pieces (another reason it's a good idea to cut off a small piece to cook from time to time). Bring the water in a large steamer to a simmer. Place the desalted beef in the steamer basket and set over the simmering water. Cover and let steam gently for 2½ to 3 hours, until the meat is tender. The corned beef is now ready to eat.

MENTAL NOSH

Why is it called corned beef if there is no corn in it? Corn *is an old English word that means "grain," and "corned beef" is so called because the salt used to preserve it comes in grains. Being corny, as I am, has nothing to do with it.*

stuffed breast of veal

THE JEWISH FOOD I GREW UP ON wasn't exactly elegant. Delicious? Yes. Satisfying? Yes. Attractive? Well, not always. Sophisticated? Only on the rare occasion. Of course, you could always bake a kugel in a glass dish and set it in a beautiful sterling silver holder, as my mother often did for company. But when you looked long and hard at what you were eating, it usually wasn't pretty. This stuffed breast of veal recipe is an exception. It is an elegant entree for a large group celebrating a special occasion, a relief from the holy trinity of brisket, roast chicken, and prime rib.

Order a whole breast of veal on the bone and have your butcher cut a pocket in the flesh between the top flap of meat and the rack of bones. If the incision for the pocket is made along one of the short ends, you can stuff the entire length of the breast to produce beautiful slices once it's cooked. Don't be daunted by the size of the piece of meat—a lot of it is bone and other waste. Like my mother, I use a potato stuffing, not unlike the filling for knishes on page 222, but just about any stuffing or filling will work (bread or matzo, page 246; or even kasha, page 225). While the breast bakes, the fat and juices of the veal are absorbed by the stuffing, making it irresistible. As one friend who was picking at the crisp top layer of meat before I sliced it remarked, "I guess this is as close to suckling pig as Jews get."

a bissel advice

You think I'm a surgeon? Carving the breast of veal can be daunting, especially hot out of the oven. The trick is not to cut the slices too thin, and not to be afraid to reassemble the slices on the serving plate should they fall apart. A sharp knife helps, too. Also, have your butcher crack through the bones along the thicker side of the breast to make carving easier. If you make the veal in advance and cool it completely, it is easier to slice (chilled it cuts like a dream), but the veal has a tendency to dry out when you reheat it. To reheat, cover slices with aluminum foil and bake in a 300°F. oven 20 to 30 minutes, until heated through.

So much meat? This is a dish for a large group—there is no getting around it. You can have your butcher sell you a piece of a breast, but it is harder to keep the stuffing inside, and the presentation isn't as dramatic. Wrap the leftovers in aluminum foil and refrigerate. Carve and reheat as directed above.

kosher status FLEISHIG, if the filling is made with schmaltz or oil
TRAIF, if like my mother, you use butter

In a large sauté pan, heat the fat over medium-high heat. Add the chopped celery, chopped onions, and shredded carrots, and sauté until tender and just slightly golden brown, about 15 minutes. Stir in the kosher salt and the pepper. Combine this mixture with the mashed potatoes, and the eggs and matzo meal, and mix well. Taste and adjust the seasoning with more salt and pepper if necessary.

Preheat the oven to 350°F.

Place the roughly chopped onions and smashed garlic in the bottom of a large roasting pan. Place the veal breast rib side up in the pan on top of the onions. Season with half of the salt, pepper, garlic powder, and paprika. Turn the breast over and season the other side with the remaining spices. Using a long spoon or spatula, fill the veal with the potato mixture evenly throughout the length of the breast. Stuff the pocket until it is full, but not bulging, as the stuffing will expand as it cooks. (The pocket may bust anyway, but it's not a big deal.) If you have leftover stuffing, place it in a greased baking dish and bake it at 350°F. for 40 minutes to serve alongside the veal.

Tightly cover the roasting pan with a lid or heavy-duty aluminum foil. Place in the preheated oven and bake for 2½ hours. Remove the cover, turn up the oven to 400°F., and continue baking for an additional hour, until the top of the breast is a deep, crisp brown. Remove from the oven and let sit 15 to 30 minutes before carving. If any stuffing has burst out of the pocket, scoop it out of the pan into a serving bowl along with some of the onions from the bottom of the pan.

Using a sharp serrated knife, cut the veal breast in half through the center. With a spatula and a large fork, lift half out of the pan onto a cutting board. Cut the meat into slices about ½ inch thick, straight through the meat and stuffing and parallel to the bones. If you get to a bone that you cannot cut through, simply leave it behind. The meat should be soft enough to separate easily from the bone. Arrange the slices on a large platter and spoon some of the onions from the pan on top.

FOR THE STUFFING

½ cup Chicken Schmaltz (page 236), unsalted butter, peanut oil, or any combination

2 large celery stalks, chopped (1 cup)

2 large yellow onions (1 pound), chopped (3 cups)

2 medium carrots (about 6 ounces), shredded on a handheld grater (1 cup)

3 pounds Yukon Gold potatoes, peeled, cut into 2-inch chunks, boiled in salted water, and mashed

1 tablespoon kosher salt

1 teaspoon freshly ground black pepper

2 large eggs

¼ cup matzo meal or bread crumbs

FOR THE BREAST OF VEAL

4 large yellow onions (2 pounds), roughly chopped

4 large garlic cloves, smashed

1 (7- to 9-pound) breast of veal, cleaned and trimmed with a pocket for stuffing cut between the rack of bones and the meat

4 teaspoons kosher salt

1 teaspoon freshly ground black pepper

1 teaspoon granulated garlic powder

½ teaspoon paprika

SPECIAL EQUIPMENT

Potato masher

Large roasting pan to fit veal with cover or heavy-duty aluminum foil

roast chicken

THIS IS IT. ROAST CHICKEN. The *ne plus ultra* of Jewish entrees, or at least right next to brisket in prominence. My mother has eaten so much roast chicken in her life she wondered aloud recently if she weren't going to start laying eggs. The reason she eats so much of it is that her roast chicken is amazing; my siblings and I ask for it every time we go home. It is always down-right juicy, flavorful, and so tender it falls off the bone. We used to think the secret was in the roasting pan—she always uses an oval-shaped aluminum prewar beauty that came from my grandfather's house. But then we saw her work her magic in a newfangled glass baking dish. Then we were sure it was the chicken. But she makes as good a roasted chicken from a jaundiced, mass-produced, supermarket-bought bird as she does from a pristine, plump one that comes from an exclusive kosher butcher.

After studying her make roast chicken in my own New York kitchen (she lives in Toronto), the secret emerged. She cooks it covered, breast side down, on a bed of a lot of onions for a long time so that the chicken actually steams. Then she removes the cover, turns up the heat and browns the underside to a crisp. A final browning of the breast side produces an exemplary roast chicken— deliciously overcooked but moist and yummy. No basting. No special treatment. Be warned: once you master this technique, you may start sprouting feathers.

a bissel advice

How do you cut up a chicken? A good question. I find it easiest to use a pair of sharp poultry shears or kitchen scissors, and I do it in the roasting pan to avoid making a mess on the counter. Position the roasting pan so you are looking at the rear end of the chicken. Use the shears to cut through the center of the breast, starting at the cavity and ending at the neck. This will expose the backbone, which is the ridge in the middle of the bottom of the cavity. Cut along both sides of the backbone to separate the chicken into two halves. Place one half on a plate. Snip the leg off the thigh at the joint (find it by wiggling the leg). You should be able to separate the thigh from the breast just by pulling it. Remove the wing the same way you removed the leg, at the joint. Cut the breast in half to produce two equal portions. Repeat this process with the remaining half chicken. You should end up with 10 pieces.

2 large onions (1 pound), chopped

1 large garlic clove, minced

1 (4½-pound) roasting chicken

1 tablespoon kosher salt

½ teaspoon granulated garlic

½ teaspoon freshly ground black pepper

½ teaspoon ground paprika

1½ pounds (4 medium) Yukon Gold potatoes, peeled and cut into 2-inch chunks (*optional*)

SPECIAL EQUIPMENT

1 roasting pan with a tight-fitting lid or heavy-duty aluminum foil

preheat the oven to 350°F. Place the onions and minced garlic in the bottom of the roasting pan. Set the chicken breast side up on the onions. Sprinkle ½ tablespoon of the salt, ¼ teaspoon of the granulated garlic, ¼ teaspoon of the black pepper, and ¼ teaspoon of the paprika on the chicken and in the cavity. Turn it over, breast side down, and sprinkle with the remaining spices. Cover the chicken with a lid or aluminum foil and set in the oven for 1 hour.

Remove the cover or foil and scatter the potatoes (if using) in the onions and cooking juice around the base of the chicken. Raise the oven temperature to 400°F. and continue roasting until the skin begins to brown, 15 to 25 minutes. Using two large forks or a pair of tongs, turn the chicken over so the breast is facing up. Continue to roast for an additional 30 minutes, until the skin has browned and crisped. The potatoes should be fork-tender. Remove from the oven and let cool for about 10 minutes before cutting up the chicken to serve.

nana's chicken acropolis

AS I'M SURE YOU'VE ALREADY guessed, there is a story behind the name of this dish. When I went to cook Mitteleuropean Jewish dishes with my friend Daňo in upstate New York (who isn't Jewish, by the way), he wanted to show me a special type of cholent that he remembered the Jewish families he grew up with in Slovakia making before

the Sabbath. They would stuff a chicken and bury it in a pot of beans that they would take to the village baker, who would cook it in his oven overnight. Daňo couldn't find the right beans where he lives, so he asked me to bring them from the city. "I want big—no, giant beans . . . and check it," he said assuredly. Assuming he literally meant giant beans, or Greek "gigantes" beans, that's what I brought. As he instructed, I made sure I had it right by "checking it." Daňo took one look at the beans and said they were the wrong ones. He hadn't meant "check it," he'd meant "checked" or speckled beans, but I didn't understand his accent. He was a little distraught, but we made the dish anyway.

While we were cooking together, I made a comment about how a lot of the Jewish dishes he was showing me seemed like they might have come from Italian Jews. It became a running joke over the next few days that here was this Ukrainian-born, Czechoslovakian-raised Christian chef—who started cooking while he was a ballet dancer in

Vienna—showing me Jewish-Italian recipes. When I asked what he called the chicken and bean dish, he said it was "cholent." I said I didn't think calling it cholent would do the dish justice because cholent is much less fussy (see my recipe on page 70). Then, to gibe me for my earlier comment, he referred to it as "chicken milanese." As long as we are naming it, I said, it ought to be a Greek name, for the beans I brought—and which we both loved—were Greek. So Daňo suggested either "chicken Acropolis" or "Nana Mouskouri's chicken," after the international singing sensation from Greece. I thought we should use both. Nana's Chicken Acropolis it is. And in the spirit of "Jewish is as Jewish does," this dish was born and named (without a *bris*). Serve stuffed on a bed of giant beans, the chicken makes for a dramatic presentation.

Note that although you will have more beans than only four people can consume, the beans make a fantastic soup the next day. I've given a recipe for the leftovers on page 83.

FOR THE BEANS

2 pounds giant dried beans (known in Greek as "gigantes")

3 tablespoons peanut oil or Chicken Schmaltz (page 236)

1 large yellow onion (½ pound), chopped (1 cup)

2 garlic cloves, minced

1 tablespoon kosher salt

½ teaspoon freshly ground black pepper

2 bay leaves

½ teaspoon dried marjoram

¼ cup red wine vinegar

FOR THE STUFFING

4 or 5 slices stale white bread (about 6 ounces)

3 tablespoons peanut oil or Chicken Schmaltz (page 236)

1 large yellow onion (½ pound), chopped

1 celery stalk, chopped

1 small carrot, grated

3 mushrooms (2 ounces), sliced

1 large egg

1 teaspoon kosher salt

¼ teaspoon freshly ground black pepper

¼ cup chopped parsley

FOR THE CHICKEN

1 (4½-pound) roasting chicken

1 tablespoon kosher salt

½ teaspoon freshly ground black pepper

2 tablespoons peanut oil or Chicken Schmaltz (page 236)

2 cups chicken stock or water

SPECIAL EQUIPMENT

Large, deep roasting pan with a tight-fitting lid or heavy-duty aluminum foil

o prepare the beans, pick them over to remove any stones or any shriveled-up or discolored beans. Place them in a bowl or container and cover with cold water at least 2 inches above the level of the beans. Let soak at room temperature for 12 hours or overnight. Drain.

In a large 5- or 6-quart saucepan, heat the oil or schmaltz over high heat. Add the onion and sauté until golden brown, about 8 minutes. Add the garlic and sauté an additional minute or two. Add the drained beans, salt, pepper, bay leaves, marjoram, vinegar, and 8 cups of cold water. Bring to a boil, then turn down the heat and simmer, uncovered, until the beans are plump and tender, about 1 hour 20 minutes. The beans should have a soft, creamy texture inside, but should still hold their shape and not burst. Better to err on the side of underdone because they will cook more later on.

MENTAL NOSH

Who is this Nana Mouskouri, anyway? *Nana Mouskouri is a Greek singer who is popular in Europe and became a sensation in America after recording the title song to the film* Never on Sunday. *She also sings many Jewish folk songs, including "Chava Nagihla." Touring with Harry Belafonte from 1964 to 1966 made her a star. At one time I think she had sold more records than any living performer, or something like that. My siblings and I came to know her from cheesy late-night television commercials for her albums, the kind with the running list of song titles, the one being played highlighted in yellow, and bad B-roll footage of her concerts in the background. Whenever we would make fun of her, my mother would get angry because apparently Nana has a fantastic voice—too bad she couldn't do anything about those black-rimmed glasses! Anyway, Nana is famous for being able to sing in many languages. One day my sisters and I realized that we could order food in just as many languages, and we started to make up songs by stringing together foreign menu items. We thought it was very funny. I'll understand if you don't.*

recipe continues →

nana's chicken acropolis

(continued)

a bissel advice

What a production! Although each step is easy, all together they do take some time. To make it a little less complicated, you can skip the stuffing completely and just roast chicken pieces in the beans. Use an assortment of breasts and legs or thighs and season with salt and pepper. Brown them in a sauté pan in hot oil and bury them in the beans. Roast, covered, for about 1 hour and 30 minutes, until the meat is tender and falls off the bone.

So many beans, are you crazy? As I said before, you can use the leftover beans to make a terrific soup. Here's what you do. Place the beans in a large pot along with the chicken carcass; 1 large onion, roughly chopped; 2 celery stalks, with the leaves; 1 large carrot, sliced; and a sprig or two of fresh herbs, such as rosemary or thyme. Cover the beans with cold water, ½ to 1 inch above the top level of the beans. Bring to a boil, turn down the heat, and simmer for about 1 hour, until the vegetables are very tender. Using a slotted spoon or kitchen tongs, remove the chicken carcass and any of the bones that may have dislodged. Puree the soup in small batches in a food processor fitted with a metal chopping blade or blender. Pass the puree through a wire sieve to remove any lumps or unwanted pieces of bone that you didn't find before. Adjust the seasoning with salt and pepper. The giant beans have a creamy texture that makes this soup divine.

For the stuffing, place the bread in a bowl and cover with water. Soak for just a minute. Dump out the water, squeeze out the bread to remove any excess moisture, and return it to the bowl. Set aside. Heat the oil or schmaltz in a small sauté pan set over high heat. Add about three-quarters of the chopped onion and sauté until golden brown, about 8 minutes. Add the celery and carrot and cook until soft, another 4 or 5 minutes. Add the mushrooms and cook just until they have turned brown and given off their juice, 2 minutes more. Add this mixture to the soaked bread along with the remaining raw ¼ onion. Mix in the egg, salt, pepper, and chopped parsley and stir to blend, breaking up the bread if necessary until the mixture is uniform. Set aside.

To finish assembling the dish, preheat the oven to 450°F. Remove the neck, liver, and gizzard package from the chicken and rinse the bird. Pat dry with paper towel. Cut off the tail and trim any excess fat. Season the chicken with the salt and pepper, being sure to season the cavity also. Place the oil or schmaltz in a large sauté pan and heat over high until very hot. Put the chicken in the hot pan right side up to brown the skin on the bottom. Just let the chicken sizzle away and brown for 8 to 10 minutes. Remove from the pan. Fill the cavity with the stuffing, packing in as much as it will hold.

Dump the cooked beans into the roasting pan, along with any cooking liquid they might have. Make a depression in the middle of the pan where the chicken will sit. Transfer the chicken to the roasting pan, and sort of wiggle it until it is somewhat buried in the beans. Pour the chicken stock or water into the pan. Place the roasting pan in the preheated oven for 20 minutes to brown the top of the chicken. Turn down the temperature to 350°F., cover the roasting pan tightly with its cover or with heavy-duty aluminum foil, and continue roasting for 1 hour 30 minutes, until the meat is tender enough to fall off the bone. Present the chicken at the table on the beans. It's easiest to carve the bird while it is sitting on the beans (see page 80 for a good carving technique).

stewed chicken

A SIMPLE, HOMEY DISH, THIS CHICKEN benefits from a long cooking time and a day or two's rest in the refrigerator. I've been told that it isn't the most attractive dish, but everyone who's told me that has waited until after the bowl was licked clean. Although I suggest cooking potatoes in the liquid, you might still want to serve it with buttered egg noodles, or maybe even mashed potatoes for some variety. Of course, you could serve a vegetable, also, but that wouldn't be very Jewish.

a bissel advice

But I don't have any wine? Just leave it out and add more water. How come my Jewish dishes have basically the same ingredients? It beats me. I don't know what we had to cook with in the desert, but there must have been a lot of onions and mushrooms around.

MAKES **4** TO **6** SERVINGS

kosher status FLEISHIG

In a wide bowl or resealable plastic bag, combine the flour with 1 tablespoon of the salt and the pepper, and mix well. Dump a few pieces of the chicken into this mixture and stir to coat. Tap off any excess flour and set aside. Repeat with the remaining chicken until all of the pieces are well coated.

Meanwhile, heat 6 tablespoons of the fat in a large (10- to 12-inch) frying pan set over medium-high heat. Place the chicken skin side down into the hot fat, being sure not to crowd the pan so much that the chicken will not brown. Cook until golden brown and crisp, but not cooked through. Remove from the pan and drain on paper towels. In a heavy, medium-size saucepan, heat the remaining 2 tablespoons of fat over medium-high heat. Add the sliced onion and garlic and sauté until translucent, about 8 minutes. Add the browned chicken along with the mushrooms, tomato paste, white wine, bay leaf, paprika, potatoes, and 7 cups of cold water. Bring to a boil, turn down the heat to a simmer, partially cover, and cook for 1 hour and 10 minutes, or until the meat begins to fall off the bone.

1 cup all-purpose flour

1 tablespoon plus 2 teaspoons kosher salt

1 teaspoon freshly ground black pepper

1 (4½-pound) roasting chicken; have a
    butcher cut it into 10 pieces or buy an
    equivalent amount of chicken pieces

8 tablespoons Chicken Schmaltz (page 236)
    or peanut oil

1 large yellow onion (½ pound), sliced

1 garlic clove, minced

½ pound button mushrooms, portobellos, or
    a combination, sliced

1 heaping tablespoon tomato paste

¾ cup dry white wine

1 bay leaf

¼ teaspoon ground paprika

2 to 3 Yukon Gold or Red Bliss potatoes
    (1 pound), peeled and cut into 2-inch
    chunks

roast turkey

THINK OF IT AS A BIG CHICKEN, only it's actually easier to make. The one time a year when everyone is supposed to make turkey—Thanksgiving—everybody panics. The Butterball hotline rings off the hook. It's madness. The truth is, when you roast a turkey, the oven does all the work—except of course for the lifting in and out of the oven,

which requires strong arms. Just in case there wasn't enough food—which happened never—my mother would sometimes throw a turkey in the oven for large gatherings in addition to her brisket and chicken wings and all of the other dishes.

My preference is for fresh-killed (i.e., not frozen) turkey. But the truth is that sometimes frozen turkeys are juicier. (If you ordered a fresh-killed turkey from the butcher shop I used to work at, we needed a day's notice so we had time to defrost one for you.) Frozen Empire brand kosher turkeys are good. The koshering process, which involves the application of a lot of salt, isn't too far off from the current culinary craze of brining turkeys in saltwater overnight before roasting them. If you buy a frozen turkey, defrost it in the refrigerator. It will take 2 or 3 days, so plan accordingly. Just letting it sit on the counter overnight provides the perfect incubator for all sorts of bacteria. You can safely speed up the defrosting process by soaking the turkey in cold, running water, but you will have to tie up a sink or a bathtub for 5 or 6 hours in the process.

Although I've heard some people recommend ½ pound of whole, uncooked turkey per person, that just wouldn't ever do in my family. If you like having leftovers or your friends are big eaters, figure 1 pound per person. A giant bird makes for a dramatic presentation, but if you need a turkey bigger than 20 pounds, you are probably better off buying two smaller ones.

a bissel advice

Well, that was easy, but how do I make gravy? If you are using an aluminum roasting pan, transfer everything that's left in the bottom of the roasting pan, including any browned bits that you can scrape off the bottom, to a saucepan. If you are using a real roasting pan, you can just set it directly on the stove. Add 2 or 3 cups of water or chicken soup or dry white wine, or a combination, and bring to a simmer. If you saved the neck and the giblets, you can add them to the pan. While it simmers, scrape the bottom of the roasting pan to remove any brown bits—these have a lot flavor. Let this simmer for about 20 minutes. While it cooks, mix equal parts butter (or schmaltz or peanut oil) and all-purpose flour, about ¼ cup of each, to make a paste. Set aside. Strain the simmering pan juices into a clean saucepan and set over medium heat. Using a large metal spoon, skim off any fat that floats to the top. Whisk in the fat-and-flour mixture in small beads and continue cooking until it thickens—add more if necessary, but be sure to let it cook out to remove any taste of raw flour. Adjust the seasoning with salt and pepper and serve.

To stuff or not to stuff? That is the question. It is true that stuffing cooked inside a turkey is delicious because it absorbs all the juices as the turkey cooks. But it can also be deadly. Inside a turkey, stuffing should reach a temperature of at least 165°F., all around, by which time your turkey breast is probably dry and overcooked. Even before everyone was afraid of salmonella, my mother used to cook her stuffing in a casserole on the side. If you don't stuff the turkey, fill the cavity with chunks of onion, some whole cloves of garlic, carrots, a handful of parsley, half of a lemon, and whatever else you think might lend a nice flavor to the meat.

I never truss my bird, so I don't recommend it. I think sticking the drumsticks through the band of skin left at the bird's tail keeps the turkey compact enough. If you only make a turkey once a year, buy an aluminum roasting pan at the grocery store that you can throw away without cleaning after dinner. Just be careful while transporting the turkey into and out of the oven because the aluminum has a tendency to buckle. For support, put it on a cookie sheet. If you are making turkey more often, you may want to invest in a serious roasting pan (be sure it fits in your oven!). They are expensive, but they are not only good for the turkey, they are also good for the gravy.

MAKES 10 TO 14 SERVINGS

kosher status FLEISHIG
TRAIF, if you use butter in the gravy

4 large onions (2 pounds), roughly chopped

5 garlic cloves, smashed

1 (12- to 14-pound) turkey, defrosted, giblets and neck removed, rinsed under cold water and patted dry

¼ cup peanut oil, softened butter, or Chicken Schmaltz (page 236)

2 tablespoons kosher salt

1½ teaspoons freshly ground black pepper

1 teaspoon granulated garlic *(optional)*

½ teaspoon paprika

SPECIAL EQUIPMENT

Large aluminum roasting pan and cookie sheet or large roasting pan

Instant-read thermometer

preheat the oven to 325°F.

Place the onions on the bottom of the roasting pan and scatter the garlic around. Lay the turkey, breast side up, on the onions. If you have a roasting rack, you can put the rack on the onions and the turkey on top of the rack. Rub the skin all over with the peanut oil, butter, or schmaltz. Season the turkey inside and out with the salt, pepper, garlic (if using), and paprika. You can stuff the bird at this point, packing the stuffing inside the main cavity and also in the space where the neck was removed — you'll need about 8 cups of stuffing, or 1 batch of the recipe on page 122. Remember that the stuffing will expand as it cooks, so don't pack it too tightly. Otherwise, put a handful of the onions and garlic and whatever else you have lying around in the cavity.

recipe continues →

roast turkey

(continued)

Tuck the drumsticks into the band of skin left from where the tail was removed.

Place the turkey in the preheated oven. Conventional wisdom has it that the bird will take about 14 minutes per pound, but I find it usually takes a little longer, especially if it is stuffed. I put it in the oven for about 3½ hours, basting it every ½ hour or so, and then I start checking it for doneness. The only way to know for certain if the turkey is cooked is to poke it all over with an instant-read thermometer; it should register at least 165°F. against the bone and in the thickest part of the meat; the drumstick should wiggle freely and the juices should run clear. If you are uncertain, better to err on the side of dry meat. The skin should be nicely browned, but if it's not, crank up the oven to 425°F. and let it roast for another 10 to 15 minutes, until the skin achieves the tan you desire.

Remove the turkey from the oven and let it sit on the counter for at least 30 minutes before carving (be sure to factor that time into your schedule). I find it easiest to carve the turkey in the roasting pan (which also catches the juices so you can make a good gravy). First cut the skin that's holding the legs. Scoop out anything in the cavity, whether stuffing or onions. Remove the legs and the thighs, which should separate easily at the joints, and cut the meat off the bone into large morsels. Make a horizontal cut into the lower side of the breast and slice the breast meat vertically to that cut; the slices should fall off in nice pieces.

baked fish in sweet-and-sour sauce

THIS IS ONE OF THE RARE FISH dishes that can be prepared in advance. In fact, the sauce can be made several days before assembling the dish, and the fish can actually be baked up to a day or two before serving. It can also be reheated and served warm. The secret is to strike a good balance between the sweetness and sourness of the sauce.

MAKES **6** SERVINGS

kosher status PAREVE

to prepare the sauce, heat the oil in a large sauté pan or saucepan set over high heat. Add the onion and sauté until golden brown, 6 to 8 minutes. Add the garlic and continue cooking for an additional minute or two. Add the carrots. Squeeze the tomatoes into the pot, breaking them up into smaller pieces between your fingers. Add all of the juice from the tomatoes, plus about ¼ cup of water that you use to rinse out the can. Add the brown sugar, vinegar, salt, pepper, and bay leaves, and bring to a boil. Turn down the heat to a simmer and cook for 10 minutes. Add the chopped green pepper, stir, cover, and let simmer for about 5 minutes, until the pepper is wilted. Stir in the raisins. Cool to room temperature.

For the fish, heat the oil in a large sauté pan set over high heat. Dredge the fish fillets in flour and place in the hot oil. Don't crowd the pan. Season the fillets with salt and pepper while they fry until very light brown, no more than 2 or 3 minutes. Flip and cook for another 2 minutes or so. Remove from the pan and pat dry with paper towels.

To assemble, preheat the oven to 350° F. Spoon some of the sauce onto the bottom of a 2-quart rectangular baking dish. Arrange the fried fish fillets on top in a single layer. Pour the remaining sauce over the fish. Bake in the preheated oven until cooked through, about 20 minutes. Serve warm or at room temperature.

FOR THE SAUCE

3 tablespoons light olive oil, peanut oil, or
     vegetable oil
1 large yellow onion (½ pound), finely
     chopped (1 cup)
2 garlic cloves, minced (1 tablespoon)
2 large carrots (⅓ pound), grated (1 cup)
1 (28-ounce) can peeled tomatoes
½ cup dark brown sugar
¼ cup plus 1 tablespoon red wine vinegar
½ teaspoon kosher salt
¼ teaspoon freshly ground black pepper
2 large bay leaves
1 medium green pepper, roughly chopped
     (1 cup)
¼ cup golden raisins, roughly chopped

FOR THE FISH

½ cup light olive oil, peanut oil, or
     vegetable oil
1½ pounds skinless and boneless whitefish
     fillets, such as cod, sole, haddock, or
     halibut
½ cup all-purpose flour, for dredging
½ teaspoon kosher salt
¼ teaspoon freshly ground black pepper

SPECIAL EQUIPMENT

2-quart rectangular baking dish

falafel

ALTHOUGH NOT PART OF THE ASHKENAZI culinary tradition per se, the Jewish neighborhood in north Toronto where I grew up was nevertheless crowded with falafel restaurants. Today, after the recent immigration of many Israelis to Canada, this neighborhood — where my mother still lives — has a falafel place on almost every corner. That said, I have to confess that the best falafel I have ever eaten comes from a place in Paris in the old Jewish section on Rue des Rosiers called L'As du Falafel. Now, I know my point is moot because I haven't been to Israel, where falafel is the national dish and it is said to be superb. But Lenny Kravitz's picture hangs on the wall of L'As du Falafel, and on it he has given his own seal of approval. If it's good enough for Lenny Kravitz . . . enough said. In truth, it's not the falafel itself that is so good (although it is good), it is the array of garnishes they put inside the falafel sandwich that makes it stand out: pickled turnips, beets, cabbage salad, tomatoes, fresh parsley, mint, tahini sauce, and fiery hot sauce.

The mix for falafel is made from dried chickpeas that have been soaked overnight in water to soften. You can used dried fava beans instead to make an Egyptian specialty known as *tamiya*. Then the soaked beans are chopped in a food processor or meat grinder with seasonings, formed into balls or patties, and fried. I add soaked bulgur wheat to the mix to make them extra crunchy, but you can leave it out if you prefer. Stuff the balls into a pita and experiment with your own sandwich fixin's to find a combination that you like.

a bissel advice

What if I can't find bulgur wheat? Bulgur is used to make tabbouleh. It shouldn't be too hard to find — it comes in small boxes or in bulk and is always available in health-food stores, if not in the grain section of the grocery store. You can substitute about 3 tablespoons of unflavored bread crumbs for the bulgur and the all-purpose flour or just leave it out altogether for a softer falafel. *How come my falafel are falling apart?* The beans weren't soaked enough, or they weren't ground enough, or the mixture isn't moist enough. Put it back in the food processor and add a tablespoon of water. If it still won't hold together, stir in an egg white. *How come my falafel are burned on the outside but mushy on the inside?* Your oil is too hot. Turn down the heat and let the falafel take their time to get browned. When cooked properly, the falafel should be crisp on the outside and moist in the center.

½ pound (about 1¼ cups) dried chick-peas
   or dried, shelled fava beans (sometimes
   called broad beans)

3 tablespoons bulgur wheat or bread crumbs
   (optional)

2 garlic cloves

1 large shallot or ½ small onion

2 tablespoons all-purpose flour

1½ teaspoons ground cumin

2 teaspoons kosher salt

¼ teaspoon cayenne pepper (or to taste)

¼ teaspoon freshly ground black pepper

½ cup chopped fresh flat-leaf parsley

2 cups vegetable oil for frying

SPECIAL EQUIPMENT

Food processor or meat grinder

Pick over the dried chick-peas or fava beans to remove any stones or unusable beans. Place them in a large bowl and cover with cold water at least 2 inches above the level of the beans. Let sit for 12 hours or overnight at room temperature. The next day, place the bulgur, if using, in a small bowl and cover with warm water. Let sit about 1 hour. Drain both the beans and the bulgur of any excess water.

In the bowl of a food processor fitted with a metal chopping blade, place the garlic and the onion. Pulse until they are chopped fine, scraping down the sides to be sure no pieces are left too large. Add the drained beans, bulgur, or bread crumbs, if using, flour, cumin, salt, cayenne, and black pepper, and pulse until the beans have ground into a fine meal and the mixture is well blended and holds its shape when pinched. Scrape down the sides once or twice again to be sure the mixture is evenly ground. Add the parsley and pulse to combine. Alternately, you can grind the garlic, onion, and beans in a meat grinder and stir in the remaining ingredients. The falafel mixture can be made 2 or 3 days in advance and refrigerated until ready to use.

To cook the falafel, heat about 1 inch of oil in the bottom of a heavy sauté pan (I use cast iron) set over medium-high heat. The oil should reach about 350°F. Scoop a heaping tablespoon of the falafel mixture into the palm of your hand and gently shape it into a flattened ball. Set it into the hot oil, using a spoon to transfer the falafel to the oil if you are afraid of burning yourself. The oil should sizzle if it is hot enough. Repeat, rinsing your hands occasionally. Alternately, you can use a small, 1-ounce ice-cream scoop with a release. Fry the falafel in batches of 12 to 14 in the hot oil. Turn over the falafel occasionally while they cook, until they are nicely brown and crisp all around, 6 or 7 minutes total. Remove from the oil and drain on paper towels. Serve in pita sandwiches or on platters with Hummus (page 12) and Tahini Sauce (page 201).

falafel-crusted salmon

THIS DISH BECAME THE SIGNATURE of a small seafood restaurant called Aquagrill in New York City's SoHo neighborhood. Although I'm not sure how the chef there makes his rendition, one day when I had some falafel mix lying around I began to experiment. The results were delicious. Use the falafel recipe on page 90 for the crust and follow my directions below. Instead of salmon, why not try chicken or veal cutlets, too.

a bissel advice

How do I prepare the salmon fillets? **Remove the skin and any bone from the salmon fillet. Lay the salmon fillets skin side down on the work surface. Run your fingertips over the surface of the flesh to try to find any pin bones that may not have been removed when the salmon was filleted. Use tweezers or a pair of needle-nose pliers to yank out these bones in the direction of the grain of the flesh. Insert a sharp knife between the skin and the flesh at the narrow end of one of the fillets. Grab onto the skin and hold it tightly with your left hand. With the knife slightly angled toward the work surface away from you, run the blade along the skin to separate the flesh. Discard the skin. Trim off any dark spots from the fillet, especially from the side that was closest to the skin. Repeat with the remaining fillets.**

Can I use other types of fish? **No. Well, yes, you can use any fish. But salmon has a strong flavor and firm texture that won't be overpowered by the flavorful falafel crust. More delicate fish will get lost in the crust.**

Can I do anything else with this technique? **For an alternative to ordinary falafel sandwiches, cut salmon in strips and fry them as directed. Stuff the salmon strips into pita and garnish them as you would an ordinary falafel sandwich.**

I f any of the fillets are too big for one serving, trim them to equal size. Place the eggs in a small, wide bowl and beat with 1 tablespoon of cold water until light. Place the flour on a plate and dump half the falafel mixture on another plate. Dredge the first fillet in the flour and dust off any excess. Drop it into the egg mixture. Be sure it is well coated with egg, then let any excess drip off back into the bowl. Lay the fillet on the falafel mixture. Turn it over and pack an even layer of falafel on top. Flip this side onto a spatula, and be sure the fish is evenly covered with the falafel mixture. Use the spatula to transfer the fillet onto a clean plate or cookie sheet. Repeat with the remaining salmon. At this point the salmon can be wrapped in plastic and chilled for up to 6 hours before frying. Save any leftover falafel mixture.

Preheat the oven to 300°F. Line a cookie sheet with paper towels. Heat the oil in a large, heavy frying pan (I like to use cast iron) over medium-high heat. You should have about ¼ inch of oil on the bottom of the pan. Cook the thicker fillets first. Use a spatula to lift the fish fillets off the plate or cookie sheet and slide them into the hot oil. If the crust has broken in any place, use some of the leftover falafel mixture to patch it. Fry the salmon in the hot oil for about 5 minutes on each side, until the crust has browned and crisped (cook it longer if you like your fish well done). When both sides are done, remove the salmon to the paper-towel-lined pan. Because you have fried the thicker fillets first, you can place the tray in the preheated oven while you finish cooking the others. When all of the salmon is fried, pat off any excess oil and serve immediately. The salmon is delicious with a dollop of Hummus (page 12) and a drizzle of Tahini Sauce (page 201).

1½ pounds skinless salmon fillets (not steaks), cut into 6 equal pieces
1 batch uncooked Falafel mix (page 90), about 2½ cups
3 large eggs
1 cup all-purpose flour
½ cup vegetable oil

SPECIAL EQUIPMENT
Tweezers or needle-nose pliers
Sharp knife

breaded fish

MY MOTHER BREADED JUST ABOUT everything in matzo meal and fried it in butter. It's a recipe for success, especially when you have fillets of a delicate fish such as flounder, sole, or turbot. Don't confuse this with nouvelle cuisine—the fish should be well-cooked, not rare, but because of the butter it will remain moist and tender.

Like her mother and grandmother before her, my mother always served breaded fish with Jewish Spaghetti (page 100). And steamed broccoli was usually not far behind. To prevent the butter from burning while the fish fries, I cut it with peanut oil, which also has a pleasant, buttery flavor.

a bissel advice

Fish cooked in advance? Okay, I know it sounds crazy, but my mother used to fry her fish early in the day (about the same time she would make her Jewish Spaghetti), keep it at room temperature all day, and reheat it in the oven before dinner. Maybe it was all of that butter, but the fish didn't really dry out, at least not in an unappealing way. Besides, plenty of Jewish "appetizing" stores sell breaded fish all day long. Whether you make your fish in advance or just before you serve it, be sure to pat away any excess fat so it isn't greasy.

Can I do anything with the leftover breading? My mother (and her grandmother before her) mixes together the leftover egg mixture and matzo meal, shapes it into a pancake, and fries it in whatever butter is left in the pan. In some circles this is called a *bubbeleh,* or "cute little thing that grandma does." That's also the same word older Jewish women say when they pinch a child's cheeks until it hurts.

½ cup all-purpose flour

2 large eggs, beaten with 1 tablespoon water

1 cup matzo meal

2 teaspoons kosher salt

½ teaspoon freshly ground black pepper

1½ pounds fish fillets, preferably a delicate
    white fish, such as flounder, turbot,
    or sole

4 tablespoons unsalted butter

4 tablespoons peanut oil

place the flour on a dinner plate and the beaten eggs in a separate, wide, shallow bowl. Place the matzo meal on yet another plate, and stir in the salt and black pepper. Cut the fish fillets to appropriate serving sizes, 4 or 5 ounces each. Dredge the first fillet in flour and dust off any excess. Dip it in the beaten egg and drain off any excess. Place the fillet on the seasoned matzo meal, and using a fork or your fingers, cover it on all sides with the matzo meal. Place the breaded fillet on a clean plate and repeat with the remaining fish until all of it is breaded.

Line a cookie sheet or tray with paper towels. In a large, heavy-gauge sauté pan (e.g., cast iron), heat 2 tablespoons of the butter with 2 table-spoons of the peanut oil over medium-high heat. When the fat is hot—you can tell because the butter will sizzle—add the fillets, paying attention not to crowd the pan. (Adding the fish before the fat is hot enough will cause the fish to soak up a lot of fat.) Fry until golden brown, 7 or 8 minutes. Using a wide spatula, carefully flip to cook the other side. If the fat has been absorbed, add more as needed in the same proportions—equal amounts of butter and peanut oil. Continue frying until golden brown and crisp, an additional 5 or 6 minutes. Remove to the paper-towel-lined tray and pat to remove any excess fat. If you have more fish to fry, so to speak, place the tray of cooked fish in a 250°F. oven to keep warm.

breaded veal

YOU CAN USE the same breading and frying technique on pounded veal chops scaloppine for a tasty entree. Substitute the same amount of veal (use a little more if you are using chops with bones) for the fish. Pound the veal between two sheets of plastic wrap with the bottom of the frying pan or a meat pounder, or have your butcher pound it for you until it is thin. Dip the veal in the flour, egg, and matzo meal as described above, and fry in oil, schmaltz, butter *(Oy, vey!),* or a combination until golden brown.

fish patties

I WAS NEVER A FAN OF THE salmon patties my mother would make from canned salmon for the occasional milchig dinner. Although she used only red sockeye salmon and she painstakingly removed any evidence of skin or bone from the flesh, I just found the whole idea of canned-and-then-fried fish unappealing (like cat food!). Many years

later I was flipping through an issue of *Cook's Illustrated* magazine and I saw a recipe for salmon patties that used fresh fish. Given that I spend my life contemplating, discussing, cooking, and eating food, I can't explain why the idea had never occurred to me. I was eager to tell my colleagues at work about my discovery, but they, for whom patties from fresh fish were not news, were not as enthusiastic. Still, for me, that night, when for the first time I made salmon patties from fresh salmon,

my world was changed forever.

Using a similar method, I have since made delicious fish patties with tuna, trout, and various combinations of fresh and smoked fish. You can dip them in flour, egg, and bread crumbs before frying, but I find it isn't necessary. With some good tartar sauce and a squirt of lemon, fish patties are delicious as a light main course at dinner or as the star attraction in a sandwich.

a bissel advice

Can I combine fish? **You can, but I wouldn't advise it. Make salmon patties or tuna patties or trout patties, but don't mix different fish. The flavor of fish is so subtle that I wouldn't want to confound it. The same holds true with the smoked fish: use fresh and smoked salmon, or fresh and smoked tuna (yes, you can buy smoked tuna!), or trout, but not in combination.**

What if I bought salmon steaks instead of fillets? **No problem, but you'll have to clean them a little differently. First cut them in half horizontally and remove the white, circular bone in the middle. Pull out any pin bones you can feel with your fingertips. Place the dark skin side of each half on the cutting board. Using a sharp knife, trim away the white, belly side of the skin (which should be facing up). Then, holding the trimmed skin, turn the knife in the opposite direction and slide it under the flesh to remove the darker skin. Chop the flesh as indicated above.**

breaded fish patties

PREPARE THE RECIPE as indicated, but shape the patties in advance and let them chill on a parchment- or waxed-paper-lined cookie sheet. Carefully dip the chilled patties in flour, then beaten egg, then matzo meal or bread crumbs (Japanese panko bread crumbs work really well) to coat. Use a slotted spoon to carefully transfer the patties between dips without breaking them. Fry the patties as directed. Breading gives them a nice crunchy exterior.

kosher status MILCHIG, if made with milk
PAREVE, if made with water or wine

2 slices stale white bread, crusts removed
(2 ounces without the crusts)

⅔ to ¾ cup milk, stock, diluted dry white
wine, or water

1¼ pounds fresh fish fillets: salmon, tuna, or
trout, or a combination of fresh and
smoked fish, the smoked fish not
exceeding ¼ pound (4 ounces)

1 tablespoon mayonnaise

1 large egg

1 large shallot or ½ small yellow onion,
minced (3 tablespoons)

2 tablespoons finely chopped fresh flat-leaf
parsley

1 teaspoon kosher salt

¼ teaspoon freshly ground black or white
pepper

Juice from ½ lemon (1 to 2 tablespoons)

½ cup peanut or vegetable oil

SPECIAL EQUIPMENT

Tweezers or small, needle-nose pliers

Sharp knife

place the stale slices of bread in a mixing bowl and pour over the milk or whichever liquid you are using. Once the bread has soaked up as much of the liquid as it can, squeeze it out and discard the liquid. Return the soaked and squeezed bread to the bowl, breaking it up into little pieces.

Lay the fish skin side down on a cutting board. Run your fingers over the flesh side to try to locate any pin bones that may not have been removed. Use tweezers or needle-nose pliers to remove the bones, firmly yanking them out in the direction of the grain of the fish. Insert a sharp knife between the skin and the flesh and, holding the skin tightly, run the knife down the length of the fillet with the blade angled slightly down toward the work surface. The flesh should easily separate. If any flesh remains on the skin, scrape it off with the blade of the knife. Chop the fish and the smoked fish (if using) into very fine dice, about ¼ inch. I find that slicing the fish into thin strips, like julienne, then chopping the strips into dice works best. You'll have a little more than 2 cups of chopped fish.

To the soaked bread add the chopped fish, mayonnaise, egg, minced shallot or onion, parsley, salt, pepper, and lemon juice. Stir to evenly distribute the ingredients. Chill for about 30 minutes or until you are ready to cook the fish.

Heat the oil in the large skillet (by now you know I prefer cast iron for frying) over medium-high heat. When the oil is hot (a drop of water should sizzle like mad), shape the patties. Use a ¼-cup measure to scoop out some of the fish mixture and shape it in the palm of your hands into a flat, ¾-inch-thick round patty the size of a small hamburger. Carefully lay the patty in the hot oil and repeat, working quickly, to fill the pan.

The patties should take 4 or 5 minutes to turn deep golden brown. Carefully flip them with a spatula and continue cooking the second side for the same amount of time. Remove the cooked patties to a paper-towel-lined plate and pat with additional paper towel to remove any excess oil.

chapter 4

side dishes

and

vegetables

I Was Afraid There Wouldn't Be Enough to Eat

How much

is enough food? If the infantry happens to pass in front of our house around dinnertime, will we have what we need to feed them? These were the unspoken questions that must have occupied my mother's mind whenever she was planning a special meal while we were growing up. Although I've already said she liked to offer a selection of meats, her trump card was the side dishes. Every food group needed to be represented: potatoes, noodles, kasha. There was the occasional green vegetable, but it was usually just some steamed broccoli or a salad—and because her salad bowl was too big to fit on the table, we would often just put it on the sideboard and forget about it.

IN MY OPINION, STARCHES ARE WHERE Jewish cooking really shines. I think I could live on farfel and kasha. Lokshen kugel begins with one of my favorite foods, egg noodles, and adds all sorts of fattening things to it—what could be bad? There are symbolic side dishes, such as latkes—I'm fully aware that many people serve them as an appetizer—and their secular counterparts, such as potatoes roasted in schmaltz.

WHY LIMIT YOUR MENU PLANNING to a meat and two veg? Pile on the options and your guests won't be disappointed. Oh, and don't forget about that salad; your guests are going to need all the help (and health) they can get.

jewish spaghetti

WELL, IF THERE IS ANY recipe in this book that could stand as a totem for the kind of food I grew up on, it is Jewish Spaghetti. To this day, it serves as the ultimate comfort food for every member of my family. It was so much a part of our vernacular that we thought it was a recipe shared by Jews throughout the Diaspora. When I realized that no one at school had the foggiest idea what I was talking about when I referred to it casually in conversation, I was crushed like a Hunt's tomato.

Jewish Spaghetti is a recipe that originated with my great-grandmother Eva. It was made by my grandmother and her three sisters. It is made regularly by my mother. I can't think of a piece of sole breaded in matzo meal and fried in butter (see page 94) without a scoop of Jewish Spaghetti on the side. It isn't really spaghetti, or even Jewish, for that matter, at all. But never you mind.

If anything, Jewish Spaghetti probably has its roots in Italy. I had a revelation once when I was cooking in Italy and the chef for whom I was working was preparing the employee meal—spaghetti in tomato sauce. I was in Piedmont at the time, and in that region every pasta dish is finished with a generous dose of butter. The tomato sauce had been made fresh from those sweet Sicilian tomatoes that are hung to dry slightly, to concentrate their flavor and sugar content. Made with fresh pasta, the end result was as close to Jewish Spaghetti as you could get. I was so excited that I telephoned home to share my discovery with my family. Everyone at the restaurant in Italy thought I was *pazzo*.

Unlike its Italian cousin, Jewish Spaghetti is best if it is made in the morning and reheated at night. You can reheat it in a pot on the stove, or in a casserole that you bake in the oven. My mother dots the top with a little extra butter before she heats it up. It is also good cold from the fridge.

a bissel advice

It isn't even spaghetti! Truth be told, you can use just about any shape of pasta to make this dish, but I prefer the smaller shapes. My mother's favorite shape these days is rotini. But like the flavor of every can of tomato sauce, the name of every shape of pasta changes among brands. One company's rotini is another company's fusilli. Find a shape you like and stick with it. If you want to use spaghetti, break it up into smaller pieces as you put it in the boiling water to cook.

Do you get kickbacks from Hunt's? Nope. But over the years, my family has tried every brand of tomato sauce on the market. And the only one that gives Jewish Spaghetti its characteristic sweet, tomatoey flavor is the one made by Hunt's.

How much should I make? This dish is good at any temperature: hot, cold, lukewarm. Because my mother always let it sit on the stove all day, she had to make extra to compensate for the tastes we would sneak whenever we'd pass through the kitchen.

1 pound dried pasta, preferably a small, compact shape, such as rotini, fusilli, elbow macaroni, ditalini, tubettti, or shells

½ cup (1 stick) unsalted butter

2¼ cups (1 15-ounce can plus 1 8-ounce can) Hunt's Tomato Sauce—not Italian style, not salt-free, just the regular one

4 to 6 tablespoons sugar

½ teaspoon kosher salt, or to taste

Pinch of freshly ground black pepper

b ring a large pot of salted water (about 4 quarts water with 1½ tablespoons kosher salt) to a boil. Add the pasta, stir, and cook until just past al dente, about 10 minutes. Drain. Do not rinse.

In a medium saucepan, melt the butter over medium-low heat. Add the tomato sauce, sugar, salt, and pepper. The amount of sugar necessary will depend on the sweetness of the tomato sauce—yes, in this modern, standardized, industrialized age, every can of tomato sauce still has a slightly different flavor. Add the drained noodles and stir to coat. Turn off the heat, cover, and let sit several hours at room temperature so that the noodles absorb the sauce.

To serve, reheat in one of two ways: (1), transfer the pasta to a 2-quart baking dish. Dot the top with a tablespoon or so of butter, cover with aluminum foil, and bake in a preheated 350°F. oven for about 30 minutes. Remove the cover and bake a few more minutes until crisp on top. Or (2), you can just reheat the pasta over low heat on top of the stove, stirring frequently to prevent burning.

sonny's special potato latkes

SO THIS IS MY MOTHER'S famous, award-winning latke recipe. For various reasons I shouldn't need to explain, these are my favorite latkes (even though they are less traditional, according to some Judaica scholars, than the grated latkes on page 104). I am not alone. This recipe took me to the top of the latke world—with it I won the first annual James Beard Foundation latke cook-off in 1995. I beat famous chefs and other culinarians

a bissel advice

Isn't using a food processor sacrilege? **Some** *bubbes* **and other Jewish cooks will tell you that if you don't grate the potatoes by hand, you can't make latkes. Perhaps the bits of knuckle and other body parts that end up in the mix when you use a handheld grater improve the flavor. But I actually prefer the texture of latkes made from potatoes grated in the food processor, as long as the strands of potato are kept long and thin. Still, if you'd prefer to use a hand grater, use a box grater and grate the potatoes on the side with the largest holes. Mince the onion on a cutting board with a chef's knife. Combine the two, wring out in a dish towel, and proceed with the recipe as indicated. But if you nick your finger on the grater, don't forget the latkes will be fleishig.**

Can't I make them in advance? **I don't recommend it, but I know that if you are having guests, sometimes you have to prepare them ahead. Once the latkes are cooked, drain them well and place them on a wire rack to cool. Preheat the oven to 275°F. Place the wire rack on a cookie sheet and arrange the latkes on top so that they are close but not touching. Set the cookie sheet in the oven. The rack allows the hot air to circulate around the entire surface of the latkes, which keeps them crisp (a trick learned from my friend Bonnie). The latkes should be heated through in about 20 minutes, depending on their thickness.**

with my mother's formula of one onion for every two potatoes. I even wrote an article for a national food magazine about them. Start with good, large Russet or Yukon Gold potatoes. Make sure the onions are big, too. You can peel the potatoes in the morning and let them sit covered with cold water until you are ready to use, but once grated, they can't be kept for any length of time.

the whole meshpucha

You can increase the recipe as you need, as long as you maintain the ratio of one onion for every two potatoes.

kosher status PAREVE, but beware of sour cream
PESADICH

4 potatoes (2 pounds), such as Russet or Yukon Gold, peeled and cut into large chunks

2 large onions (1 pound), halved

2 large eggs, lightly beaten

¼ cup matzo meal

2 to 3 teaspoons salt, to taste

½ teaspoon freshly ground black pepper

About ¾ cup peanut oil, for frying

SPECIAL EQUIPMENT

Food processor with a shredding disk

Using the medium shredding blade of a food processor, grate a couple of pieces of potato, laying them horizontally in the feed tube to maximize the length of the strands. Next, grate half an onion. Alternate the potatoes and onions in the feed tube until everything is grated. The onions will turn to mush, but their juices will help keep the potatoes from turning brown. Pick out any ungrated pieces.

Lay a clean dish towel inside a large bowl and transfer the grated mixture into the towel. Roll up the towel lengthwise and wring out as much liquid as possible (you can do this over the bowl or right over the sink).

Transfer the grated mixture to a clean bowl. Add the eggs, matzo meal, salt, and pepper, and mix well. In a large cast-iron or nonstick skillet, pour about ⅛ inch of oil and heat on medium high. The oil is hot enough when a piece of potato sizzles when added. Form a trial latke with a tablespoon of the mixture. Fry until brown, taste, and adjust the seasoning.

To form the latkes, scoop up about ½ cup of the mixture with your hands and loosely pat it into a pancake about ½ inch thick, leaving a few straggly strands along the edge. (As you work, liquid will accumulate in the bowl. Squeeze out the excess to form a compact pancake.) After shaping each latke, slip it into the hot oil and flatten it gently with the back of a spatula. Fry until deep golden brown, at least 10 minutes on each side to be sure the center is fully cooked. The latkes may take more or less time depending on how many you fit into your pan and how hot your stove is, but I've never been able to get the total cooking time under 15 to 20 minutes a batch. If the edges darken very quickly, lower the heat. To prevent excess oil absorption, flip each latke only once. Add oil between batches as needed, making sure the oil heats up again before frying more latkes. Drain the latkes on paper towels or a clean brown paper bag. Serve immediately with Chunky Applesauce (page 212) and/or sour cream. I like ketchup, too.

MENTAL NOSH

I have learned that the first latke (and I don't mean Andy Kaufman) was probably made with cheese (see page 106). The potato isn't the point here (although in common English usage latke *has come to connote potato pancake), it's the oil. The oil represents the oil found by the Maccabees after their Temple in Jerusalem was destroyed. There was only enough oil to last for one day, but it lasted miraculously for eight days—hence the eight days of Chanukah. Anyway, anything fried in oil is good for Chanukah (and good to eat). So don't go trying to pass off the baked latkes that were popular a couple of years ago as traditional Chanukah fare. They are the product of the very contemporary American aversion to fat.*

grated-potato latkes

THIS IS NOT HOW MY mother made her latkes (for her recipe, see page 102), and I used to think the grated-potato latke was limp and bland. But that was before I tried Steve Gold's latkes. Steve is the proprietor of Murray's Chickens, and I watched him take top honors with this recipe at the James Beard Foundation's Third Annual Latke Lovers' Cook-Off.

Although some Jewish grandmothers will attest that a scraped knuckle or two makes the finished product more authentic, like my mother, Steve chooses to make his latkes in the food processor rather than by hand. He leaves the skin on the potatoes and on his knuckles, and adds a drop of self-rising flour to make a light, potatoey latke that I think is delicious. (Don't skimp on the salt, which helps bring out the flavor.) Because you don't peel the potatoes, the batter is easy to work with, and the latkes fry up quickly, this recipe is ideal when cooking latkes for a crowd.

a bissel advice

How far in advance can I make these latkes? **As with any pancake, they are best right out of the pan. But because this mixture is more like a batter than a heap of shredded potatoes, you can actually keep it about 30 minutes before you intend to fry them. Once cooked, if you must, the latkes can be reheated on a rack in a 300°F. oven. See "advice" on page 102.**

the whole meshpucha

Because this mixture pours easily and is a pleasure to work with, I like to use it if I have a whole lot of latkes to make. Increase all of the ingredients proportionately.

kosher status PAREVE

2 large Russet potatoes (1 pound), unpeeled, washed well, and cut into quarters

1 large onion (½ pound), peeled and cut into quarters

1 large egg plus 1 egg yolk

4 tablespoons self-rising cake flour or
   4 tablespoons all-purpose flour with
   ½ teaspoon baking powder and
   ¼ teaspoon kosher salt

1 teaspoon kosher salt

¼ teaspoon freshly ground black pepper

¾ cup vegetable oil, for frying

Using a food processor fitted with a coarse shredding disk, shred the potatoes and the onion. The potatoes should come out in long strands, while the onions will turn to mush. Transfer to a clean bowl. Fit the food processor with the metal chopping blade and return the shredded potatoes and onions to the bowl. Pulse four or five times, until the potatoes are finely chopped. Add the egg and egg yolk and pulse just until combined. Working quickly, so as not to let the potatoes oxidize and turn brown, transfer the mixture to a large mixing bowl and add the self-rising flour (or substitute), salt, and pepper. Mix just until the flour disappears.

Set a medium cast-iron or other heavy-bottom sauté pan over medium-high heat. Pour in about ¼ inch of vegetable oil. Once the oil is hot (test it by placing a drop or two of batter into the pan to see if it sizzles), use a tablespoon to scoop the batter into the hot pan. Flatten and shape immediately with the back of the spoon. When the edges of the latke are brown and crisp, about 5 minutes, flip. Cook until the second side is browned, remove from the pan, and drain on paper towels. Serve with applesauce and/or sour cream.

cheese latkes

IT WASN'T UNTIL THE JAMES Beard Foundation started holding latke contests in 1995 that I delved into latke lore. And there I found out that the first latkes are actually thought to have been made from cheese, not potato. (Actually, in one of the first competitions a contestant made a cheese latke that baffled the judges.) The reason for

eating cheese latkes extends beyond just frying any old thing in oil. It seems that during the war that led to the destruction of the Temple, a widow, Judith, attracted the general of the Assyrian army (Holofernes). One night while he tried to seduce her, she fed him cheese and wine that made him sleepy. While he was asleep, she cut off his head, and his army fled. So, that's why on Chanukah some people, although not my people, eat cheese latkes. Of course, since then, I have heard of, seen, and tasted many cheese latkes. They are sweet, breakfast-like pancakes that happen to be delicious, although I can't say I much care for them at the end of a heavy Chanukah meal. Here is a recipe for a light, sweet cheese latke that is yummy whenever you choose to eat it. I like them sprinkled with cinnamon sugar or doused in maple syrup.

Because of the combination of ingredients in this recipe, these are one of the few types of pancakes that are almost as good reheated as they are freshly made.

a bissel advice

How come my batter got gloppy? **As the batter sits, the matzo meal swells up and thickens it. As the latkes cook, the batter will loosen again, but the quicker you can fry them, the better. You may have to flatten the pancakes with the back of a spoon as indicated in the recipe. If you have leftover batter that you want to save, you can keep it in the refrigerator for up to 3 days. Because the batter will have thickened a lot, you can either drop it into the hot pan and use a spatula dipped in cold water to flatten the pancakes, or else you can wet your hands and shape the batter into pancakes before you put it in the pan.**

Can I make these latkes in advance and reheat them? **As with any latke or pancake, they are best hot out of the pan. But because these latkes are rich with cheese, they actually reheat pretty well. The easiest thing to do is to put them in a microwave for 30 to 40 seconds per pancake. Alternatively, you can line a cookie sheet with a dish towel and cover the latkes with another. Set them in a 300°F. oven to warm up to the appropriate temperature.**

kosher status MILCHIG
PESADICH

1 cup (7.5 ounces) farmer cheese

¼ cup (2 ounces) cream cheese, at room
temperature

3 eggs

1 cup milk

1 cup matzo meal

1 teaspoon kosher salt

¼ cup (4 tablespoons) sugar

1 teaspoon pure vanilla extract

5 tablespoons unsalted butter, for frying

Cinnamon Sugar (page 239), for dusting

In a mixing bowl, combine the farmer cheese with the cream cheese, mixing with a wooden spoon until smooth. Beat in the eggs, milk, matzo meal, salt, sugar, and vanilla.

Heat 1 tablespoon of the butter in a large frying pan (I think cast iron works best) set over medium-high heat. Drop ¼-cupfuls of batter into the pan to form pancakes, being careful not to crowd the pan. When the pancakes have browned on the bottom and begun to bubble slightly, about 4 minutes, carefully flip them over to cook the second side. They should take an additional 2 or 3 minutes of cooking. Remove to a clean plate or cookie sheet and keep warm. Continue frying the latkes, adding more butter as necessary and being sure not to let the pan get so hot that the latkes burn before they are cooked through. (I take the pan off the heat for a minute or two between batches.) The batter will thicken as it sits, so you may have to spoon the last few latkes into the pan and spread them out a little with the back of a spoon. Serve dusted with Cinnamon Sugar.

sweet potato latkes

WITH A FEW MODIFICATIONS TO my grated-potato latke recipe (page 104), sweet potatoes can be substituted to produce another delicious latke variation. Because sweet potatoes do not brown after they are peeled, the latke mixture can be kept for about a day after it is made before the latkes are fried. Note that although sweet potatoes require roughly the same amount of cooking time as regular potatoes, their higher sugar content gives them a tendency to burn more quickly. Keep your eye on them while they brown, and lower the heat if necessary.

a bissel advice

I can make these in advance? **Sort of. You can make the mixture up to a day in advance, but you should fry them just before serving.**

the whole meshpucha
Because of the mixture's holding potential, these are good latkes to make for a crowd.

kosher status PAREVE
PESADICH

2 large sweet potatoes (1½ pounds), peeled and cut into large chunks

1 large yellow onion (½ pound), halved

2 large eggs

⅓ cup matzo meal

½ teaspoon kosher salt

¼ teaspoon ground mace

Pinch of freshly ground black pepper

About ¾ cup peanut oil, for frying

Using the medium shredding blade of a food processor, shred the potatoes, laying them lengthwise in the feed tube to maximize the length of the strands. Grate the onion on top of the sweet potatoes. Pick out any ungrated pieces of onion or sweet potato. Lay a clean dish towel inside a large bowl and transfer the grated mixture to the towel. Roll the towel lengthwise and wring out as much liquid as possible. Discard the liquid and return the shredded mixture to the bowl. Add the eggs, matzo meal, salt, mace, and pepper, and mix well.

In a large cast-iron or nonstick skillet, heat about ⅛ inch of oil over high heat. The oil is hot enough when a piece of potato sizzles when added. Form a trial latke with a tablespoon of the mixture. Fry until golden brown on both sides. Taste and adjust the seasoning with more salt and pepper if necessary.

To form the latkes, scoop up about ⅓ cup of the mixture with your hands and loosely pat it into a pancake about ½ inch thick, squeezing out any excess liquid. Slip the latke into the hot oil and flatten gently with the back of a spatula. Fry until deep golden brown, about 10 minutes on each side to be sure the center is fully cooked. If the edges darken very quickly, lower the heat. To prevent excess oil absorption, flip each latke only once. Add oil between batches as needed, making sure the oil heats up again before adding more latkes to the pan. Drain the latkes on paper towels or a clean brown paper bag. Serve immediately.

farfel

FOR MY ENTIRE LIFE I have heard my mother tell the story of the farfel served at her wedding. My great-grandmother Eva, who was the first great cook in our family, had made the farfel by hand for 80 people. As was her technique, she rolled out the sheets of pasta dough, dried them until they could be cut into tiny squares, toasted the squares in the oven, and stored them in brown paper bags. It was a lot of work, but according to my grandmother, my mother was worth it (she was the only grandchild interested in learning her grandmother's cooking secrets). Problem was, a day or two before the wedding, somebody mistook the brown bags for garbage and threw away all the farfel. My great-grandmother remade it, but my mother swears the work almost killed her.

Although I knew this story backward and forward, never having tasted or tried to make farfel by hand, I couldn't really relate to the emotional pull of the narrative. So when my mother came to visit to help me get down some of the family recipes on paper, we wanted to try to make farfel the way my mother remembered her grandmother doing it.

Farfel is sometimes translated into English as "egg barley," I presume because it is made with egg pasta and, depending on how you form it, it has the approximate shape of barley. It is otherwise completely unrelated to barley. It seems to me more closely related to other small, toasted, pellet-shaped pastas, such as Hungarian tarhonya,

Greek trahana, and Turkish tarhana, which are all made with flour (sometimes semolina) and milk (often soured), and then dried in the sun or in a slow oven.

There are numerous techniques people use to shape farfel made by hand. Some, like my grandmother, dry the dough out in sheets, cut it into strips, then into little squares that are toasted in the oven. Others form the stiff dough into balls, let the balls dry, and grate them directly into boiling salted water or simmering soup to cook. For reasons that are perhaps beyond anyone's control, I have the best success making farfel the way my great-grandmother did.

I believe the affinity people have for one technique over another has led to a couple of different types of commercially made farfel in the marketplace. There is farfel that comes in little beads like barley (from Manischewitz, for example), and farfel that looks like little toasted misshapen pieces of dough (from Streitz's or Goodman's). The latter more closely resembles homemade farfel. Some commercially prepared farfel is toasted, some isn't.

If you buy farfel or egg barley that isn't toasted (you'll only know by looking; toasted farfel has a dark beige or tan color) you can toast it in a 350°F. oven for 25 to 30 minutes to give it that characteristic nutty, toasted flavor. Otherwise you can just cook it out of the bag.

Whether you make it yourself or buy it, toast it or not, farfel is cooked like noodles, in boiling salted water until tender. It makes a delicious garnish for soup. Some people cook it like rice pilaf, with sautéed onions and a measured amount of liquid. But because different farfels soak up liquid at different rates, I've never had much luck with this method. We ate farfel most often mixed with sautéed mushrooms and onions and baked in a casserole like a stuffing.

Matzo farfel is available at Passover time. Really just tiny pieces of matzo, it can be treated like regular farfel except that instead of boiling it, you just moisten it with water or soup before you mix it with sautéed mushrooms and onions and bake it. Stirring in some beaten egg turns matzo farfel into a Passover kugel.

Here is the recipe that "almost killed my great-grandmother" at my mother's wedding. When you make it for eight people, it is a lot less hassle. If you are feeling industrious, you can make a double or triple batch and store it for up to a year.

a bissel advice

What if I'm impatient? **You really have to take the time to let the dough dry out, both when you roll it out initially, and then after you cut it into strips. Otherwise, the little pieces of farfel stick together, and instead of cute little pellets of farfel, you make a mess. Some farfel is going to stick together anyway, but once toasted, you can easily break it apart. So if you're impatient, don't make your own farfel. Just buy it.**

recipe continues →

farfel

(continued)

1¾ to 2 cups unbleached all-purpose flour

½ teaspoon kosher salt

3 large eggs

MAKES ¾ POUND (2½ CUPS) DRIED,
ABOUT **6** SERVINGS COOKED

kosher status PAREVE

In a small mixing bowl, combine 1¾ cups of the flour and salt. Break in the eggs, add 1 teaspoon water, and using a fork, mix to form a shaggy dough. (Alternately, you can make a well with the flour on the counter, crack the eggs in the center, and stir with a fork to form a dough, as my grandmother did.) Don't worry if all of the flour isn't incorporated. Turn the mixture out onto a clean work surface. Knead to form a stiff dough, incorporating any stray flour or pieces of dough as you work. Add more flour if necessary to make it firm, not sticky, and smooth. Divide the dough into quarters and shape each quarter into a little ball.

Roll each quarter out to a rectangle, about 9 inches by 7 inches. Lay out the rectangles on a floured surface or cloth to dry out for about an hour, until the surface of the dough is leathery to the touch. Turn the dough over a couple of times to be sure it dries out evenly. With a sharp knife, cut the dough into thin strips, less than ¼ inch wide, and let the strips dry for another 20 minutes or so. This second drying prevents the farfel from sticking together when you cut it. Cut the strips crosswise to form small squares. Transfer the squares to a cookie sheet and continue to let dry while you finish cutting the rest.

Preheat the oven to 300°F. Set the cookie sheet of farfel in the oven and toast for between 20 and 25 minutes, raking it frequently with a spoon or spatula, until the noodles are light brown. Remove from the oven and cool to room temperature. You can cook the farfel immediately, but if you intend to store it, you need to dry it out further. Leave it on the trays at room temperature for at least 24 hours. You can store the toasted and dried farfel in brown paper bags, as my great-grandmother did, but you risk it being mistaken for trash and thrown away. Alternatively, you can store the farfel in a canister or jar. It will keep for about a year.

matzo farfel

THIS IS THE PASSOVER EQUIVALENT of farfel, made from tiny pieces of toasted matzo instead of tiny pieces of toasted noodle dough. Matzo farfel is available in boxes in the Jewish section of grocery stores around Passover time. I have never seen it at other times of the year; but then again, I haven't been looking. You can just take regular matzo and break them up into tiny pieces, but I find that the already made matzo farfel has a lighter texture. Unlike regular farfel, matzo farfel doesn't have to be boiled to be eaten—it is just soaked briefly in water and then mixed with other flavorings and baked. Because little tiny pieces of matzo just taste like matzo, I always use a lot of sautéed mushrooms and onions (made with a lot of butter) to doctor it up. Some people like to use a lot of egg to make the matzo farfel more like a kugel, but I use only a little egg because I think it keeps the dish light and fluffy.

a bissel advice
Matzo farfel sounds weird. It's not really. Think of it as similar to puffed rice and experiment with it. You can use soaked matzo farfel in stuffings, pancakes, dumplings, and a whole slew of other recipes. You've got 8 days to mess around with it. Go crazy.

MAKES **2** QUARTS, ENOUGH FOR **12** TO **14** SIDE-DISH SERVINGS

kosher status FLEISHIG, if you made your mushrooms and onions with oil or schmaltz
TRAIF, if like me, you used butter

1 pound matzo farfel

4 cups (2 batches) **Mushrooms and Onions** (page 244)

3 cups chicken soup or stock

2 large eggs

1 tablespoon salt

½ teaspoon freshly ground black pepper

SPECIAL EQUIPMENT

Colander

2-quart baking dish

Preheat the oven to 350°F.

Place the matzo farfel in a large bowl and cover with cold water. Quickly dump it into a colander to drain. Return the farfel to the bowl. Stir in the sautéed mushrooms and onions, chicken soup, eggs, salt, and pepper. Taste and adjust the seasoning. Transfer to a 2-quart baking dish. The matzo farfel can be made up to this point and stored, covered, for a day in the refrigerator.

Bake the matzo farfel for 40 to 50 minutes, until it has heated through, set, and browned on top. Remove from the oven and serve.

farfel with mushrooms and onions

WHETHER OR NOT YOU MAKE your own farfel (page 110), this is a recipe for a delicious side dish. I prefer to use toasted farfel or egg barley, which has a nutty flavor. Not all of the commercially prepared farfel comes toasted. I have given directions for toasting in the advice section below. As far as cooking the farfel, there are two options.

You can sauté the mushrooms and onions in a saucepan, add the farfel and a measured amount of liquid, and simmer it, like a pilaf, until the farfel is tender and all of the liquid has been absorbed. I don't like the results I get with this technique, because I find it difficult to judge the amount of liquid to use (each brand seems to absorb a different amount), and after the mushrooms and onions have boiled for so long with the farfel, they have an unappealingly mushy texture. Instead, I prefer to cook all of the elements separately: I boil the farfel in salted water, I sauté the mushrooms and onions in a frying pan, and then I combine everything.

You also have a couple of options when it comes to serving farfel. Once everything is combined, you can just heat it up in a pot or pan on top of the stove, or even in a microwave. For company, I usually lay it out in a baking dish, dot the top with butter, spoon some soup broth over top, and bake it in the oven until the top is crisp. Sometimes I stir a couple of eggs and some soup broth into the farfel before I bake it, making it into more of a kugel. Experiment until you find a technique that you like best.

a bissel advice

And now, a toast! You should be able to tell if your farfel or egg barley is untoasted by the color: untoasted, it has the pale yellow color similar to other egg noodles; toasted, it is somewhere between beige and golden brown. If yours is untoasted, you should toast it before you proceed with this recipe: Preheat the oven to 300°F. Spread the farfel out on a cookie sheet and set in the oven for 15 to 20 minutes, until the pasta has turned a dark beige or golden brown. Periodically rake the pasta with a large spoon or spatula to ensure it toasts evenly. Remove from the oven and cool to room temperature before proceeding.

kosher status PAREVE, without butter and chicken soup
FLEISHIG, without butter, but with chicken soup
TRAIF, with butter and chicken soup

12 ounces (2 to 2½ cups, depending on the
   size) farfel or egg barley, toasted (see
   "advice," previous page)
1 batch (2 cups) Mushrooms and Onions
   (page 244)
Kosher salt, to taste
Freshly ground black pepper, to taste
1 large egg *(optional)*
¼ cup chicken soup or stock *(optional)*
1 tablespoon unsalted butter *(optional)*

bring a large pot of salted water (4 quarts water with 1 tablespoon kosher salt) to a boil. Add the toasted farfel and cook until tender, about 10 minutes. Drain, but do not rinse. Stir in the sautéed mushrooms and onions and adjust the seasoning with salt and pepper. Reheat on top of the stove or in the microwave before serving.

If you are going to bake the farfel, stir in the egg (if using). Transfer to a greased 2-quart baking dish. You can store the farfel covered in the refrigerator at this point for up to 2 days. Before serving, preheat the oven to 350°F. Spoon the chicken soup or stock over the top and dot with butter (if using). Bake for about 30 minutes, until the top browns and the farfel is heated through.

kasha

TOASTED BUCKWHEAT GROATS. YOU EITHER love 'em or you hate 'em. Me, I love 'em. I grew up

eating kasha: plain as a side dish or gussied up with pasta bow-ties and mushroom and onions—a.k.a. Kasha

Varnishkes (page 118)—for company. Buckwheat has a distinct earthy flavor (some say grassy) that detractors cite as

the reason to pass it over. I say phooey on them. Kasha makes a delicious filling for Knishes (page 22). And Kasha Varnishkes made with homemade noodles are sublime. Although they are a little bit more of a production, if you are serving kasha to people you think might not appreciate it, Kasha Varnishkes is the way to go. With enough butter and mushrooms and onions and pasta, you can get someone to eat almost anything.

You can prepare basic kasha in just about any quantity, as long as you increase the amount of liquid proportionately. If you want to halve the recipe to make less than I've suggested, just use an egg yolk or egg white instead of the whole egg. Be sure to have the liquid boiling hot. And use enough salt to bring out the true flavor of the grain.

a bissel advice

Which kasha? Kasha is available in three or four different granulations, depending on the producer: fine, medium, coarse, and whole. I alternate using all of them depending on who's eating. Fine kasha is usually preferred by people who don't love kasha in the first place. Medium is just that, medium. I think my favorite is coarse. Whole kasha is for serious kasha lovers. The whole grain takes longer to cook and has a slightly chewier texture. Play it safe with medium granulation and you should be fine, so to speak.

Do I have to toast it? By definition, kasha is toasted buckwheat groats. But I follow the directions recommended on the box that advise toasting it again with egg. You can omit the egg, toast it dry, and add the hot water. But I think the egg makes it fluffier and more flavorful.

kosher status PAREVE, without the butter or chicken soup
MILCHIG, with butter and water
TRAIF, with butter and soup

2 cups boiling water, stock, or chicken soup

2 tablespoons unsalted butter *(optional)*

1 teaspoon kosher salt

1 cup dry kasha

1 large egg or 2 egg whites, slightly beaten

¼ teaspoon freshly ground black pepper

SPECIAL EQUIPMENT

A wide saucepan or sauté pan with a tight-fitting lid

In a small saucepan, heat the water or soup, butter (if using), and salt until boiling.

Place the kasha in the wide saucepan or sauté pan. Add the egg and stir it into the kasha to distribute. The kasha will clump together, but don't worry about it. Set over medium-high heat and stir the kasha continuously to toast. As it heats, the clumps should break apart into individual grains and the kasha should give off a distinct aroma of buckwheat. Once the kasha has browned slightly, about 5 minutes, pour in the hot liquid. Add the black pepper, cover, turn down the heat, and simmer until all of the water has been absorbed and the kasha has plumped, 7 or 8 minutes. Remove from the heat, fluff with a fork, and serve.

kasha varnishkes

WHEN YOU DRESS UP YOUR kasha with pasta bow-ties and sautéed mushroom and onions, you transform it from a Russian peasant dish to formal dinner-party fare. The original Kasha Varnishkes was made with little squares of homemade pasta. But the advent of commercially prepared noodles must have brought on a need to get fancy with pasta shapes.

After consulting with a Judaica professor who in turn consulted with two other professors, I was unable to come up with a meaning for the Yiddish word *varnishkes*. (Actually, they don't even think it's a Yiddish word!) Several theories were espoused but there was not enough evidence to draw a conclusion beyond the fact that Kasha Varnishkes are (is?) delicious.

Since Kasha Varnishkes is (are?) really a dish for company, I'm giving you the proportions for a decent amount—based on ½ pound of bow-ties. (Actually, I usually make a whole pound of pasta, but I *really* love this dish.) I defy anyone to hate kasha in this form. If you want a smaller amount, you can cut the recipe in half. If you just want a little Kasha Varnishkes for yourself, do what I do and order it from the Second Avenue Deli.

a bissel advice

Goyish or Jewish bow-ties? Just about every pasta manufacturer makes pasta in the shape of bow-ties. In Italian, the shape is called farfalle. The only difference between the two is that Jewish versions (such as Manischewitz) are usually made with egg pasta, whereas Italian versions are just basic flour-and-water pasta. And the Jewish varieties tend to cook up softer than the others.

Oy, such a production? To make Kasha Varnishkes less of a production, you can prepare each component—the kasha, the mushrooms and onions, and the pasta—in advance. You can skip the pasta altogether and just add mushrooms and onions to regular kasha, too.

What about the old-fashioned way? Just for the heck of it, one day I made my own lokshen (egg noodles) cut into squares, and used them to make Kasha Varnishkes. I never should have done it, though, because the resulting dish was so delicious I now try to make my own pasta whenever I make Kasha Varnishkes. If you are feeling industrious, make ½ pound of square noodles using half the proportions for 1 pound of Egg Noodles (page 240). Roll the dough out until paper thin as directed in the recipe, and cut into 1½-inch squares. Toss the squares with flour and store on a cookie sheet until ready to use. Prepare the Kasha Varnishkes as directed, decreasing the cooking time for the homemade noodles to about 2 minutes total.

kosher status MILCHIG, if you use butter in your mushrooms and onions
FLEISHIG, if you use chicken schmaltz
PAREVE, if you use peanut oil
TRAIF, if you do what I do and use butter and chicken stock

½ **pound pasta bow-ties (a.k.a. farfalle)**

4 cups (1 batch) cooked Kasha (page 116)

2 cups (1 batch) Mushrooms and Onions (page 244)

Kosher salt, to taste

Freshly ground black pepper, to taste

½ **to 1 cup vegetable, chicken, or beef stock**

bring a large pot of salted water to a boil (about 4 quarts water with 1½ tablespoons kosher salt). Cook the pasta until just past al dente — the pinched area in the center of the bow-tie should be soft. Drain. In a large bowl or pot, toss the noodles with the cooked kasha and sautéed mushrooms and onions. Adjust the seasoning with salt and pepper.

You can eat the Kasha Varnishkes as is or heat them up in a pot on the stove, but I like to make them in the morning and reheat them in the oven before dinner. Transfer the mixture to a large, 2- or 3-quart baking dish. Pour over about half a cup of chicken stock or soup. Cover with aluminum foil and set in a 325°F. oven. Heat for about 25 minutes. Remove the cover. If the mixture looks dry, pour over another half cup of stock. Turn up the heat to 375°F. Continue baking for about 15 to 20 minutes, until the noodles on top begin to brown. Remove from the oven and serve.

savory yeast dumplings

MY FRIEND DAÑO SERVES THESE dumplings alongside braised or roasted meat at his restaurant in upstate New York. His original recipe calls for butter and milk, and it's delicious. But because I thought that might seem too traif even for some of my readers, I tried substituting schmaltz and chicken soup. The result was also delicious. In concept and texture, these dumplings fall somewhere between steamed Chinese dim-sum buns and brioche. For something a little more sophisticated, you can stuff the dumplings with any of the savory fillings on pages 220 to 225. But the plain, doughy dumplings are just as satisfying.

To save time, use quick-rising, instant, or rapid-rise yeast (three adjectives that describe basically the same product). Most grocery stores carry it and display it alongside other types of yeast. This type can be combined with other ingredients without proofing it beforehand.

The dumplings can be made up to 2 days in advance and reheated before serving. Though it is hard for me to say it, they reheat best in the microwave. If you prefer the old-fashioned way, you can reheat them in a steamer over boiling water. Serve them with braised meat, stew, or anything that has a nice gravy.

Daño also makes a delicious sweet variation, filled with prune spread and topped with melted butter, ground poppy seeds, and powdered sugar. See page 150 for that recipe.

a bissel advice

My little dumpling? Not exactly. These dumplings are kind of big, but they are light and delicate, so don't worry about stuffing your guests.

Looks complicated, nu? Not if you have an electric mixer with a dough hook. If you don't, I would suggest not making these dumplings. (What about a nice matzo ball?) The directions look more difficult than they actually are; it just takes a lot of words to describe what you have to do.

How about something sweet? Turn to page 150 for a prune-filled variation that makes a delicious dessert.

kosher status Depends on the fat and whether you use milk or not. I prefer the dumplings made with milk and butter, but then they are traif when served with meat.

h eat the fat in a small sauté pan and add the onion. Sauté until lightly golden brown, about 5 minutes. Pour in the milk or soup and bring to a boil. Turn off the heat, add the salt and sugar, and let cool until just warm to the touch (about 110°F.).

Meanwhile, combine the flour and yeast in the bowl of an electric mixer. Pour the warm liquid and onion into the flour and mix, using the dough hook, to form a soft dough. Let the dough hook knead the dough for at least 5 minutes, until the dough is smooth and shiny. It shouldn't be sticky, so if it is, add 1 to 2 tablespoons more flour and continue kneading. Turn the dough out onto a lightly floured work surface and knead five or six times to form a ball. Place a drop of oil in the bottom of a clean mixing bowl and place the dough inside. Move it around to coat it with oil. Cover the bowl with plastic wrap and let rise for about 1½ hours, until doubled in bulk.

Punch down the dough. Divide it into 10 equal portions and shape each into a ball by pinching the edges underneath. Cup your hand and roll the ball of dough between the work surface and your cupped palm to make it smooth and tight. Place the dough balls on a cookie sheet. Cover with a clean paper towel and let rise in a warm place while the water comes to a boil.

Bring a large, wide pot of salted water to a boil (about 4 quarts water with 1 tablespoon kosher salt). Use the remaining ¾ teaspoon oil to coat the bottom of a plastic container. Plop five of the dough balls into the boiling water. Cover tightly and let boil for exactly 5 minutes. Have a sharp paring knife at the ready. After 5 minutes, remove the lid and use the paring knife to poke three or four holes in each dumpling to help prevent deflating. Using a slotted spoon, lift the poked dumplings out of the water and place them into the oiled container. Repeat with the remaining dumplings. Cool to room temperature. The dumplings can be covered tightly and stored for up to 3 days. To reheat, place the dumplings on clean plates and microwave on medium power for whatever the total of 50 seconds per dumpling works out to be.

4 tablespoons unsalted butter, schmaltz, peanut oil, or a combination

½ large yellow onion (¼ pound), finely chopped

1¼ cups milk, chicken soup, or stock

2 teaspoons kosher salt

1 tablespoon sugar

3 cups unbleached all-purpose flour

2 packages (4½ teaspoons) active dry yeast

1 teaspoon peanut or vegetable oil

SPECIAL EQUIPMENT
Electric mixer with a dough hook
Wide 8-quart pot with a tight-fitting lid
Sharp paring knife

stuffing

IN THE SAME WAY THAT we still say that we "dial" a telephone number when what we actually do is push buttons, we call moistened bread mixed with egg, onion, and other flavorings "stuffing" when in fact it is rarely stuffed into anything at all. "Dressing" is no better. For some, my sister Leslie included, stuffing isn't stuffing without the flavor of sage and thyme. But since our mother didn't use herbs, I associate stuffing more with the flavor of celery. (This just proves a point we used to fight over when we were little, that we weren't related—now, if only we didn't look so much alike.) Anyway, whether you add sage or not, this is a basic, all-purpose stuffing that can be served with meat or fish. It is practically identical to the stuffing used in the Nana's Chicken Acropolis (page 82), except that I bake it in a casserole and serve it alongside roast turkey or chicken. Substituting matzo for the bread makes a perfectly delicious Passover stuffing.

a bissel advice

Can I use this inside a bird? Of course. But be sure to cook it very well to avoid food poisoning from salmonella or its friends. An instant-read thermometer inserted into the center of the stuffing in the cavity of whatever you have stuffed should read at least 165°F. to avoid any possible food-borne illness. The problem is that at this point, whatever you've stuffed is probably overcooked and dry. Better safe than sorry.

the whole meshpucha

This recipe can be increased or decreased proportionately as necessary.

kosher status MILCHIG, with butter
FLEISHIG, with schmaltz
PAREVE, with oil
PESADICH, with matzo
TRAIF, with butter and chicken soup

1 pound (1 large loaf) stale white bread, torn into pieces (about 12 cups), or 1 pound box plain matzo, broken into pieces (about 8 cups)

½ cup (1 stick) unsalted butter, Chicken Schmaltz (page 236), peanut oil, or a combination

2 large onions (½ pound), finely chopped

2 large celery stalks (⅓ pound), finely chopped

2 large carrots (⅓ pound), shredded

5 medium leaves fresh sage, minced, or ½ teaspoon ground sage *(optional)*

1 teaspoon fresh thyme, chopped, or ¼ teaspoon dried

¼ pound assorted mushrooms, chopped (2 cups)

2 tablespoons kosher salt

1 teaspoon freshly ground black pepper

4 large eggs, slightly beaten

½ cup minced flat-leaf parsley

4 scallions, chopped (about ½ cup)

SPECIAL EQUIPMENT
2-quart baking dish

Preheat the oven to 350°F. Grease the baking dish.

Place the bread or matzo pieces in a large bowl and cover with cold water or a combination of water and chicken stock (if you have extra lying around), about 2 quarts. Let sit for 1 minute. Drain, using a strainer if necessary, and pressing against the side of the bowl to squeeze out as much excess liquid as possible. Set aside.

In a large sauté pan set over medium-high heat, heat the fat. Add the chopped onions and sauté until translucent, about 5 minutes. Add the celery and carrots, and continue cooking until somewhat tender, about 5 minutes more. Add the fresh sage and thyme (if using), and cook for 1 minute (if using dried, add it later). Add the mushrooms and cook until they have softened and shrunk, about 2 minutes. Stir in 1 tablespoon of the salt and all of the pepper. Cool. Add this mixture to the soaked bread or matzo. Stir in the beaten eggs, parsley, scallions, dried sage and thyme (if using), and the remaining tablespoon of salt. Transfer this mixture to the greased baking dish. The stuffing can be made up to this point, covered, and refrigerated a day in advance, if desired.

Bake at 350°F. until the stuffing has set and the top has browned, about 45 minutes. If you have to keep the stuffing in a warm oven longer, baste with some chicken soup or some of the pan juices of the roast turkey or chicken.

spätzle

THOUGH AUSTRIAN IN ORIGIN, THESE tender, eggy noodles are a delicious Old World side dish that everybody loves. They are close to the quick lokshen my mother made once in a while for chicken soup, and in fact you can drip them directly into the soup to cook. (I prefer to cook them in a separate pot of boiling water and transfer them when they are done to the soup.) This is another dish from my friend Daňo, but Daňo doesn't ever use a recipe, and it took me a while to figure out the right proportions to achieve the proper consistency—somewhere between pancake batter and dough. My favorite way to serve spätzle once they are boiled is to fry them in butter with onions (see page 126). They are also delicious stirred into scrambled eggs and topped with melted cheese for breakfast. You can make a batch of spätzle, toss them with a drop or two of oil, and keep them in the fridge for up to a week. Then whenever you want to eat them, you can just grab a handful and toss them into a frying pan with some butter.

a bissel advice

What on earth is a spätzle maker? Imagine a cross between a grater and a funnel. You pour the batter into the funnel part and then slide it back and forth over the grater part so that short drips of batter fall into the boiling water. You can create the same effect by using a coarse potato ricer or a colander with wide holes and a wooden spoon. Add more egg or water to make the batter thinner. Pour the batter into the colander and run the wooden spoon over it to force the batter through the holes.

1½ cups unbleached all-purpose flour

6 to 7 large eggs

1 tablespoon peanut or vegetable oil, for
   storing

SPECIAL EQUIPMENT

Spätzle maker or a colander with large holes

Using a mixing bowl and a strong whisk, or an electric mixer fitted with a paddle attachment, combine the flour with 6 eggs. Beat to form a loose batter, slightly thicker than pancake batter. Depending on the humidity of the flour, you may need an additional egg to achieve the right consistency. The batter should be pourable, but still have a slightly springy quality (the result of the gluten in the flour and the eggs). Let this batter sit at room temperature while the water comes to a boil.

Bring 3 or 4 quarts of water to a boil with 1½ tablespoons of kosher salt in it. Fill a large bowl with ice water. Hold the spätzle maker or colander over the pot of boiling water and ladle about ¾ cup of the batter into it. Move it around so that the batter flows through the holes into the boiling water. If the batter is too thick to go through the holes, return it to the bowl and beat in 1 to 2 tablespoons of water. Don't overcrowd the pot. Stir it around a couple of times to keep the spätzle from clumping. The noodles will sink to the bottom of the pan and then float to the top and puff up when they start cooking. Once the water comes back up to a boil, cook for 2 minutes. Remove the spätzle from the water with a small sieve or slotted spoon and plunge them into the ice water. The spätzle will shrivel up while they cool. Repeat with the remaining batter. I find it takes me three batches to cook this much batter. Drain the spätzle in a colander and remove any ice that hasn't melted. Toss the drained spätzle with the oil to coat and store in the refrigerator for up to 1 week until ready to use.

buttered lokshen or spätzle

SERIOUS COMFORT FOOD. THAT'S WHAT freshly made lokshen or egg noodles and spätzle become when they are fried in butter. For a savory dish, I sauté an onion in the butter before I add the noodles. You can add sautéed cabbage, too. For something sweet, I flavor the noodles with sugar and cinnamon. Adding large-curd cottage or farmer cheese makes the kind of baby food grown-ups enjoy. Even if you don't make the noodles yourself, this type of dish is always a treat. Although you can certainly substitute schmaltz for butter when making the savory version, I would recommend using butter for the sweet.

FOR SAVORY NOODLES

2 tablespoons unsalted butter or schmaltz

½ medium onion (4 ounces), chopped

2 cups (⅓ pound) shredded green cabbage (optional)

2 cups cooked Egg Noodles (page 240), Spätzle (page 124), or other small noodles

Pinch of kosher salt

Pinch of freshly ground black pepper

½ cup large-curd cottage cheese, drained, or farmer cheese (optional)

FOR SWEET NOODLES

2 tablespoons unsalted butter

2 cups cooked Egg Noodles (page 240), Spätzle (page 124), or other small noodles

1 tablespoon Cinnamon Sugar (page 239), or to taste

½ cup large-curd cottage cheese, drained, or farmer cheese (optional)

MAKES **2** TO **4** SERVINGS

kosher status MILCHIG, with the butter and cheese
You can use schmaltz and leave out the cheese to make the savory noodles FLEISHIG, but using oil is not advised

for the savory noodles, heat the butter or schmaltz in a large frying pan set over medium heat. Add the onion and sauté until soft and very lightly golden brown, about 6 minutes. Add the cabbage (if using), and continue sautéing until the cabbage is wilted and tender, about 10 minutes. Add the cooked noodles and toss to coat with the fat. Add the seasoning and stir in the cheese (if using). Continue cooking until the noodles are heated through.

For the sweet noodles, heat the butter in a large frying pan set over medium heat. Add the noodles and toss to coat. Stir in the cinnamon sugar and cottage cheese (if using), and continue cooking until the noodles are heated through.

a bissel advice

You call that a dish? **This combination of noodles and cheese has virtually the same medicinal properties as chicken soup: it makes everything better. Some people eat it only when they are sick. But the savory version also makes a nice accompaniment to braised roasts or meats.**

roasted potatoes

BECAUSE NO MEAL AT MY MOTHER'S HOUSE is complete without a selection of starches — never just one — Roasted Potatoes were a common accompaniment to dinner. They are pretty easy to make, but you have to be sure to allow enough time for them to roast. Even though we aren't concerned about the proscription of butter with

meat, my mother likes to baste her potatoes with chicken schmaltz while they roast because she (and all of us) likes the flavor. If she doesn't have any schmaltz around, she uses sweet butter.

You can make these potatoes in any quantity, provided you don't fill the pan so much that they don't get browned and crisp. I prefer the roasted potatoes hot out of the oven; they don't reheat very well. But for advance preparation, you can peel and cut them up beforehand; be sure to keep them submerged in cold water to prevent discoloration.

a bissel advice

What can I do in advance? Not much. Peel and chunk the potatoes and submerge them in cold water until you are ready to roast them.

MAKES **8** SERVINGS

kosher status MILCHIG, with butter
FLEISHIG, with schmaltz

3 pounds (6 large) starchy potatoes, such as Yukon Gold or Red Bliss potatoes, peeled and cut into 1½-inch chunks

4 teaspoons kosher salt

½ teaspoon freshly ground black pepper

¼ teaspoon paprika

½ cup Chicken Schmaltz (page 236) or 1 stick (¼ pound) unsalted butter, cut into chunks

SPECIAL EQUIPMENT

Cookie sheet with sides or jelly roll pan (nonstick is a bonus).

Preheat the oven to 350°F.

Lay the potatoes out on a cookie sheet so that they are not touching. Season with the salt, pepper, and paprika and toss to coat evenly. Drop spoonfuls of schmaltz or chunks of butter around the cookie sheet and set in the oven. After about 10 minutes, baste the potatoes with the melted fat (you may have to tilt the pan to one side to be able to get a good spoonful). Continue roasting for 1 to 1¼ hours, basting every 15 minutes or so, until the potatoes are soft and browned around the edges. Turn the potatoes around on their side once or twice while they are cooking to ensure even browning. Remove from the oven, and using a spatula to be sure you scrape all the crisp bits off the pan, transfer the hot roasted potatoes to a serving dish.

apple-orange lokshen kugel

KUGEL (KOO-GUHL) MEANS "PUDDING" IN Yiddish, but not in the sense of chocolate or butterscotch. Think bread pudding, only substitute noodles (lokshen) or potatoes and you'll have a better idea of what I am talking about. A WASP might call it a baked casserole. In the Jewish culinary canon, kugels come in two different forms: sweet

and savory. Interestingly, both are eaten as accompaniments to the meal, not as desserts or main courses. And in my experience, they are usually served just slightly warmer than room temperature, although they are pretty good hot out of the oven or cold out of the refrigerator. When I was a kid I used to sneak pieces of my mother's Cherry–Cheese Lokshen Kugel (page 165) out of the freezer and eat them frozen.

Some people find a piece of sweet noodle kugel—rich with eggs, butter, apples, and raisins—an odd thing on a plate with a piece of roast beef or brisket. Although this combination recalls the Ashkenazi tradition of mixing sweet and savory (see Tzimmes on page 134), you can eat your kugel whenever you please. At a large holiday spread I always save the piece of sweet noodle pudding on my plate until the end, as a sort of pre-dessert.

If you have time to make your own egg noodles (page 240) you won't regret it. In fact, if you do it once, you'll have to do it every time after that. Savory noodle kugels and potato kugels (like a latke that's baked in a casserole), on the other hand, are served like stuffing. And I happen to like a sweet noodle pudding cold for breakfast.

Anyway, the point is that you should a kugel the next time you are looking for a bulky dish to round out a meal. Because they are easy to transport and can be served at room temperature, they are also perfect to cart along to a potluck dinner.

This is a recipe from my Tante Paula's repertoire. Though not my real aunt, Paula was a neighbor of ours in Teaneck, New Jersey. Originally from Poland, she was an excellent cook, and my mother made several of her recipes family standards. For a slightly different but equally delicious flavor, you can substitute crushed pineapple for the applesauce.

a bissel advice

So sweet? I've actually decreased the amount of sugar in the original recipe. But if you still find it too sweet, decrease it further.

1 pound wide egg noodles

½ cup (1 stick), unsalted butter

6 large eggs, slightly beaten

2 cups Chunky Applesauce (page 212), or a
    1-pound jar commercially prepared
    applesauce

⅔ cup sugar

1 small can (6 ounces) frozen orange juice
    concentrate, defrosted but not diluted

½ cup golden raisins

¼ teaspoon ground cinnamon (if using
    commercially prepared applesauce)

Preheat the oven to 350°F.

Bring a large pot of salted water (about 5 quarts with 1½ tablespoons kosher salt) to a rolling boil. Cook the noodles until tender but not soft, about 8 minutes. They should remain al dente because they will be cooked further in the oven. Drain the noodles in a colander, but do not rinse. Place the noodles back in the warm pot and add the butter, stirring until it is melted. Add the remaining ingredients and stir with a wooden spoon until well combined.

Transfer the kugel mixture to a 2-quart rectangular glass baking dish or other similar ovenproof dish. The kugel can be made up to this point and either refrigerated for up to 2 days or frozen for up to 3 weeks before baking. When ready to bake the kugel, remove it from the refrigerator or freezer and let it come to room temperature. Bake in the middle of the preheated oven for 35 to 45 minutes, or until some of the noodles on the top have turned deep brown and the pudding has set. If you want to be sure, insert an instant-read thermometer in the center of the kugel (but not touching the bottom); if it reads about 180°F., the kugel is cooked.

Remove from the oven, place on a rack, and cool to room temperature before slicing. Cut into squares. Serve the kugel at room temperature or reheat in a 300°F. oven until warm.

pineapple-orange lokshen kugel

SUBSTITUTE 1 (18-ounce) can of crushed pineapple, with juice, for the applesauce. Proceed with the recipe as directed.

savory noodle kugel with greens and cheese

HERE IS A VERSATILE, SAVORY (as opposed to sweet) lokshen kugel, or "noodle pudding," that can be made with just about any variety of greens (think spinach, kale, beet tops, or chard), and any type of fresh, curd cheese, such as cottage cheese, pot cheese, or crumbled feta. Served with a salad, this kugel makes a satisfying lunch entree.

As a side dish it sort of serves two roles—starch and vegetable (not to mention fat). Like all kugels, this one can be served hot out of the oven, at room temperature, or chilled. I happen to prefer it just slightly warmer than room temperature.

And like all noodle kugels, if you make your own noodles your friends and family will love you forever.

a bissel advice

Which lokshen? Egg noodles come in three sizes: fine, medium, and wide or broad. I happen to prefer the wide noodles for most kugels, but it isn't important. What is important is to pay attention to the size of the package. Egg noodles are sold in 12-ounce (3/4 pound) or 16-ounce (1-pound) packages. This recipe calls for 12 ounces. Others in the book call for 16 ounces.

Which greens? If you are making Beefy Beet Borscht (page 50) or the Chocolate Beet Cake (page 174), purchase fresh beets with the tops and use them in this kugel. Otherwise, you can use just about anything.

3/4 to 1 pound fresh greens, such as spinach,
    kale, chard, beet tops, or collards, or one
    10-ounce package frozen greens

12 ounces dried egg noodles

6 tablespoons (3/4 stick) unsalted butter

1 large yellow onion (1/2 pound), finely
    chopped (about 1 1/4 cups)

1 tablespoon chopped fresh dill (about
    5 sprigs)

1 cup fresh curd cheese, such as cottage
    cheese, pot cheese, or crumbled feta

5 large eggs

2 1/2 teaspoons kosher salt

1/2 teaspoon freshly ground black pepper

SPECIAL EQUIPMENT

2-quart baking dish, about 2 inches deep

Preheat the oven to 350°F. Butter the baking dish and set aside.

If using fresh greens, they first must be cleaned thoroughly and blanched. To clean, fill a clean sink or large tub with cold water. Remove and discard the stems and any tough or stringy veins running through the leaves. Place the greens in the water and let soak for about 10 minutes, swishing them around periodically to be sure they are well rinsed. Lift the greens out of the water into a colander or strainer to drain. Discard the water and repeat.

To blanch, bring a large pot of salted water (about 4 quarts water and 1 tablespoon kosher salt) to a boil. Add the greens and cook until tender. Softer greens, such as spinach and chard, will take only 2 or 3 minutes; tougher greens, such as beet tops, kale, and collards, will take 10 to 15 minutes. Drain. Squeeze out as much water as you can. Chop. You should have about 1 1/2 cups.

If using frozen greens, defrost in a strainer to allow them to drain. Squeeze out any excess water and chop.

MENTAL NOSH

Depending on where your ancestors are from, you probably grew up with either sweet (as I did) or savory kugels like this one. I have heard Polish Jews like sweeter food and Russian Jews like saltier food, but I've never been able to prove this hypothesis.

Meanwhile, cook the noodles. Bring a large pot of salted water to a boil (4 quarts water with 1 1/2 tablespoons kosher salt). Cook the egg noodles until just past al dente, about 10 minutes. (If using homemade noodles, 2 minutes will suffice.) Drain.

Melt the butter in a large sauté pan over medium-high heat. Add the chopped onion and sauté until soft, about 8 minutes. Stir in the chopped dill. In a large mixing bowl, combine the chopped greens and sautéed onion mixture with the cheese, eggs, salt, and pepper, and mix well. Transfer to the buttered baking dish, even out the top with the back of a spoon, and set in the preheated oven. Bake for 45 minutes, or until the kugel has set (firm to the touch) and the top has browned. Remove and cool to room temperature. Cut into rectangles or squares to serve.

potato kugel

WE NEVER ATE POTATO KUGEL at home because my family preferred to take our potatoes and onions in the form of latkes. While I was talking to my mother one evening trying to come up with a recipe for a potato kugel that wasn't heavy, greasy, or unappealingly gray, as most of them are, the phone rang. It was Mimi Sheraton, author of one of my favorite Jewish cookbooks, *From My Mother's Kitchen,* who had just written a new book on the bialy. Her call reminded me to consult her older book only to find that she and her family didn't like potato kugels much either, for the same unappetizing reasons.

At takeout shops in the Hasidic section of Crown Heights, Brooklyn, I've tried potato kugels that look like they were baked in large tubs. They are sold by the pound. The black crust and unappetizing gray color are off-putting at first. And the texture is a little oily. But the flavor, salty and potatoey, can be truly delicious.

I began experimenting. And to everyone's surprise, I created a potato kugel that is light, oniony, and delicious, with a pleasant, discernible potato flavor. Two things are key: the way you chop the potatoes (I use a two-step food-processor technique); and the addition of potato starch, a staple around Passover that you can keep throughout the year. Even my mother enjoyed this potato kugel. I haven't had the chance to serve it to Mimi yet.

a bissel advice

Something special? To make individual kugels, use a non-stick muffin tin. Bake them at the same temperature, but for only 30 minutes, depending on the size of the muffin tins and how filled they are. To be sure they are done, use an instant-read thermometer.

the whole meshpucha

You can increase the ingredients in this recipe proportionately. Be sure to use an appropriately sized baking dish so that the kugel is no more than 1½ to 2 inches thick.

kosher status MILCHIG, with butter
FLEISHIG, with schmaltz
PAREVE, with oil

3 pounds (6 large) Yukon Gold potatoes, cut into 3-inch large chunks

2 large yellow onions (1 pound), halved

7 large eggs

4 tablespoons schmaltz or unsalted butter, melted and cooled, or peanut oil

1 tablespoon kosher salt

2 teaspoons baking powder

2 tablespoons potato starch

6 tablespoons all-purpose flour

½ teaspoon freshly ground black pepper

SPECIAL EQUIPMENT

Food processor

Deep 2-quart baking dish

Clean dish towel

preheat the oven to 400°F. Grease and flour a deep 2-quart baking dish. Using a food processor fitted with a shredding disk, shred about half of the potatoes into long strands. On top of the shredded potatoes, shred half of the onions. The onion juice will help keep the potatoes from turning brown. Turn this mixture out of the work bowl into the center of a clean dish towel. Roll up the towel lengthwise and wring the mixture over the sink to squeeze out as much water as possible. Place in a bowl and set aside. Repeat with the remaining potatoes and onions, being sure to wring them out well. Change the blade of the processor to the metal chopping blade. Working with half the mixture at a time, pulse the shredded potatoes and onions with until finely chopped, about ten 1-second pulses in all. Repeat with the remaining mixture. Combine in a clean bowl.

Stir in the eggs, fat, salt, baking powder, potato starch, flour, and pepper, and mix well. Transfer to the greased and floured baking dish and even out the top with a spatula or the back of a spoon. Bake for 45 minutes to an hour, until the kugel has set, browned, and cooked through. An instant-read thermometer should register about 185°F. when the kugel is done. Remove and cool to room temperature before serving.

carrot and sweet potato tzimmes

TZIMMES IS BOTH A DISH and a Yiddish word that means "a little of everything all mixed up together"—in short, "a mess." I suspect the meaning comes from the fact that tzimmes often contains sweet and savory elements, sometimes meat, vegetables, dried fruit, and all sorts of other things. Truth be told, I do not love tzimmes with too many different things, and I find the combination of meat cooked with sweet unappealing. That's why I like this tzimmes, which is just sweet potatoes and carrots with prunes and flavorings. It's sweet, and you still serve it with the main meal, not as dessert, but it is a pleasant addition to a big holiday spread. If you don't overcook it, each element retains its own texture and flavor, while somehow still coming together to make a unified dish. You can increase the proportions to make it any size. If you do not want to use the butter because you are serving the tzimmes with meat, simply omit it; don't try to substitute margarine or oil—that is gross.

1½ pounds (3 medium) sweet potatoes,
    peeled and cut into 2-inch chunks
¾ pound (5 large) carrots, cut into 2-inch
    chunks
½ pound (1 large) sweet white onion (such
    as Vidalia or Maui), cut into 1-inch
    chunks
¼ pound (¾ cup) pitted prunes
⅓ cup honey or sugar
¾ cup orange juice
½ stick (2 ounces) unsalted butter *(optional)*
2 2½-inch sticks cinnamon
1 small piece (1 point) star anise
1 teaspoon kosher salt
Pinch of white pepper

SPECIAL EQUIPMENT

2-quart baking dish with cover or heavy-duty
    aluminum foil

MAKES **2 QUARTS, OR 10 SERVINGS**

kosher status MILCHIG, with butter
PAREVE, without

Preheat the oven to 350°F. In the baking dish, combine the sweet potatoes, carrots, onion, prunes, honey or sugar, orange juice, butter (if using), cinnamon, star anise, salt, and pepper. Toss everything around a couple of times to be sure the ingredients are evenly distributed. Cover the baking dish. Set in the preheated oven and roast for 1 hour and 30 minutes, or until the vegetables are tender.

a bissel advice

Can I make it in advance? You can assemble the tzimmes, cover it, and refrigerate it for a couple of days. Then you can bake it the day you intend to serve it. But because the vegetables are very well cooked, I wouldn't advise cooking it days in advance; once you reheat it, the tzimmes turns to mush.

braised sauerkraut with mushrooms

THIS IS A QUICK, SIMPLE side dish that has a particular warming quality on cold winter nights. Of course, if you make your own sauerkraut (see page 198), the dish is that much better. But you can use commercially made sauerkraut along with a few extra spices to produce fine results. Without the wine, I use this recipe to make a filling for Pierogi (page 17) or Knishes (page 22).

MAKES 2¹/₂ CUPS, ABOUT 4 SIDE-DISH SERVINGS

kosher status Choose your fat wisely

In a medium saucepan, heat the fat over medium-high heat. Add the sliced onion and sauté until soft and translucent, 6 to 8 minutes. Add the mushrooms and continue cooking until they give off some water and soften. Add the sauerkraut and wine, and the juniper, caraway, and bay leaf (if using). Turn down the heat and simmer, uncovered, until the sauerkraut is soft and about one quarter of the liquid has evaporated, approximately 10 minutes. Adjust the seasoning with salt and pepper.

3 tablespoons Chicken Schmaltz (page 236), duck fat, unsalted butter, or peanut oil
1 large yellow onion (¹/₂ pound), thinly sliced
¹/₄ pound button mushrooms, thinly sliced
2 to 2¹/₄ cups sauerkraut (1 pound), rinsed under cold water and drained
¹/₄ cup dry Riesling or Gewürztraminer
2 juniper berries *(optional)*
¹/₄ teaspoon caraway seeds *(optional)*
¹/₂ bay leaf *(optional)*
¹/₄ teaspoon kosher salt *(optional)*
¹/₄ teaspoon freshly ground black pepper

MENTAL NOSH

Choucroute garni is French for "garnished sauerkraut," and it is a classic dish of the Alsace region of France. To make it, sauerkraut is braised with wine, sausages, potatoes, onion, and other aromatics. Although my version of braised sauerkraut is less involved, it was inspired by this traditional dish, one of my favorites of all of French cooking. People in Alsace love sauerkraut. In the fall, men with sharp blades used to go door to door to shred the cabbage that households would then use to make their sauerkraut for the season. Unfortunately, people living in New York City in the third millennium have to do it themselves. To find out how, see page 198.

bean salad

ALTHOUGH MOST PEOPLE JUST COOK beans in water until they are soft and then use the cooked beans as an ingredient in salads and other preparations, my chef-friend Daño cooks his with the vegetables and other aromatics that will later become the salad. Once the beans are chilled, he adds raw vegetables to provide contrasting textures and seasoning to balance the flavors. I now use this technique of simmering beans with all sorts of things—vegetables, vinegar, spices—whenever I cook them, whether I am going to serve them plain as a side dish, or use them in other dishes, such as Nana's Chicken Acropolis (page 82) or Herring in Sour Cream with Potatoes and Beans (page 32).

a bissel advice

How do you pick over the beans? I find it easiest to dump the dried beans on one side of a cookie sheet and pass them to the other side while looking for stones or dark and disfigured beans. By the time all of the beans are on the opposite side of the cookie sheet, they are ready to soak.

Cook the beans with salt—are you crazy? Contrary to conventional wisdom, I prefer the texture of beans cooked with salt. True, they are somewhat more toothsome, but in the way al dente pasta is better than mushy pasta, that toothsomeness is desirable. The only time I would cook beans without salt is if I intend to puree them—for instance, if I were making a smooth soup or hummus or something like that.

to prepare the beans, the night before you intend to cook them, pick them over to remove any stones or any dark or disfigured beans. Place the beans in a large bowl and cover with tepid water, making sure the water level comes at least 2 inches above the beans. Let soak for 12 hours or overnight, until plump and wrinkled, adding more water if necessary to be sure the beans remain submerged. Drain.

Heat the oil in a large saucepan set over high heat. Add the onion and cook until golden brown, 6 to 8 minutes. Add the salt, pepper, and garlic, and cook an additional 2 minutes. Add the mushrooms and cook until they have turned brown and shrunk, 2 minutes. Add the soaked and drained beans along with the white wine, chicken stock or water, red wine vinegar, bay leaf, and thyme. Bring to a boil. Don't worry about the froth that rises to the surface. Turn down the heat and simmer, uncovered, for about 45 minutes. Add the celery, carrots, parsnip, green pepper, and red pepper. Continue cooking for another hour, or until the beans are tender but not mushy. If necessary, add more water or stock to be sure the beans are submerged in liquid while they cook. Cool to room temperature. Chill.

To finish the salad, add the cucumbers, green pepper, vinegar, olive oil, parsley, salt, and pepper to the beans and chill. The salad is best after it has chilled for 4 or 5 hours.

MENTAL NOSH

Beans, as well as broccoli, cabbage, and brussels sprouts, contain complex sugars called oligosaccharides that some people have difficulty digesting. As the beans pass through the system, bacteria in the colon consume these sugars, producing by-products of hydrogen and carbon dioxide, which have to go somewhere. Many oligosaccharides are water soluble, so soaking beans overnight helps both to soften them so they cook better and to make them more digestible. But be sure to dump out the soaking water before you cook the beans, or all of that good stuff that's dissolved in the water will end up back in your system, anyway.

FOR THE BEANS

1 pound white beans (2 cups), such as northern or cannellini

3 tablespoons peanut or vegetable oil

1 medium yellow onion (6 ounces), chopped (about 1 cup)

2 teaspoons kosher salt

¼ teaspoon freshly ground black pepper

2 medium garlic cloves, minced

3 or 4 button mushrooms (2 ounces), sliced (1 cup)

1 cup dry white wine

4 cups chicken stock or water

½ cup red wine vinegar

1 large bay leaf

3 sprigs fresh thyme, or ¼ teaspoon dried thyme

2 large celery stalks, sliced ¼ inch thick (1 cup)

2 large carrots, sliced ¼ inch thick (1 cup)

1 small parsnip, diced (½ cup)

1 green pepper, coarsely chopped (1 cup)

1 red pepper, coarsely chopped (1 cup)

FOR THE SALAD

1 large or 2 small cucumbers, peeled, seeded, and sliced ¼ inch thick

1 green pepper, seeded and chopped

⅓ cup red wine vinegar

¼ cup extra-virgin olive oil

¼ cup chopped fresh parsley

Kosher salt, to taste

Freshly ground black pepper, to taste

creamy coleslaw

IF YOU ARE LIKE MY CULTURALLY Jewish but not kosher friends and me, somewhere in your unconscious you think that mayonnaise contains milk. We know it doesn't, but sometimes just the suggestion of its white creaminess is unappetizing: think of a corned beef sandwich with mayonnaise—perfectly acceptable under the laws of kashrut, but almost as unappealing as steak with a glass of milk. And yet coleslaw made creamy with mayonnaise is somewhat of a deli staple. (Note that New York City's Second Avenue Deli serves an oil-and-vinegar coleslaw, I suspect for the irrational aversion I've explained above.) My version of creamy coleslaw, a variation on my mother's, is a basic recipe that can be used as a starting point for your whims of culinary fancy—shredded apples, nuts, jicama, what have you. The only thing that distinguishes it is that I wilt the cabbage with salt before making the slaw, a practice that used to be more common, but must have fallen out of favor in this fast-paced world we live in because it requires a couple of hours of waiting. Still, I believe the resulting coleslaw has a better texture and is more easily digested.

a bissel advice

I like creamy, but . . . If the coleslaw is too creamy for your taste, dilute the mayonnaise mixture by adding equal parts white vinegar and water.

the whole meshpucha

This recipe can be increased proportionately for however much coleslaw you need. If you are planning a really large barbecue, you can do what my friend Sharla's father does and mix it in a large, heavy-duty garbage bag.

kosher status PAREVE. Equally delicious with corned beef or grilled-cheese sandwiches.

1 small head green cabbage (2 pounds), quartered and cored

2 tablespoons kosher salt

1 cup Hellmann's (or Best Foods) mayonnaise

2 tablespoons cider vinegar

1 tablespoon sugar

¼ teaspoon freshly ground white pepper

¼ teaspoon celery seed

2 large carrots (⅓ pound), shredded

SPECIAL EQUIPMENT

Japanese mandoline or food processor *(optional)*

I like to shred the cabbage using a handheld Japanese mandoline. Alternatively, you can use the thickest slicing disk of a food processor (not the shredding disk, which will make the cabbage too fine), an electric meat slicer, or a large chef's knife. Be sure to remove any tough outer leaves and the core.

Place the shredded cabbage in a large bowl. Sprinkle the salt over the cabbage and toss it around with your hands to be sure the salt is distributed evenly. Cover with a plate to weight down the cabbage, and let sit at room temperature for about 2 hours, until the cabbage has wilted and given off a good amount of water. Drain the cabbage, rinse quickly with cold water, and drain again. Return to the large bowl.

In a small bowl, whisk together the mayonnaise, vinegar, sugar, white pepper, and celery seed with 2 tablespoons water until smooth and creamy. Pour this mixture over the cabbage. Add the shredded carrots and stir until combined. For best results, refrigerate overnight before serving. Adjust the seasoning with salt and freshly ground black pepper.

deli-style oil-and-vinegar coleslaw

WHEN YOU SIT DOWN AT the Second Avenue Deli, the first thing they bring to your table is a bowl of coleslaw. Unlike the creamy mayonnaise variety popular at family barbecues (see page 138 for a recipe), this is a light, slightly sweet, oil-and-vinegar-dressed cabbage and carrot salad. I've often wondered if this type of coleslaw is preferred in kosher delicatessens because creamy coleslaw, though perfectly pareve, seems like it should be milchig. My sister Carrie has perfected this recipe for deli-style coleslaw. In fact, though it's hard for me to admit, I prefer hers now to the one served at the Second Avenue Deli, in part because she takes the time to wilt the cabbage before dressing it, a step that I think makes the finished salad more appetizing and easier to digest.

a bissel advice
What else can you say? If you like, add some shredded green pepper or celery to the mix for added color and flavor.

FOR THE SALAD

2½ pounds green cabbage, quartered and cored

2 large carrots (⅓ pound), shredded (about 1 cup)

½ small onion (3 ounces), very thinly sliced

1 small garlic clove, minced

2 teaspoons sugar

½ teaspoon kosher salt

FOR THE DRESSING

¼ cup mild vegetable oil, such as soybean or peanut oil

½ cup white vinegar (5 percent acidity)

½ teaspoon kosher salt

Freshly ground black or white pepper to taste

SPECIAL EQUIPMENT

Japanese mandoline or food processor (optional)

MAKES SLIGHTLY MORE THAN 2 CUPS

kosher status PAREVE

Shred the cabbage by slicing it on a mandoline or in the food processor (with the thickest slicing disk, not the shredding disk). You can also slice it very thin by hand with a sharp knife. It should be in long, thin strands. In a large bowl, combine the cabbage, carrots, onion, and garlic. Sprinkle with the sugar and salt, and toss. Place a large plate on top of the vegetables to cover and press them down. Let sit at room temperature for 1 to 2 hours to wilt. Pour off any liquid that has been released.

In a small bowl, whisk together the oil, vinegar, salt, and pepper. Combine this dressing with the salad and stir to coat. Transfer to a wide container and chill for at least 3 or 4 hours. Once chilled, taste the coleslaw and adjust the seasoning with more sugar, salt, or pepper to taste.

carrot and raisin salad

THIS IS A SALAD FOR those times when you forget to make a vegetable and you can't get back to the store. Chances are you have a bag of carrots and a jar of mayonnaise in the fridge. Though simple, the salad is delicious. And the bright color makes it a welcome addition to any spread. My sister Carrie, who devised the recipe, uses dark raisins because of their contrasting color (she happens to be an art teacher), but if golden raisins are all you have lying around, they will work fine. Since I usually have currants on my baking shelf, I use them sometimes, too. The salad is best if it chills for a couple of hours so the raisins plump and the flavors have time to blend, but it can also be eaten as soon as it is made.

a bissel advice

Great grating. **If you are using whole carrots, peel them and cut off the pointed tip, but leave the wide, dark end intact. Use this end to grip the carrots while you grate them on a handheld box grater. This technique enables you to maximize the amount of carrot you can grate without grating your fingers. If you are using already-peeled baby carrots, you are better off using a food processor to grate them so you can keep your knuckles attached to your fingers and thereby keep the salad pareve.**

MAKES 4 SIDE-DISH SERVINGS

kosher status PAREVE

In a medium mixing bowl, combine the shredded carrots, raisins or currants, mayonnaise, lemon juice, salt, pepper, and 2 tablespoons of water, and stir with a fork until blended. If time permits, cover and refrigerate until chilled, at least 2 hours. Before serving, adjust the seasoning with salt, pepper, and more lemon, if needed.

1 pound carrots, peeled and shredded, or
    1 12-ounce bag baby carrots, shredded
    (about 2½ cups)
¼ cup raisins or dried currants
⅓ cup mayonnaise
Juice of ½ lemon (about 1 tablespoon)
½ teaspoon kosher salt, plus more to taste
Freshly ground black pepper to taste

SPECIAL EQUIPMENT
Handheld grater or food processor

You Call That a Piece of Cake?

chapter **5**

desserts, sweets,

and some other things

you can eat

for breakfast

I hate

to rely on Jackie Mason for my schtick, but he happens to have some funny jokes about food. There's the one about the Jews and Gentiles in the restaurant: the meal is over and the waiter brings a piece of cake to the table for dessert. The serving of cake is so big the Gentiles start singing "Happy Birthday." The Jews want to know what happened to the size of the portions; they're getting smaller all the time.

ALTHOUGH IT'S A GROSS GENERALIZATION, "a piece of cake" is to Jews what cocktails are to WASPs: something you can consume while you socialize with friends and acquaintances. We always had a freezer full of cake "just in case somebody stopped by." (Interestingly, I think my mother still has unopened bottles of alcohol hanging around her home that are older than I am.) Although at first it seems like an unusual juxtaposition, many people I know get a slight buzz after a slice of a good crumb cake. A handful of cream cheese rugelach and they are so limbered up there is no telling what might happen. Who needs a martini? Not Jews.

WHAT THIS MEANS IS THAT JEWISH desserts, though often consumed at the end of a big meal, aren't limited to that time slot. Like WASP cocktails, they can be enjoyed at breakfast, lunch, with coffee in the afternoon—just about any time is appropriate to nosh on a little something sweet.

KEEPING KOSHER ADDS A LEVEL of logistic complexity that some find difficult to navigate. Since, without question, the best sweets are made with butter, and often cream or cheese, eating them after a big dinner of meat is not a kosher option. (Some rabbis would have you wait four to six hours for dessert! A travesty!) Luckily, in our nonkosher home, butter was considered pareve—inasmuch as my mother used it to cook everything, even meat. And ice cream or whipped cream were sort of *hors de classe*. Make your own rules and you're guaranteed not to break them.

cream cheese rugelach

THESE FLAKY, BUTTERY COOKIES—ROLLED with nuts and jam or prunes or chocolate—are, like bagels, quickly losing their ethnic identity. Rugelach are sold in coffee shops and cookie stores around the country without any reference to 5,000 years of Jewish persecution. Eating these ersatz, de-ethnicized rugelach is torture enough. They are usually hard, dry, overstuffed, and flavorless, distinguishable only in shape from the oversized biscotti inevitably stored in a glass jar somewhere nearby.

Ah, but there are several varieties of true rugelach, the name of which seems to be Yiddish for "little rolled things" (*rugelach* is plural; one is correctly called a *rugel*). The difference is in the dough. The most popular homemade rugelach calls for a dough enriched with cream cheese and plenty of butter. Then there's one made with a sweet yeast dough tenderized by the addition of sour cream. These rugelach are similar to the German *schneken,* or snails. I've even heard of one rugelach recipe made with ice cream! Pareve rugelach are made without any milk products. For the fat, I have taken to using sweet chicken schmaltz, rendered with a vanilla bean (see page 237), which makes the pareve rugelach flakier than if I use plain old margarine. In fact, it also makes them fleishig. Alternatively, you can use peanut oil.

As for the fillings, rugelach provide a good venue for using up the remains of the jars of jams and marmalades that, if you are anything like me, crowd the second shelf of your refrigerator. As a

a bissel advice

How do you choose a filling? First, take a look at pages 226 through 235. The classic for this dough is the Streusel Filling. I also like the Lemon and Almond Filling, a favorite combination of my friend Bonnie. Chocolate works pretty well, but the dough is almost too rich for cheese.

But I took geometry twenty years ago! An isosceles triangle has two sides of equal length and one, the base, that is shorter. I find that I can't get all of the triangles to be the right shape from a circle so, I call on my spatial-relations skills to cut the dough into shapes that look like they will roll up into crescents. Don't worry if your rugelach aren't perfectly shaped. That's how everyone will know they are homemade.

Rugelach in a pinch? I like to make and shape the cookies and freeze them before they are baked. Lay them out on the cookie sheet and freeze them until firm. Then transfer the rugelach to a resealable plastic bag and keep them in the freezer for up to 2 months. You can take out a handful of cookies at a time and bake them as you need them, in a 425°F. oven for a little bit longer than the recipe says.

What else can I do with this cream cheese dough? This is one of the easiest and most delicious doughs that bakers in my family (and many other families) make. I use it as a mock puff pastry to line tart shells. I dab little squares with apricot jam and bake them as cookies like my great-aunt May used to make. Because it isn't sweet, you can also use it for savory treats like hors d'oeuvres or vegetable tarts.

rule, I like to have something to spread, something to sprinkle, and something to bite in each filling combination. This means I might spread some jam, sprinkle some cinnamon sugar or orange zest, and add some nuts or raisins. So in addition to providing you with recipes for the three types of dough, I've given a number of sweet fillings (see pages 226–235). But don't let my limited list squelch your creativity.

Finally, there is the question of shape. Homemade rugelach are usually shaped into crescents. The dough is rolled out into a circle and covered with the filling. Then the circle is cut into isosceles triangles and each triangle is rolled up from the wide end to the point. The resulting roll is bent to form a crescent, then baked. Bakery-bought rugelach are usually shaped more like snails. The dough is rolled out into a rectangle that is then covered with the filling. Then the rectangle is rolled up from the wide end like a jelly roll. The dough is refrigerated and then cut into 1-inch pieces and baked.

Whatever combination of fillings, doughs, and shapes you choose, make plenty because nobody can resist fresh-baked rugelach. My friend Bonnie Stern, who runs a cooking school, Internet store, and consulting business in Toronto, always has plenty of rugelach on hand during holiday time to give as gifts to friends and colleagues.

MAKES **4** DOZEN

kosher status MILCHIG and pretty good with a cold glass of milk, I might add

6 ounces (2 small packages or ¾ cup) cream cheese, at room temperature

½ pound or 1 cup (2 sticks) unsalted butter, at room temperature

1½ cups unbleached all-purpose flour, plus additional for rolling

About 2 cups sweet filling (choose one from pages 226–235)

1 egg beaten with 1 teaspoon cold water

2 tablespoons crystallized sugar or Sugar in the Raw

SPECIAL EQUIPMENT

2 cookie sheets lined with parchment or a nonstick silicone mat

Pastry brush

p lace the cream cheese and butter in a large mixing bowl and combine with a wooden spoon. Alternatively, you can use the paddle attachment of an electric mixer. Add the flour and mix to form a soft dough. Chill for at least 2 hours before rolling out and shaping. The dough can also be frozen for up to 2 months and defrosted in the refrigerator before using.

To shape, divide the dough into quarters. Refrigerate all but the quarter you are working with. Roll out the first quarter to a 10-inch circle, using a generous amount of flour to keep the dough from sticking. Once the circle is the right size, use a pastry brush to remove any excess flour. If you are using Streusel (page 227) or Lemon and Almond Filling (page 228), spread the circle with one quarter of the jam, about 2 tablespoons, and sprinkle with the nuts or raisins (or whatever else you've chosen). If you are using

recipe continues →

cream cheese rugelach

(continued)

chocolate (page 226), prune (page 232), sweet cheese (page 224), or poppy seed (page 230) fillings, just use ¼ of the batch. Cut the circle in half, and then each half into half again. Divide each of these quarters into three equal isosceles triangles. Roll up each triangle, starting from the base and working toward the point. Bend to shape into crescents and place on a parchment- or silicone-mat-lined cookie sheet, making sure the point of the dough triangle stays tucked underneath. Repeat with the remaining dough and filling. You will probably need two cookie sheets to accommodate all of the cookies. Leave about 1 inch between the cookies because they will rise and straighten out while they bake.

Preheat the oven to 425°F.

Brush the cookies with the egg wash and sprinkle with the crystallized sugar. Bake for 15 to 20 minutes, until the dough has puffed and the cookies have browned. Some of the filling will no doubt seep out while baking, but not enough to worry about. Using a spatula, remove the rugelach from the pan while they are still warm so the melted jam and/or sugar doesn't harden to the cookie sheet. Let cool completely on a wire rack. Store in an airtight container for up to 5 days.

MENTAL NOSH

Many people consider rugelach—particularly cream cheese rugelach—a traditional Chanukah food. Not my family. But I suspect the tradition is a relatively modern one stemming from the legend of Judith, who fed an enemy general copious amounts of cheese to make him sleepy, and then she cut off his head. (For more about this story, see the Cheese Latkes recipe on page 106.) The reason I think it must be somewhat modern is that cream cheese was first invented and marketed in the late 19th century. Until then, milk or sour cream or quark (a fresh curd cheese) would have been the likely ingredients. And none of these products is really cheese, anyway. The rugelach shape, however, is a tradition that goes way back to 18th-century Vienna. Regardless of their history, rugelach are now popular year-round.

yeast-raised rugelach

THESE RUGELACH ARE MORE LIKE the ones you find in commerical bakeries than the Cream Cheese Rugelach (page 144) or Pareve Rugelach (page 148).

a bissel advice

This sounds like what my aunt Zelda called schnecken. It's close, especially if you choose the Streusel Filling (page 227). They are like a miniature version of cinnamon buns.

How do you choose a filling? Check out the options on pages 226-235. Just about anything will work in this versatile dough. My favorites, though, for Yeast-Raised Rugelach are the chocolate and the streusel fillings. Prune is delicious, too. Cheese and poppy seed are better left for coffee cakes.

MAKES **4** DOZEN

kosher status MILCHIG

1 recipe Sweet Yeast Dough (page 256)

About 2 cups sweet filling (see pages 226–235)

1 tablespoon milk *(optional)*

1 tablespoon sugar

SPECIAL EQUIPMENT

Parchment paper or nonstick silicone mat

Punch down the dough. Divide into quarters and let sit for about 15 minutes. Preheat the oven to 400°F.

Roll out each quarter of dough to a rectangle roughly 12 inches by 9 inches. Spread and sprinkle the dough with one quarter of the filling, being sure to go right to the edges along the shorter sides of the rectangle but leaving ¼ inch of dough clean along the longer sides. Beginning on the longer side, roll up tightly like a jelly roll to form a log. With a sharp serrated knife, cut the log into 1-inch pieces and place on a cookie sheet lined with a piece of parchment, a silicone mat, or another nonstick surface. Lightly brush the surface with milk (if using) or water, and sprinkle with sugar. Bake for 15 to 20 minutes, until risen and browned. While still warm, remove from the baking sheet to a wire rack and allow to cool completely.

pareve rugelach

THIS RUGELACH DOUGH IS SIMILAR to the knish dough on page 22. The difference is that I like to use a sweet chicken schmaltz that I make by rendering the fat with a vanilla bean (page 237). Okay, you caught me—the fat makes these fleishig rugelach, but I thought that sounded unappetizing. Anyway, the only reason to want pareve rugelach in the first place is that you want to eat them with or after a fleishig meal. Besides, if you don't want to use the schmaltz, you can substitute peanut oil for a very tasty result.

a bissel advice

Sweet chicken schmaltz? Are you crazy? Nope. Traditionally, much Eastern European baking used animal fats. They produce a product with good flavor and a flaky texture. (Those of you who have eaten such things might think of pie crust made with lard as a comparison.)

MAKES 4 DOZEN

kosher status FLEISHIG, with schmaltz
PAREVE, with only peanut oil

2 large eggs

2 tablespoons Sweet Chicken Schmaltz
(page 237), at room temperature, or
2 tablespoons peanut oil

2 additional tablespoons peanut oil

2 tablespoons sugar

2 teaspoons baking powder

½ teaspoon kosher salt

1⅔ cups unbleached all-purpose flour

About 2 cups sweet filling (pages 226–235)

1 egg beaten with 1 teaspoon cold water

2 tablespoons crystallized sugar or Sugar in
the Raw

In a medium bowl, beat the eggs with a fork or small whisk. Beat in the schmaltz or peanut oil and the additional peanut oil, plus the sugar, baking powder, and salt, and continue beating until combined. Stir in the flour to make a firm dough. Turn out onto a clean work surface and knead for 2 or 3 minutes, until the dough is smooth and elastic. Place in a clean bowl, cover with plastic wrap, and let sit for about 30 minutes to allow the gluten to soften.

Divide the dough into quarters. Roll out each quarter to form a 9-inch circle. Spread and sprinkle the circle of dough with one quarter of the filling. Cut the circle in half and cut each half into six isosceles triangles (see page 144). Roll up each triangle beginning at the base and ending at the point. Place on a cookie sheet lined with parchment, a silicone mat, or any other nonstick surface. Repeat with the remaining dough.

Preheat the oven to 400°F.

Brush the rugelach with the egg wash and sprinkle with the crystallized sugar. Bake for 18 to 20 minutes, until slightly risen and browned. Remove from the cookie sheets while still warm and let cool completely on wire racks.

MENTAL NOSH

Award-winning Jewish cookbook author, rabbi, and cultural historian Gil Marks links the origin of rugelach to Austria, where in 1793 bakers apparently invented crescent-shaped pastries to celebrate the end of the Turkish siege of Vienna — a crescent shape was prominent on the Ottoman flag.

prune dumplings

THIS IS THE SWEET VARIATION of my friend Daňo's Savory Yeast Dumplings (page 120). Of all the recipes I gathered and perfected while doing research for this book, this is one of my favorites. The dumplings are unlike any American dessert you've ever been served, but there is something still so soft and warm and sweet and comforting about them that they seem familiar. For best results, use quick-rising, instant, or rapid-rise yeast, which doesn't require proofing. Because of these dumplings' size, they are probably best eaten in the afternoon with coffee or even for breakfast. Like the savory dumplings, they can be made in advance, stored in the refrigerator, and reheated in the microwave.

a bissel advice

What is lekvar? As I explain in the recipe for Prune Filling (page 232), lekvar is a Hungarian prune spread that can be purchased in many gourmet stores. Although my Hungarian friends tell me lekvar can actually refer to any kind of fruit spread, here in the New World it almost always means prune.

But I hate prunes! You can use any fruit spread, such as apple butter, apricot jam, cherry pie filling—you name it. In fact, almost any of my sweet fillings (pages 226–235) can also be used; the poppy seed filling works especially well. But Daňo and I think the lekvar is the best filling for these dumplings. Call us traditionalists.

How do I grind poppy seeds? You will need a coffee grinder. Check out my recipe for Poppy Seed Filling on page 230 for the technique. I would advise against thinking you can get away without grinding them. Except on bagels or challah, whole poppy seeds just aren't very palatable. If you can't swing a grinder, just dust the dumplings with confectioners' sugar and call it a day.

Can I make them in advance? The dumplings can be covered lightly and stored in the refrigerator for up to 3 days. To reheat, place them on clean plates and microwave on medium power for whatever the total of 50 seconds per dumpling works out to be. Otherwise you can steam them for 2 to 3 minutes over, but not touching, boiling water.

kosher status MILCHIG. Soy milk doesn't work so well.

1¼ cups milk

4 tablespoons unsalted butter

1 teaspoon kosher salt

2 tablespoons granulated sugar

3 cups unbleached all-purpose flour

2 packages (4½ teaspoons) quick-rising, instant, or rapid-rise active dry yeast

1 teaspoon peanut or vegetable oil

1 cup lekvar (prune butter) or Fresh Plum Conserve (page 215)

FOR THE GARNISH

4 tablespoons unsalted butter, melted and kept warm

3 tablespoons poppy seeds, ground (see "advice" on previous page)

3 tablespoons confectioners' sugar

SPECIAL EQUIPMENT

Electric mixer with a dough hook

Wide 8-quart pot with a tight-fitting lid

h eat the milk and butter in a small saucepan over medium heat until just about boiling. Turn off the heat, add the salt and sugar, and let cool until just warm to the touch (about 110°F.).

Meanwhile, combine the flour and yeast in the bowl of an electric mixer. Pour the warm milk mixture into the flour mixture and mix, using the dough hook, to form a soft dough. Knead the dough for at least 5 minutes, until the dough is smooth and shiny. It shouldn't be sticky, so if it is, add 1 to 2 tablespoons more flour and continue kneading.

Turn the dough out onto a lightly floured work surface and knead five or six times to form a ball. Place a drop of oil in the bottom of a clean mixing bowl and place the dough inside. Move it around to coat it with oil. Cover the bowl with plastic wrap and let rise for about 1½ hours, until doubled in bulk.

Punch down the dough. Flatten the dough into a rectangle approximately 15 by 6 inches and ½ inch thick. Cut the dough into 10 equal squares. Working with one square at a time, use your fingertips to flatten the four edges of the square, creating a flat ¾-inch border around a little puffed center. On the center, place 1 tablespoon or so of the lekvar or plum conserve. Draw up the corners over the filling and pinch to seal. Nudge the dumpling into a spherical shape. Invert the dumpling on a cookie sheet, seam side down. Cover with a clean dish towel and repeat to form the remaining dumplings.

Bring a large, wide pot of water (about 4 quarts) to a boil. Place the remaining ¾ teaspoon oil in a plastic container, and have a sharp paring knife at the ready. Plop five of the dough balls into the boiling water. Cover tightly and let boil for exactly 5 minutes. After 5 minutes, remove the lid and use the paring knife to poke three or four holes in each dumpling. This will help prevent them from deflating. Using a slotted spoon, lift the poked dumplings out of the water and place them into the oiled container if you intend to store them. Repeat with the remaining dumplings. To serve, microwave or steam the dumplings until warm. Pour the melted butter over the warm dumplings and dust with the ground poppy seeds and confectioners' sugar.

mandel bread

MANDEL IS GERMAN for "almond"; *brot* means "bread." The truth is these cookies should be called mandelbrot in German or *mandlbroyt* in Yiddish, but my family always used the English-German compound. Why we mixed up the two languages and didn't use the Yiddish I'm not sure. A friend once suggested we just call them *biscotti judaica,* Italian for "Jewish cookies." After all, they look, taste, and are even made like Italian biscotti. (At least one food authority thinks they may have originated in the ghetto of Venice.) You should have seen my sister Carrie and me trying to teach my mother the word *biscotti.* Just when we thought she had it, she flubbed the word *spaghetti* instead. Anyway, these cookies are terrific.

Mandel bread comes in many varieties. Some have chocolate chips, others are made with matzo cake meal so they can be eaten on Passover. Although I've seen "mandel bread" made with hazelnuts, the phrase "hazelnut mandel bread" is actually an oxymoron.

The trick is that the cookies are baked twice. First they are shaped into logs and baked until set. Then they are sliced into cookies and baked again to dry out. The resulting cookie is a little bit like a rock—in a good way. They are best dunked in coffee (an Italian might use vin santo). Despite these numerous steps, they are easy to make. My mother, who lost her sight several years ago, can literally make them without looking. And hers are always delicious.

There are several secrets to these cookies, not the least important of which is using fresh, good-quality almonds. My mother sprinkles the dough with vanilla sugar, available in small packets from Germany's Dr. Oetker, or made simply by putting vanilla beans in a canister of sugar and letting them sit for a few weeks. Alternatively, you can roll the cookies in cinnamon sugar before the second baking.

a bissel advice

Why Crisco oil? I just like it better. Crisco makes a neutral-tasting soybean oil. As I've said before, I find both canola oil and corn oil to have distinct flavors and oiliness when used in desserts (or anything, for that matter). Although I usually recommend cooking or baking with peanut oil, I find the peanut flavor fights with the almonds for dominance in these cookies. But pay attention to the label because Crisco also makes a 100 percent canola oil. *Can I make these in advance?* Once cooled, transfer the cookies to an airtight container. They will keep for up to 3 weeks on the counter or you can freeze them for up to 2 months.

Preheat the oven to 350ºF. Toast the almonds on a cookie sheet in the preheated oven for 8 to 10 minutes, until they give off a pleasant, almondy aroma. Cool. Transfer to a food processor and pulse about 15 times to chop coarsely—the pieces should not be uniform.

In a large mixing bowl, whisk together the orange juice concentrate, vanilla extract, vegetable oil, eggs, sugar, and salt until well blended. Using a wooden spoon, stir in about 2 cups of the flour with 2 teaspoons of the baking powder and half of the almonds until blended. Add another 2 cups of flour and the remaining baking powder and almonds. The dough should have the consistency of loose Play-doh—it should hold its shape without looking dry. You can add up to ½ cup flour, until it holds its shape.

Using a large spoon, scoop about half of the dough into a log shape down the center of one of the cookie sheets. With the back of your spoon or a flexible spatula, shape the dough into an even log about 2 inches across, 1 inch thick, and 12 to 15 inches long. Repeat with the remaining dough on the second cookie sheet. Smooth out the logs so they look uniform. Don't try to crowd two logs on one sheet. If using vanilla sugar, sprinkle one whole package over the surface of each of the logs to cover. Set in the middle of the oven and bake for 20 to 25 minutes, until the logs are somewhat firm to the touch and look cooked through (slight hairline cracks on the surface will indicate that they are ready). Remove from the oven and cool. Turn down the oven to 250ºF.

Transfer the logs to a cutting board. Using a sharp serrated knife, slice the logs on an angle about ½ inch thick to produce biscotti-shaped cookies. Lay the cookies sliced side down on the parchment-lined cookies sheets (you may need an extra cookie sheet in order to have enough room). If you didn't use the vanilla sugar, place the cinnamon sugar in a wide soup bowl. As you cut the cookies, roll them in the cinnamon sugar before placing them on the cookie sheet. Return the cookies to the 250ºF. oven for 20 minutes to dry out. Turn each cookie over and continue baking for another 20 minutes. Remove from the oven and cool.

2 cups whole almonds, with skins

½ cup frozen orange juice concentrate (about 1 small 6-ounce can), defrosted but not diluted

1 tablespoon pure vanilla extract

1 cup Crisco vegetable (100% soybean) oil

4 large eggs

1 cup sugar

Pinch of salt

4 cups all-purpose flour, plus an additional ½ cup if necessary

4 teaspoons baking powder

2 packages (about 3 tablespoons) vanilla sugar (see headnote) or ¾ cup Cinnamon Sugar (page 239)

SPECIAL EQUIPMENT

2 cookie sheets lined with parchment paper or well greased

Food processor

chocolate-dipped macaroons

ALTHOUGH MOST JEWS RELEGATE COCONUT macaroons to Passover time, I think they are delicious year-round. They also happen to be just about the easiest cookie known to man (or woman). I find that the best coconut to use is the standard sweetened and flaked coconut available in the grocery store. This coconut has a tender texture and buttery taste that people often mistake for butter in the recipe. As you can see, there isn't any, so the joke is on them. By contrast, I find unsweetened coconut dry, stringy, and pretty tasteless, unless you can find a terrifically fresh source—which most health-food stores are not. Dipping the cookies in chocolate is also simple, but it *looks* really impressive. Use a high-quality dark chocolate.

a bissel advice

What if I don't want to bother with the chocolate? **Don't. Plain macaroons are delicious, too, and the fact that you made them yourself is impressive enough.**

Do they keep? **You can store the dipped macaroons for a day or two at room temperature, about a week in the fridge, or up to a month in the freezer.**

kosher status PAREVE, but watch out for any milk content in the chocolate
PESADICH

2½ cups (12 ounces) sweetened, flaked
   coconut

2 large egg whites

⅓ cup sugar

1 teaspoon pure vanilla extract

Pinch of kosher salt

4 ounces bittersweet or white chocolate,
   coarsely chopped

SPECIAL EQUIPMENT
Parchment paper or silicone mat

Preheat the oven to 350°F.

Line a cookie sheet with parchment paper or a silicone mat and grease it lightly with butter or peanut oil. In a small mixing bowl, combine the coconut, egg whites, sugar, vanilla, and salt, and stir to mix well. To shape the cookies, dip your fingertips in a bowl of cold water. Grab about 2 or 3 tablespoons of the coconut mixture and shape it into a mound on the cookie sheet. Space the mounds out evenly on the sheet. The macaroons won't spread while they cook, but if they are too close they won't brown evenly. Bake for about 15 minutes, until the coconut has begun to brown on top and the bottoms are an even, golden brown. Remove from the oven and cool for about 5 minutes on the pan before removing them carefully with a spatula to finish cooling on a wire rack.

Line a clean cookie sheet with parchment paper. When the macaroons are completely cool, melt the chocolate in the top of a double boiler, or in a stainless steel bowl set over simmering water, or in the microwave. Be careful not to get any moisture into the chocolate, particularly from the condensation of steam. Stir the melted chocolate until smooth. Holding the macaroons on one side, dip half into the melted chocolate. Place the dipped macaroons on the parchment paper and continue until all are half dipped. You can alternate white chocolate and dark, or double-dip in the same chocolate once the first dipping has hardened.

You also can drizzle the macaroons with the melted chocolate. Place the melted chocolate in a small plastic sandwich bag. Close the bag tightly. Using a pair of scissors snip off one of the corners to produce a tiny hole. While the macaroons are still on the cooling rack, but completely cooled, squeeze the chocolate out of the hole in the bag while zigzagging it over the macaroons. You can repeat this process with melted white chocolate to produce an attractive two-toned effect.

Place the macaroons in the refrigerator for about 30 minutes to harden the chocolate, and then transfer them to an airtight container to store.

chocolate-caramel matzo crunch

THIS RECIPE WAS FIRST GIVEN to me by my friend Jennifer, a food scholar, a former caterer, and a good cook who doesn't believe it is ethical for Passover desserts to resemble regularly leavened sweets. Jennifer brought some of this crunch to a class and I'd never tasted any homemade Passover *nosherei* that I thought was as good. Like a cross between a cookie and a candy, it is a nice thing to serve alongside other holiday desserts. Always looking for a way to make a good thing better, my friend Bonnie started making it with white chocolate, too. My sister Carrie does patches of white and dark chocolate on the same batch. Together, the dark and white chocolates make for an attractive presentation.

a bissel advice

How do you grate or chop chocolate? I first like to be sure my chocolate is very firm, so I stick it in the refrigerator for an hour or so. Using the large-hole side of a box grater, you can grate the chocolate into small pieces. But if, like me, your hands are very warm, this technique makes a big mess. Alternatively, use a large, sharp chef's knife to chop the chocolate on a cutting board. Use two hands to apply pressure to the blade, and be careful not to get your fingers caught below it. I find that if I have a large block of chocolate, making a cut every ¼ inch or so causes the chocolate to break up into tiny pieces.

5 square matzos

½ pound (2 sticks) unsalted butter

1 cup light brown sugar

12 ounces bittersweet or white chocolate, or
a combination, grated or chopped finely

½ cup sliced almonds, toasted *(optional)*

reheat the oven to 350°F.

Line a large cookie sheet with aluminum foil. Lay the matzos in a single layer in the cookie sheet (it's okay if some edges overlap). Melt the butter in a heavy, nonstick sauté pan set over medium-high heat. Add the brown sugar and stir to combine. As the sugar begins to melt, start to whisk the mixture to blend. Keep whisking until the butter and sugar form a light caramel.

Pour the caramel over the matzos and spread it out evenly with a spatula. Set the sheet pan in the preheated oven and bake for 6 to 7 minutes, until the caramel has been absorbed somewhat into the matzo and is bubbly. Remove from the oven. While hot, dust with an even layer of chocolate. You can make a pattern with the dark and white chocolate or make patches of dark and white chocolate to create a variety of different flavors and designs. As the chocolate melts on the hot matzos, spread the chocolate out evenly with a spatula to coat. Sprinkle with the toasted almonds at this point, if using. Cool completely and break into bite-size pieces.

hamentaschen

EVERY YEAR A BOX OF MY mother's Hamentaschen arrives unexpectedly at my office. (These are unexpected because I never remember when Purim is.) Because of Canada Post's snail-paced service, they are usually stale. But my colleagues and I enjoy them anyway. It's the thought (and a lot of butter) that counts. Hamentaschen are shaped into triangles to symbolize Hamen's tricorn hat. My friend Peggy was recently out in the wilds of Queens, New York, and saw a sign in a coffee shop advertising "humantaschen." Perhaps they were taking the metaphor of eating Hamen's hat a step further.

The most traditional filling is poppy seed or mohn, but I like them with chocolate, prune, apple, and cheese, too (see pages 226 through 235 for sweet filling ideas). Although I have made them with many doughs, including Sweet Yeast Dough (page 256), I find the cookies made from the same dough I use for my Apple Cake (page 162) are irresistible. A rabbi recently told me they were the best Hamentaschen he'd ever had. I'm not sure in whose good graces that will get me, but it was nice to hear.

a bissel advice

Triangular pegs in round holes? I was never good in geometry, but I do know that if you fold up three sides of a circle, you can make a triangle. Jewish bakers have been doing it for years.

kosher status MILCHIG, or PAREVE; it depends on the fat
you use for your dough and your filling

1 batch Apple Cake dough (page 162), chilled

4 cups Sweet Filling, such as chocolate,
prune, poppy seed, or cheese (pages
226–235)

SPECIAL EQUIPMENT

Parchment paper or nonstick silicone mats

3¼-inch round cookie cutter

Pastry brush

Preheat the oven to 400°F. Grease two cookie sheets or line them with parchment paper or silicone mats.

Cut the chilled dough into quarters and refrigerate all but the one you are working with. Generously flour the work surface. Shape the dough into a disk and generously flour it. Roll out until just under ¼ inch thick, using more flour if necessary to prevent sticking. Cut with a 3¼-inch round cookie cutter. Because the dough is delicate, I like to work one cookie at a time. Using a thin spatula or a flexible knife, loosen the dough from the work surface and move to a lightly floured area.

Place 1 heaping teaspoon of filling in a mound in the center of the disk of dough. Dip your finger in a little cold water and dab the circumference of the circle with water. Using the same spatula or knife, flip one edge of the circle onto the mound of filling about halfway up the side. Repeat two other times with opposing sides to produce an equilateral triangle. Pinch the corners together to seal, leaving the center open to expose the filling. Brush off any excess flour. Repeat with the remaining dough.

Carefully place the cookies on the prepared cookie sheets. This dough has such a high proportion of fat that you can rework the scraps three or four times and still get good results. Leave about 1 inch between the cookies to account for spreading (the cheese filling spreads more than the others), and bake for 20 to 25 minutes until the edges are browned.

Let cool 5 minutes on the cookie sheets and then with a spatula transfer to a wire rack to finish cooling. Store in an airtight container for 2 to 3 days or freeze for up to 1 month. You can crisp up the cookies by reheating them in a 325°F. oven for 5 to 7 minutes and letting them cool.

doughnuts

HERE'S A TECHNIQUE FOR MAKING simple doughnuts or *sufganyot* (in Hebrew) to serve at Chanukah. There are three basic types of dough for doughnuts: yeast doughnuts, which rise because of the action of yeast; cake doughnuts, which rise because of the action of baking powder; and doughnuts made from cream puff paste *(pâte à choux),* which rise because of the action of steam. Because I have included recipes for two types of dough already in the book (Sweet Yeast Dough, page 256, and Cream Puff Paste, page 258), I thought I'd better not complicate things by adding a third. Although these two different doughs produce completely different types of doughnuts, they are both delicious. The yeast doughnuts can be shaped with a hole in the center or into little balls; the cream puff doughnuts should just be shaped like little balls. (If you're good with a pastry bag, you could pipe them into French crullers.) Both doughs can be made a day or two in advance and fried just before they are served.

A word of warning: If you are a fan of Krispy-Kreme doughnuts (which I think are completely overrated) you might not like these denser, homemade doughnuts. Treat them like apples and oranges to avoid disappointment.

a bissel advice

What on earth is a doughnut cutter? It's like a metal bull's eye with two concentric circles, one larger and one smaller, that cuts out the doughnut and the hole in one swoop.

Can I make them in advance? Not really, about 6 hours max. Fried things just don't keep very well. But you can make the dough in advance and keep it in the refrigerator for 2 or 3 days before you shape and fry them.

1 batch Sweet Yeast Dough (page 256),
   chilled, or 1 batch Cream Puff Paste
   (page 258)

½ cup sugar

½ cup Cinnamon Sugar (page 239)

4 to 6 cups vegetable oil, for deep-frying

SPECIAL EQUIPMENT

Round doughnut cutter for yeast doughnuts,
   or a 3½-inch round cutter and a 1-inch
   round cutter (optional)

*t*o prepare the yeast doughnuts: Roll out the chilled dough until no more than ½ inch thick. Using the doughnut cutter or the 3½-inch round cutter, cut out as many doughnuts as you can. Use the smaller 1-inch cutter to make the hole if your doughnut cutter didn't do it already. You can gather the scraps, knead them into a ball, roll them out, and cut out more doughnuts, but note that these second-pass doughnuts tend to rise unevenly. Place the doughnuts and doughnut holes on a cookie sheet, cover with a clean dish towel, and let sit in a warm place until the oil comes up to frying temperature.

To prepare cream puff paste doughnuts: No advance shaping is necessary; they can be dropped from spoons right into the hot oil. One tablespoon of dough will make a 2-inch doughnut.

Frying the doughnuts: Lay out a piece of paper towel on the counter and place a wire cooling rack on top of it. Place the sugar in a small bowl and the cinnamon sugar in another.

The pot you use will determine how much oil you will need. I find I can fry 1 batch of doughnuts with 4 cups (1 quart) of oil in a pot that is 8 inches in diameter. A wider pot will require more oil. Ideally, the oil should be no less than 2 inches deep. Over medium-high heat, bring the oil up to 335°F. (use a candy or deep-frying thermometer to be sure). Place three or four yeast doughnuts and a couple of holes into the hot oil or drop 4 or 5 separate tablespoonfuls of cream puff paste into it. The doughnuts will sink to the bottom and then float to the top while they expand and bubble furiously. Using a slotted spoon or tongs, turn the doughnuts over a couple of times while they cook so that they brown evenly. They should take about 6 minutes' cooking time in total. If they are getting too brown, turn down the heat.

Remove the doughnuts from the oil and let cool on the wire rack. Fry the remaining doughnuts, also in small batches. When the doughnuts are cool enough to be handled but still warm, dip them in either one of the bowls of sugar. Be sure to coat them well, piling sugar on top so that it gets in the hole. Return to the rack to finish cooling.

MENTAL NOSH

Here's a fact to impress your friends with: the shape of a doughnut (or a bagel, or an inner tube, for that matter) is called a toroid.

apple cake

MRS. COOPER WAS A POLISH woman who lived next door to us while I was growing up in Toronto. Her granddaughter Tammy was one of my best friends. Mrs. Cooper had a knack for baking—I can still smell the sweet lemon-cinnamon scent of this cake, which she would cool in the kitchen window. When I called my mother to ask for the recipe for this book, she said, "Why don't you make Mrs. Cooper the happiest woman in the world and call and ask her yourself?" It was good advice because Mrs. Cooper was indeed happy that I called—and because she had such a personality-filled way of giving me the directions. "How much sugar do you add to the apples?" I asked, and she responded in her melodious Polish accent, "You're a cook, you taste an apple, you'll know."

I've tinkered with the recipe a little to try to make it more exact. Although Mrs. Cooper's apple cake was always made with Crisco so it was pareve, it will probably come as no surprise that I prefer the recipe with butter. I've also cut down the amount of dough that the original recipe called for. It's a versatile dough that can be made into cookies or other cakes, too. It makes the best Hamentaschen (page 158) you've ever tasted. "I make a lot of dough so I have some left over for cookies or another cake," Mrs. Cooper advised. "Don't waste any. You can keep the dough in the freezer so you have it ready."

a bissel advice

Can I make the cake in another shape? Of course. A springform pan makes the cake easy to serve, but don't use anything larger than 9 inches in diameter or else the outer edge overbakes while the center remains raw. A 9-inch springform pan will require only a little more than half of the dough. Use the scraps as indicated below.

What can I do with the scraps? This dough makes delicious cookies. Knead in a handful of chocolate chips or a teaspoon of poppy seeds, roll out, and cut into different shapes. Bake at 350°F. for 10 minutes, or until the bottoms are light brown. This is also the dough I use to make Hamentaschen (see page 158 for details).

Is it really as good if I use Crisco? Obviously, it isn't going to have a rich, buttery flavor. But the dough is still pretty good. Remember, it was with Crisco that I grew to love this cake in the first place.

either by hand with a wooden spoon or in an electric mixer with a paddle attachment, cream the butter and sugar. Add the eggs and continue beating until light and fluffy. Add the juice, vanilla, peanut oil, and salt, and beat to combine. Remove from the mixer (if using), and stir in the baking powder and flour with a wooden spoon to produce a soft dough. Wrap the dough in plastic and chill while you prepare the filling.

Place the lemon zest and juice in the bottom of a large bowl. Peel and core the apples, and cut them into ½-inch chunks, tossing them in the lemon juice to prevent the apples from discoloring while you work. Add the sugar, cinnamon, vanilla, and almond extract (if using), and toss to coat.

Preheat the oven to 350°F.

Divide the dough into two pieces, about two thirds to one third. Pat the larger piece into a rough rectangular shape and refrigerate the smaller piece until you are ready to roll it out. Because the dough is soft right after it is made, it is easiest to roll it out between two pieces of plastic wrap. Lay a large piece of plastic wrap on the counter (depending on how wide your plastic wrap is, you may have to overlap two pieces). Lightly flour the plastic wrap. Place the rectangular-shaped dough on top and lightly flour the dough. Cover with an additional piece or two of plastic wrap. Using a long rolling pin, roll out the dough between the plastic wrap until it is roughly 13 inches by 17 inches and ½ inch thick, or large enough to line the bottom and sides of your baking pan. Align the long side of the pan with the dough. Remove the top layer of plastic wrap and carefully lift the dough, flipping it over into the center of the baking dish. If the dough sticks to the plastic, use a knife or spatula to gently scrape it off. Don't be worried if the dough splits or breaks. Wet your fingertips with cold water and press the dough into the corners and sides of the pan. Pinch any cracks or seams together. If the dough doesn't completely come up the sides of the pan, work it with the tips of your fingers to make it fit. Brush off any excess flour with a pastry brush.

FOR THE DOUGH

¾ pound (3 sticks or 1½ cups) unsalted butter or Crisco vegetable shortening, at room temperature

1⅓ cups sugar

3 large eggs

2 tablespoons lemon or orange juice

1 teaspoon pure vanilla extract

1 tablespoon peanut oil

½ teaspoon kosher salt

1½ teaspoons baking powder

4 cups flour

FOR THE FILLING

Zest and juice of 1 lemon

10 large (3½ pounds) cooking apples, such as Northern Spy, Russet, Gala, Golden Delicious, or a combination

¼ cup sugar

1 teaspoon ground cinnamon

1 teaspoon pure vanilla extract

3 or 4 drops pure almond extract (optional)

Additional 2 or 3 tablespoons granulated sugar or crystallized sugar for topping

SPECIAL EQUIPMENT

9-by-13-inch baking pan

Pastry brush

Electric mixer (optional)

recipe continues →

apple cake

(continued)

Trim any overhanging dough. Fill the dough with the prepared apples and pat down to level the surface.

Similarly roll out the remaining smaller piece of dough between two pieces of floured plastic wrap, until it is a rectangle the size of the pan, 9 by 13 inches. Flip this dough on top of the cake to cover the filling. Press down the edges to seal. Trim. Poke three or four holes in the top of the dough. Place the additional sugar in a small bowl or ramekin. Wet the tips of your fingers and pick up some of the sugar. This will cause it to clump. Scatter clumps of sugar on top of the cake. Alternately, you can use crystallized sugar to decorate the top of the cake.

Bake the cake in the preheated oven for 45 minutes. Turn down the heat to 300°F. and continue baking for 20 minutes. To be sure the cake is done, an instant-read thermometer should read 190°F. when inserted into the center. You can also poke it with a toothpick to be sure the apples are tender and cooked. Remove from the oven and cool completely before eating. Note, as is often the case, the first piece of this cake is difficult to remove from the pan in one piece. But after that you shouldn't have any problem.

cherry-cheese lokshen kugel

THIS IS THE RECIPE for a lokshen kugel my mother used to make for company when we were kids. My friend Judy (not a Jew, but a lover of Jewish food) insisted that I include a recipe for it in this book because she used to like it so much. Better suited as a dessert than as a side dish for a meal, this kugel is a little bit like a cheesecake made

with noodles and topped with cherries. I remember sneaking pieces of this kugel from the freezer and eating it frozen when I was a kid. Although you could make the cherry topping yourself from delicious sour cherries when they are in season, I recall it distinctly with cherry pie filling from a can. And in fact nobody I've ever served it to seemed to mind. I guess blueberry would work fine, too.

a bissel advice

But on page 128 you said all kugels, sweet and savory, were served with main courses? That's enough out of you Mr. Smarty Pants.

MAKES **16** SERVINGS

kosher status MILCHIG

1 pound wide egg noodles

1 pound (2 cups) creamy cottage cheese

2 cups (1 pound) sour cream

5 large eggs

4 tablespoons (½ stick or 2 ounces) unsalted butter, melted

⅔ cup sugar

Zest of ½ lemon (1½ teaspoons) or ¼ teaspoon ground cinnamon

1 teaspoon pure vanilla extract

Pinch of kosher salt

1 (21-ounce) can cherry pie filling

SPECIAL EQUIPMENT

2-quart, 8-inch square baking dish

Preheat the oven to 350°F.

Generously butter a 2-quart square baking dish. Bring a large pot of salted water to a boil (5 quarts water with 1½ tablespoons kosher salt). Cook the egg noodles until just past al dente, about 10 minutes. Drain and rinse. In a mixing bowl, whisk together the cottage cheese and sour cream. Beat in the eggs, butter, sugar, lemon zest or cinnamon, vanilla, and salt. Add the noodles and mix well. Pour this mixture into the buttered baking dish.

Set in the preheated oven and bake for 1 hour and 15 minutes, until the kugel has risen and set, and is slightly brown on top. The kugel will actually rise above the edge of the pan. Remove from the oven and cool for about 10 minutes, just until the kugel has sunken below the edge of the pan. Spread the cherry pie filling on top and return to the oven to set the cherries, about 15 minutes. Remove from the oven and cool completely. Chill and cut into squares to serve.

crumb cake

I'M NOT THE KIND OF guy who sees any point in messing with perfection. As my friends will attest, this crumb cake from Nick Malgieri's *How to Bake* is about as good as crumb cake gets. I have never made it that it didn't disappear. I have changed only a couple of things: I use unbleached flour instead of bleached because that's all I have lying around, and I have made the fruit optional because I also like the crumb cake plain. If you are using prune plums, however, and you have some Fresh Plum Conserve (page 215) lying around, I would add a little to help boost the flavor.

a bissel advice

You're such a big macher? Buy Nick's book!

How do I cut out a round of parchment paper? Here's a trick. Cut the parchment paper to a square that is slightly larger than your pan. Fold the square in half and then fold the triangle in half again. Keep folding until you have a long, narrow triangle only about an inch wide at its base. Now hold the point of the triangle in the center of the pan and snip the other end so it's even with the edge. When you unfold the paper you'll have an almost round circle about the size of your pan. It's close enough and it's easy.

I love this cake, can I do anything else with it? For a satisfying variation, here's how my sister Carrie likes to make this cake: Beat together ¾ cup oef sour cream, 1 large egg, 2 tablespoons sugar, ½ teaspoon pure vanilla extract, and the finely grated zest of a lemon or orange. Pour the cake batter into the prepared pan and arrange the fruit as directed. Bake the cake like this (without the crumb mixture on top) for 20 minutes, until it starts to set. Spread the sour cream mixture on top of and around the fruit, sprinkle the top with the crumb mixture, and finish baking until done, as directed.

FOR THE TOPPING

1¼ cups unbleached all-purpose flour

½ cup sugar

¼ teaspoon ground cinnamon

½ cup (1 stick) unsalted butter, melted and
cooled

FOR THE CAKE

½ cup (1 stick) unsalted butter, plus an
additional tablespoon for greasing the
pan

¾ cup sugar

1 large egg plus 3 egg yolks

Zest of ½ small lemon (1 teaspoon)

1 teaspoon pure vanilla extract

1¼ cups unbleached all-purpose flour

1 teaspoon baking powder

2 pounds (about 9 or 10) purple prune plums
or ripe apricots, halved and pitted, or
1 quart sour cherries, pitted, or a
combination of strawberries and finely
chopped rhubarb *(optional)*

½ cup Fresh Plum Conserve (page 215)
(optional)

SPECIAL EQUIPMENT

10-inch springform pan

Parchment paper

Electric mixer fitted with a paddle
attachment

preheat the oven to 350°F.

Butter the springform pan and line the bottom with a round of parchment paper. Butter the parchment.

For the topping: Combine the flour, sugar, and cinnamon in a small bowl. Pour in the melted butter and mix to combine. Rub the mixture together between your fingertips to produce coarse crumbs. Set aside.

To prepare the cake: In the bowl of an electric mixer, cream together the butter and the sugar until light and fluffy, about 5 minutes total. Add the egg and continue beating until the color lightens even more. Add the yolks one at a time, beating after each addition. Add the lemon zest and vanilla, and mix well. Remove the bowl from the mixer, and using a wooden spoon stir in the flour and baking powder.

Pour this batter into the prepared pan and use a spatula to spread it out evenly. If using fruit, arrange the plum or apricot halves, cut side up, on top of the batter, leaving about ½ inch border free around the circumference of the pan; just scatter the cherries across the top (if using). Don't press the fruit into the batter. If using the plum conserve, spoon it around the fruit. Scatter the crumbs evenly over the top. Bake for 50 to 60 minutes in the preheated oven, until the crumbs have turned golden brown and the cake is firm to the touch. An instant-read thermometer inserted in the center should register at least 185°F. A cake made without fruit will take slightly less time, so start testing it for doneness at about 45 minutes. Remove from the oven and place the pan on a wire rack. Cool completely. To unmold, run a knife around the edge and undo the spring. Slide onto a serving plate.

passover sponge cake

IF YOU THINK THAT PASSOVER Sponge Cake should be renamed Passover Sponge or maybe Saw Dust Cake, then you haven't tried my sister's. Carrie has been making our family's Passover Sponge Cakes since she was 11 years old. That her birthday usually falls on Passover may be one reason she has a gifted touch with egg whites and

ground matzo—choking to death on a piece of cake makes for a sorry celebration, indeed. Forget the story of the Jews' expulsion from Egypt; our Seder celebrates the miracle of Carrie's moist and flavorful sponge cake.

Some of her secrets about working with egg whites are outlined in the Bissel Advice section below. But we suspect that, like my mother's matzo balls (page 43), divine intervention may also play a hand. It helps if you have a little patience. You can't be rushed or otherwise distracted on your first (or fifteenth) attempt at one of these cakes. The more you make them, the better you'll get. If you simply can't master the technique, why not make a foolproof flourless Chocolate Cloud Cake (page 176) instead?

Carrie often fills her sponge cake with lemon curd and tops it with chocolate ganache. Whipped cream and fresh strawberries turn it into a delicious simulated shortcake. Treat leftover cake like Challah French Toast (page 188) the next morning for breakfast, or do as Carrie does and make it into a mean trifle for dessert the next day.

a bissel advice

So, what's so special about working with egg whites? Herein lies the secret to good Passover sponge cake: (1) Make sure that all of the bowls and utensils you are using with the egg whites are completely free of any dirt or grease. (2) Eggs are easier to separate when they are chilled, but they should be beaten when they are at room temperature. (3) Even the slightest drop of yolk in the whites will cause the cake not to work; therefore, to separate the eggs, use a small bowl to catch the white of each egg. If the white is clean and free of any yolk, transfer it to your large mixing bowl. If there is any yolk in the white, discard it (or use if for breakfast). (4) On the other hand, it doesn't matter if any egg white has gotten into the egg yolks.

What is cake meal, anyway? Finely ground matzo. Think of it as blessed flour. But note that you can't substitute it in everything that calls for flour because the matzo baking process destroys the gluten that would have been in the flour used to make the matzo in the first place.

kosher status PAREVE, but pay attention to your accompaniments
PESADICH, obviously

1 cup matzo cake meal

¼ cup potato starch

9 large eggs, separated (see "advice" on
opposite page)

1½ cups sugar

Zest of 1 lemon or orange (about
1 tablespoon)

½ cup orange juice

Pinch of kosher salt

SPECIAL EQUIPMENT

Flour sifter or fine sieve

Electric mixer with a paddle and whisk
attachment

10-cup 10-inch tube pan, with a removable
center and little "feet" that allow you to
turn it upside down while the cake cools
(sometimes called an angel food cake
pan)

P reheat the oven to 350°F.

Sift together the cake meal and potato starch. Set aside.

Using an electric mixer fitted with a paddle attachment, beat the egg yolks on high until pale yellow, 2 or 3 minutes. Add the sugar and continue beating until the mixture has tripled in volume, at least 5 minutes. The mixture should become even paler yellow and be shiny, not grainy; when you remove the beater, a ribbon of batter should form and lazily dissolve as the mixture falls back into itself. Add the zest and orange juice and beat to incorporate. Add the sifted cake-meal mixture and beat until smooth.

In a second, perfectly clean, grease-free bowl, combine the egg whites with a pinch of salt. Using the whisk attachment, beat the egg whites until stiff but not dry, and they form firm peaks. If they begin to look grainy, stop immediately. Note that it is better for the whites to be slightly underbeaten than to overbeat them; overbeaten egg whites will produce a dry cake.

Using a large rubber spatula, fold about a third of the whites into the egg-yolk mixture to lighten it up. Add the remaining whites and fold quickly but thoroughly to incorporate without deflating. Immediately transfer the batter to an ungreased tube pan. Drop large dollops of batter around the base of the pan and smooth out with the rubber spatula. Set in the oven and bake until golden brown and firm to the touch, 50 to 60 minutes. While baking, be sure not to make any sudden loud noises that may cause the egg whites to deflate.

Remove the cake from the oven and turn the pan upside down on the counter to cool (don't worry, the cake won't fall out). When the cake has cooled completely, turn it right side up. Run a knife along the outer edge and the inner tube. Lift out the center of the pan. Slide the knife under the cake to loosen the bottom and carefully lift the cake off the insert.

cheesecake

JUST WHY CHEESECAKE BECAME ASSOCIATED with Jewish delicatessens I don't know. You couldn't

think of anything more obviously traif after a thick corned beef sandwich than a slab of cream cheese–rich cheesecake

with a butter crust. But so it is that Carnegie Deli, Lindy's, Reuben's, and Junior's became famous for their dense

cheesecakes. (Note that the kosher Second Avenue Deli serves a disappointing "cheesecake" made with tofu. It would be better labeled "tofucake.") Here is my sister Carrie's recipe for a dense, New York–style cheesecake. It has a full 2 pounds of cream cheese, and don't even think about using "light." The point of this kind of cake is that somebody makes the crack while eating it, "This is so rich it should be served on a bagel!"

a bissel advice

What if the top is too brown? **You can peel it off and cover with fresh fruit, or just top it with confectioners' sugar.**

What if it cracks? **I'm afraid there is nothing you can do. The slow cooling in the warm oven helps prevent cracking, but sometimes you do everything right and it cracks anyway. Cover the cake with a can of cherry pie filling or serve it already sliced.**

How do I slice it? **A long, thin knife dipped in hot water makes cheesecake slicing a breeze. After every cut, dip the knife and wipe off the blade.**

But I like Graham cracker crust under my cheesecake! **Don't worry, you can use the same recipe with a different crust (in fact, Graham cracker crust is even easier to make). Here's what you do: Combine 1 cup of Graham cracker crumbs with 2 tablespoons of sugar and ¼ teaspoon ground cinnamon (optional, but highly recommended). Add ¼ cup (4 tablespoons) melted and cooled sweet butter and stir to make a mixture with the consistency of wet sand. With your fingertips, pat this mixture into an even layer on the bottom of the springform pan and bake in the preheated oven for about 10 minutes to set. Cool and proceed with the recipe as directed.**

Preheat the oven to 400°F.

Butter a 9-inch springform pan. To prepare the crust, cream together the butter and sugar by hand or with an electric mixer until blended. Beat in the vanilla. Add the flour and lemon zest, and work together with a wooden spoon until the mixture produces soft crumbs. With your fingertips, pat this mixture into the bottom of the buttered springform pan. Even out the crust so that no area is thicker than another. Set the pan in the middle of the preheated oven and bake for 15 to 20 minutes, or until the crust has turned light brown. Remove from the oven and cool on a rack.

Meanwhile, prepare the filling. Cream together the cream cheese and sugar until smooth. Add the eggs, lemon juice, vanilla, and cornstarch and continue beating until well blended. Fold in the sour cream. Pour this mixture onto the cooled crust. Return to the oven and bake for 45 to 50 minutes, or until the sides have fully set and the center is just a little bit loose. If the top of the cake begins to brown, cover loosely with a sheet of aluminum foil. When the cake is done, turn off the oven and open the oven door, but do not remove the cake. Allow the cake to cool completely in the oven to prevent cracking. Refrigerate for 3 or 4 hours before serving. Serve with Blueberry Sauce.

FOR THE CRUST

1½ sticks unsalted butter, at room temperature, plus 1 tablespoon for greasing the pan

⅔ cup sugar

1 teaspoon pure vanilla extract

1½ cups unbleached all-purpose flour

Zest of 1 lemon (about 1 tablespoon)

FOR THE FILLING

2 pounds (four 8-ounce packages) cream cheese, at room temperature

1 cup sugar

2 large eggs

Juice of ½ lemon (about 1 tablespoon)

1½ teaspoons pure vanilla extract

2 tablespoons cornstarch

1 cup (½ pound) sour cream

1 recipe Blueberry Sauce (page 214) (optional)

SPECIAL EQUIPMENT

9-inch springform pan

Electric mixer fitted with a paddle attachment

russian sour cream cake

I SUSPECT THAT THIS CLASSIC coffee cake, rich with sour cream and flavored with cinnamon and walnuts, has never been served in Russia—unless there's a Starbucks in Moscow. But it is a cake that my mother has been making since before I was born. And it remains one of my family's favorites. (I always wanted my aunt Josephine's chocolate cake for my birthday, while my brother Sheldon requested this rather grown-up dessert for his.) It is a deceptively large cake that can satisfy a crowd. The cake is actually better after it has sat, tightly wrapped, for a day. It freezes well (in small hunks for convenience), and because of its broad appeal, it is a good cake to bring to a potluck or party. Slice it as close to service as possible. And don't fuss with icing or confectioners' sugar or anything. It is delicious as is.

a bissel advice

Such a big cake? **As I said, this is a cake that serves a crowd. You can halve the recipe and bake it in a loaf pan (it will still take about an hour to cook), but I usually choose instead to freeze whatever cake I don't use so that I have it on hand if anyone drops by for coffee (as Jews always seem to be doing).**

Oy, it's so rich. **Well, Peggy (see Chocolate Beet Cake, page 174) and I once had a bake-off using this recipe. She made it with low-fat yogurt and I used sour cream. Although I was skeptical, both cakes were delicious. So, if you must: substitute 2 cups plain low-fat yogurt for the sour cream and follow the recipe as indicated.**

kosher status MILCHIG; using margarine or fake sour cream would be a sin

Preheat the oven to 350°F. Butter the tube pan. Place the walnuts on a cookie sheet and set them in the oven for about 10 minutes to toast. In a small bowl, combine the walnuts, sugars, and cinnamon, and stir to blend. Set aside.

Using an electric mixer fitted with a paddle attachment or a large mixing bowl and a wooden spoon, cream the butter and sugar until light and fluffy. Add the eggs, one at a time, beating well after each addition. Stir in the vanilla, baking powder, and baking soda. If you began with an electric mixer, you're now finished with it. Use a wooden spoon to stir in the sour cream and flour, alternating each: first 1 cup of sour cream, then 2 cups of flour, until all of the ingredients are used up. Be careful not to overmix, stirring just until the previous addition is incorporated. The batter should be thick but light.

Place about a third of the batter in the bottom of the prepared pan and smooth with a spatula to form an even layer. Sprinkle with about a third of the filling. Cover with another third of the batter, dropping small spoonfuls around the circumference of the pan and carefully smoothing them out without disturbing the filling underneath. Top with another third of the filling, and top that with a layer of the remaining batter. Reserve the remaining third of the filling.

Set the cake in the preheated oven and bake for about 30 minutes. Open the oven gently and sprinkle the remaining filling evenly over the top. Close the oven and bake for an additional 40 minutes or so, until the cake has risen, browned, and set firm. A thin knife inserted into one of the cracks on the top should come out clean, and an instant-read thermometer inserted into the center of the cake should read 185°F. when it is done. Remove from the oven, place the pan on a wire rack, and let cool completely. To remove from the pan, slide a long, thin knife around the circumference of the cake and around the tube in the center. Lift the insert out of the pan. Slide the knife under the cake around the center tube. You can either slice the cake while it sits on the tube insert or lift if off the insert and slice it as needed.

FOR THE FILLING

½ cup chopped walnuts

½ cup granulated sugar

½ cup light or dark brown sugar

4 teaspoons ground cinnamon

FOR THE BATTER

½ pound or 1 cup (2 sticks) unsalted butter, at room temperature, plus 1 tablespoon for greasing the pan

2 cups granulated sugar

4 large eggs

2 teaspoons pure vanilla extract

2 teaspoons baking powder

2 teaspoons baking soda

2 cups (1 pound) sour cream

4 cups unbleached all-purpose flour

SPECIAL EQUIPMENT

10-cup, 10-inch tube pan with a removable center (sometimes called an angel food cake pan)

Electric mixer fitted with a paddle attachment (optional)

chocolate beet cake

GRANTED, THIS CAKE SOUNDS WEIRD. But trust me, people love it. The cake is dark and rich and chocolatey, with just the slightest hint of red. The beets keep it moist and add a complexity to the flavor that's almost impossible to discern until someone explains what's in it—or spills the beets, so to speak. My friends who cannot eat

dairy consider it the best chocolate dessert on the planet. And for obvious reasons, it caps off a kosher fleishig meal with finesse.

This recipe comes from my colleague and friend Peggy, a great baker who rises early before work several times a week to try out a new recipe or two. (It's no wonder I've put on weight since she started working with us at the James Beard Foundation.) Some consider Chocolate Beet Cake an ancestor to the classic American red velvet cake, which uses cocoa and red food dye to achieve a similar color. But that's where the similarities end. It was Peggy's idea to add chocolate chips, and the resulting cake is richer and better for it. There is no need to ice the cake; just sprinkle it with confectioners' sugar and serve it with a dollop of whipped cream or crème fraîche (unless you intend to keep it pareve, obviously).

Although you can substitute canned beets for fresh and thereby preempt the cooking of the beets, you can't compare the results of using fresh beets, which are sweeter and more flavorful. To help ease the process, you can puree the beets up to 3 or 4 days in advance and keep them refrigerated until you are ready to bake. For tips on how to prepare the fresh beet puree, see page 249.

a bissel advice

How many beets? If you cook and puree 2 pounds of fresh beets, you'll have a little more than the 2 cups you need for this recipe. Use the extra to make beet Horseradish (page 202). And don't forget to use the beet tops for something delicious like Savory Noodle Kugel (page 130).

What's confectioners' sugar? Confectioners' sugar (a.k.a. icing sugar, 10X sugar, or powdered sugar) is like ordinary granulated sugar that's been pulverized to a powder—ten times the fineness of regular sugar, in fact (10X).

Such a big cake? This is one of those cakes that's delicious when it's baked and gets even better after a day or two. You can also freeze it.

kosher status PAREVE, unless you use butter to grease the pan or serve it with whipped cream. Also, make sure that the semi-sweet chocolate and chocolate chips you use do not contain any milk or milk products.

1 tablespoon unsalted butter softened or vegetable oil

2 tablespoons cocoa powder or all-purpose flour

4 ounces (¼ pound) semi-sweet chocolate

1 cup chocolate chips

2 teaspoons pure vanilla extract

2 cups unbleached all-purpose flour

3 large eggs

1½ cups granulated sugar

1 cup Crisco (100% soybean) vegetable oil

2 cups beet puree (see page 249)

2 teaspoons baking soda

¼ teaspoon kosher salt

Confectioners' sugar for dusting

SPECIAL EQUIPMENT

1 (10-cup) Bundt cake pan

Electric mixer

preheat the oven to 375°F.

Using a paper towel, grease the pan with butter or oil. Add the cocoa or flour to the pan and shake it around to coat the surface. Invert over a garbage can or sink and tap to remove any excess cocoa. Set aside.

Melt the semi-sweet chocolate in a small bowl in a microwave oven (about 1 minute on medium) or in a double boiler. Cool. Place the chocolate chips in another small bowl. Add 1 teaspoon of the vanilla and toss the chips to moisten. Add about a tablespoon of the flour and toss to coat the chips. (The flour coating helps prevent the chips from sinking to the bottom of the cake.) Set aside.

With an electric mixer, beat the eggs with the sugar in a medium bowl until light and fluffy, a good 5 minutes. Slowly beat in the oil in a steady stream; the mixture will thicken as more oil is incorporated. Switch to a wooden spoon and stir in the melted chocolate, pureed beets, and the remaining teaspoon of vanilla. Add the remaining flour, the baking soda, and salt, and mix well. Stir in the prepared chocolate chips.

Pour the batter into the prepared pan and even out the surface with the back of a spoon or a spatula. Bake for 35 to 40 minutes, until the cake has risen and pulled away from the sides. A toothpick or bamboo skewer inserted in one of the cracks in the top should come out clean, save for streaks of melted chocolate from the chips. Remove from the oven and cool in the pan for 15 to 20 minutes before unmolding. Continue cooling on a rack to room temperature. To serve, dust with confectioners' sugar.

chocolate cloud cake

THIS IS A FLOURLESS CHOCOLATE cake recipe given to me by my late friend Richard Sax. Not only is it a superbly rich and beautiful cake, but because of its flourlessness it has become a Passover tradition. There is the slight problem of butter, which makes it difficult (sacrilegious, really) to serve it after a kosher meat meal. If such things are a

concern, you can figure out a time to eat it — believe me, you will want to. The cake is so dense and delicious you don't really need anything more than a sprinkling of confectioners' sugar or a spoonful of whipped cream to go with it.

a bissel advice

Are you trying to bankrupt me? Splurge on the best chocolate you can find. This cake is all about the chocolate.

You call that a piece of cake? Resist the temptation to be too generous with your portions. This cake is so rich that a sliver is all you need. (Besides, couldn't your friends stand to lose a few pounds?)

MENTAL NOSH

Just who invented the flourless chocolate cake, you ask? The answer is impossible to ascertain. In recent years, flourless chocolate cake and its underbaked cousin, the molten chocolate cake, have become ubiquitous on restaurant menus. These cakes are sometimes mislabeled soufflés, but they are more like failed soufflés than anything else. Superstar chef and cookbook author Jean-Georges Vongerichten (of Jean-Georges, Vong, Mercer Kitchen, et al.) lays claim to serving the first molten chocolate cake. But who can be sure? The thing to keep in mind is that neither underbaking nor overbaking this particular cake is desirable. It may take you one or two tries until you get the doneness just right. But don't be discouraged; this cake is always delicious. It has none of the rubberiness of other flourless chocolate cakes, and none of the uncooked-batter taste of most molten chocolate cakes.

½ pound (8 ounces) top-quality bittersweet
   chocolate (such as Lindt, Valrhona,
   Callebaut, or Sharffen Berger with
   60 percent or more cocoa content),
   coarsely chopped

½ cup (1 stick) unsalted butter, cut into
   chunks, at room temperature

6 large eggs

1 cup sugar

2 tablespoons brandy, cognac, or Grand
   Marnier

Grated zest of 1 orange (about 2 teaspoons)
   (optional)

SPECIAL EQUIPMENT

8-inch round springform pan

Parchment paper

Electric mixer or good whisk

reheat the oven to 350°F.

   Line the bottom of the 8-inch springform with a round of parchment paper (see techinique, page 166), but do not butter the paper or the pan. Melt the chopped chocolate in the top of a double boiler, or in a stainless steel bowl set over a pot of simmering water, or in the microwave. Be very careful not to get any water from condensation into the chocolate. When it is melted, remove from the heat and whisk in the butter.

   In separate mixing bowls, separate 4 of the eggs, being sure not to get any yolk in with the whites (see page 168 for some advice). Add the remaining 2 whole eggs to the yolks along with ½ cup of the sugar. Whisk until blended. Add the chocolate-and-butter mixture to the eggs. Whisk in the brandy, cognac, or Grand Marnier and the orange zest (if using). Beat until blended and set aside.

   Using an electric beater or a good whisk and a strong arm, beat the egg whites in a clean bowl until foamy, 2 or 3 minutes. Gradually add the remaining ½ cup sugar, and continue beating until the whites form soft mounds that hold their shape but are not stiff; they should look shiny and silken. Using a rubber spatula, stir about a quarter of the beaten egg-white mixture into the chocolate–egg yolk mixture to lighten it. Then dump the remaining egg whites on top of the chocolate mixture and, using the spatula, fold in the whites just until incorporated, being careful to deflate them as little as possible.

   Pour the batter into the prepared pan. Bake the cake for 35 to 40 minutes, until the top is puffed and cracked, and the mixture is no longer wobbly. Do not overbake the cake or it will be dry—better to err on the side of underdone. Cool the cake in the pan on a wire rack. The cake will sink as it cools, leaving an attractive, cracked crater in the middle. Unmold before serving by running a knife around the sides and releasing the spring. You can fill the crater if you like with whipped cream and dust with confectioners' sugar and/or cocoa.

quince upside-down honey cake

HERE IS A RECIPE FOR A HONEY CAKE from my friend Karen, an artist, pastry chef, and restaurateur who is married to my friend Daňo in upstate New York. (If you've been paying attention to the headnotes, you've already heard a lot about Daňo.) It's a great dessert for a Rosh Hashanah dinner because honey cake is traditional (it's supposed to auger a sweet New Year) and quince are in season. The quince can be poached in advance, but the cake should be baked the day it is served.

a bissel advice

What is a quince? Quince is an ancient fruit that looks like a nubby cross between an apple and a pear. Although it looks sweet and appetizing raw, quince must be peeled and cooked before being eaten. It has a core like an apple, but that core has a hard outer section that must be removed; you will know it is left because it makes a loud scraping sound when it comes into contact with your knife. Quince are used in both sweet and savory dishes.

What is cake flour? Flour is graded by protein content. Cake flour has less protein than all-purpose flour and therefore it produces a cake with a lighter, finer texture. It usually comes in a 1-pound box and is available in the baking section of most grocery stores.

What's buckwheat honey, anyway? Bees make honey from all sorts of flowers—orange blossoms, thyme, alfalfa, you name it. Honey made from buckwheat flowers (the same grain that gives us kasha) has a dark color and a deep flavor that makes this cake delicious.

How do I get all the honey out of the measuring cup? See page 180 for a good tip.

to poach the quince, in a small saucepan combine the water, sugar, wine, vanilla, and cinnamon. Bring to a boil, turn down the heat, and simmer until the sugar is dissolved and the liquid is clear. Add the quince quarters and simmer until tender but not falling apart, about 15 minutes. The quince float at first, but they begin to sink once they are almost done. Remove from the heat and cool in the liquid. Transfer to a sieve and drain.

Preheat the oven to 325°F.

Generously butter a 9-inch round cake pan or springform pan. Line the bottom with a circle of parchment paper (see page 166) and butter the paper. Slice the drained quince lengthwise into thin, even slices. Arrange the slices in a pinwheel pattern on the bottom of the parchment-lined cake pan. Remember that when the cake is unmolded, the pattern will be reversed, so channel Michelangelo and work in relief if you can.

Meanwhile, to prepare cake batter, place the honey in a small saucepan and bring to a boil. Remove from the heat and cool to room temperature. In a large mixing bowl, combine the cake flour with the baking soda, baking powder, salt, cinnamon, cloves, and nutmeg, and sift twice to blend. In the bowl of an electric mixer fitted with a paddle attachment, cream the butter and brown sugar. Add the egg and beat until very light in color, a good 5 minutes at medium-high speed. Add the cooled honey and the fresh ginger, and beat for another couple of minutes. Remove the bowl from the mixer. Using a wooden spoon, stir the dry ingredients and the milk into the egg mixture, alternating each by thirds until both are incorporated. The batter should be light and smooth. Pour over the quince and level the top with the back of the wooden spoon or a rubber spatula.

Bake in the preheated oven for 45 to 55 minutes, until the cake has risen and set, the sides have shrunk away from the pan, and an instant-read thermometer inserted in the center reads at least 185°F. Allow to cool in the pan for about 40 minutes. Run a small knife around the edge, invert on a serving plate, remove the parchment paper, and let cool completely to room temperature before serving.

FOR THE POACHED QUINCE

2 cups water

2 cups granulated sugar

1 cup dry white wine

½ vanilla bean, split

2-inch stick cinnamon

2 quince (1 pound), quartered, peeled, and cored

FOR THE CAKE

2 tablespoons unsalted butter, for greasing pan

½ cup buckwheat honey

1¾ cups cake flour, sifted

½ teaspoon baking soda

1½ teaspoons baking powder

¼ teaspoon kosher salt

½ teaspoon ground cinnamon

½ teaspoon ground cloves

½ teaspoon ground nutmeg

½ cup (1 stick) unsalted butter, at room temperature

½ cup dark brown sugar

1 large egg

½ teaspoon minced fresh ginger

⅞ cup milk

SPECIAL EQUIPMENT

9-inch round cake pan or springform pan

Parchment paper

Electric mixer

honey-walnut cake

I ALWAYS THOUGHT HONEY CAKE was for Jews what fruitcake was for Christians: you make it and you give it as a gift, but nobody really likes it. As is the tradition, every Rosh Hashanah we would have a honey cake that nobody in my family would touch. Then, just last Rosh Hashanah, my friend Peggy made a Sephardic honey cake from my late friend Richard Sax's book *Classic Home Desserts*. The cake was superb, and I went home that night to try the recipe for myself. Since then I've found a whole new appreciation for honey cakes (see another recipe for one on page 178). I realized I had just never had a good one.

This is a large cake that will keep perfectly for more than a week because the honey syrup keeps it moist. So, here is the recipe that changed my entire attitude about honey cakes. I hope it will change yours.

a bissel advice

What if I can't get all the honey out of the measuring cup? **Before you measure the honey, put a drop—about ½ teaspoon—of vegetable oil in the bottom of the cup. The honey will slide right out like it's nobody's business.**

This is enough cake for me and the Israeli army! **You can cut the recipe in half and bake it in an 8-inch-square pan.**

Don't just sit there! **Buy Richard's book.**

kosher status MILCHIG

FOR THE CAKE

4 cups walnut halves

1 cup sugar

1 cup (2 sticks) unsalted butter

1 cup (just under 1 pound) light honey, such
    as acacia or wildflower

1½ teaspoons ground cinnamon

½ teaspoon kosher salt

2½ cups unbleached all-purpose flour

1 teaspoon baking powder

1 teaspoon baking soda

FOR THE SYRUP

1 cup honey

Grated zest of 2 lemons (1 tablespoon)

Juice of 2 lemons (½ cup)

SPECIAL EQUIPMENT

9-by-13-inch cake pan

Food processor

preheat the oven to 350°F.

Butter the cake pan. To make the cake, pick out 24 of the best-looking walnut halves and set them aside. Place the remaining ugly walnut halves in the bowl of a food processor fitted with a metal chopping blade. Add the sugar. Process with 20 to 25 one-second pulses until the nuts have ground to a coarse meal. Be careful not to overprocess or the nuts will expel some of their oil and turn into a mess.

In a large, heavy saucepan, combine the butter, 2 cups water, honey, cinnamon, salt, and the ground walnut-and-sugar mixture. Set over medium-high heat and cook, stirring frequently, until the butter melts and the mixture comes to a boil. Remove from the heat. Stir in the flour, baking powder, and baking soda until blended. Pour the batter into the prepared pan and smooth out the top with the back of a spoon or a spatula. Arrange the reserved attractive walnut halves in even rows across the top of the cake. Push them down gently so they sink somewhat into the batter. Bake the cake in the preheated oven for 30 to 40 minutes, or until the top is golden brown and firm to the touch, and an instant-read thermometer inserted in the center reads at least 185°F. Place the cake pan on a wire rack and cool to lukewarm.

Meanwhile, prepare the syrup. Combine the honey with ½ cup water in a saucepan and set over medium-high heat. Add the lemon zest and continue cooking until the mixture comes to a boil. Simmer, stirring once in a while, until the mixture becomes syrupy, about 7 minutes. Remove from the heat and stir in the lemon juice. While the cake is still warm, spoon the syrup evenly over the top, letting it sink in before you pour on the next spoonful. The cake should sit for at least 4 hours to absorb the syrup, or better yet, overnight. Cut the cake into squares with a walnut half in the center of each. Eat the edges yourself, privately. Store wrapped airtight for up to 1 week.

blintzes

LIKE FRENCH CREPES OR HUNGARIAN palacsinta, blintzes are thin, delicate pancakes, stuffed with any number of different fillings and fried in butter. What could be bad? People make savory blintzes, filled with everything from potatoes to kasha, and the more common sweet blintzes, filled with cheese, fruit, poppy seeds, or chocolate. Any

of the fillings in chapter 7 will work. But if you intend to make savory blintzes, omit the sugar and vanilla from the batter.

The word *blintz* refers both to the crepe and to the finished package, filling and all, so writing about how to make them can get a little confusing. For the purposes of this recipe, I'm going to use *crepe* to refer to the pancake and *blintz* to refer to the filled package.

Perhaps the one trick to making blintzes is that the crepes are initially cooked on only one side.

a bissel advice

So much work? **This recipe reads like more of a production than it is. It's just that writing down all of the steps sort of takes up more room than just doing them.**

Which filling? **Anything is fine. Sometimes I mix and match: a little cheese and apple in the same blintz. Potato and brisket. Think of them as the original wraps.**

They are then filled with the cooked side facing in. The exposed, uncooked side is what gets fried in butter before the blintzes are served. To prevent the crepes from fusing with the inside of your pan, you should use either a nonstick sauté pan or a seasoned cast-iron crepe pan. To make pouring the batter into the pan easier, you can use a small pitcher, but a ladle works fine, too.

My recipe for batter makes about fourteen, 8-inch crepes, which requires just under 4 cups of filling, or a double batch of most of the sweet or savory filling recipes in chapter 7. Cheese blintzes are de rigueur, but instead of making a double batch of cheese filling, I usually make one batch of cheese and one batch of something else.

4 large eggs

1 cup milk

4 tablespoons unsalted butter, melted and cooled

2 cups unbleached all-purpose flour

½ teaspoon kosher salt

2 tablespoons sugar *(optional)*

½ teaspoon pure vanilla extract *(optional)*

About 4 cups filling (pages 220–235)

Additional melted unsalted butter for frying

kosher status MILCHIG. If you want to make pareve blintzes, you can substitute ¾ cup water for the milk in the batter and peanut oil for the butter. For savory fillings, try fleishig blintzes using 1⅔ cups chicken stock instead of the water and milk, and chicken schmaltz for the butter. Choose your fillings wisely.

SPECIAL EQUIPMENT

Food processor *(optional)*

8- or 9-inch nonstick sauté pan or well-seasoned, cast-iron crepe pan

Pastry brush or piece of paper towel

Water pitcher or ladle

Place the eggs, milk, ¾ cup cold water, melted butter, flour, salt, sugar, and the vanilla (if using), in the bowl of a food processor fitted with a metal chopping blade. Process for 1 or 2 minutes to produce a smooth batter. To remove any lumps, strain through a fine sieve into a bowl or a pitcher and let sit at room temperature for about 1 hour.

Alternatively, to make the batter without using a food processor, in a large mixing bowl beat the eggs, milk, ¾ cup cold water, and melted butter with a wire whisk. Mix in the flour, salt, sugar, and vanilla (if using), and continue beating until smooth. To remove any lumps, strain through a fine sieve into a bowl or a pitcher, and let sit at room temperature for about 1 hour. You can also refrigerate the batter for up to 2 days.

Place a clean dinner plate next to the stove. To cook the crepes, heat the nonstick sauté pan or crepe pan over medium heat. When hot, use a pastry brush or a piece of paper towel dipped in the melted butter to coat the pan with a very thin film of grease. Grasp the pan in your right hand (or left, if you are left-handed) and the pitcher of batter or the ladle in the other hand. Pour about 3 tablespoons of batter in the center of the pan while swirling the pan around to form a large, thin crepe the size of the entire bottom of the pan. Don't be timid. You can tilt the pan vertically, shake it back and forth, and basically do what ever you can to make the biggest, thinnest crepe possible. Don't worry, it won't fall out of the pan. If the batter is too thick to spread out across the entire bottom of the pan, add a tablespoon or two of water to thin it out. Depending

MENTAL NOSH

Warm buckwheat pancakes slathered with sweet butter and sour cream, and piled high with beluga caviar, may seem a far cry from the simple, inexpensive blintz served at Jewish dairy restaurants around the world, but etymologically speaking they are very close, indeed. The Yiddish word blintz *derives from the Russian word for pancake,* blin, *as in* blini. *Unfortunately, since sturgeon caviar is not kosher (the fish don't have scales), observant Jews have to settle for salmon eggs, or scrambled eggs, maybe with a little onion and smoked salmon? Blintzes are eaten by some people on Shevout, one tradition has it, because two blintzes side-by-side are said to resemble the tablets on which Moses' Ten Commandments were inscribed.*

recipe continues →

blintzes

(continued)

on how well you remember grade-school physics and vectors of force, it may take you a couple of attempts to end up with a round crepe.

Replace the pan on the fire and let the crepe cook for a couple of minutes until it pulls back from the edges and begins to brown. To check, you can pick up an edge and peek underneath. Once the underside of the crepe is browned, invert the pan over the dinner plate to release the crepe without damaging it. Alternatively, you can pick up the crepe with a spatula or your fingertips (I lost the feeling in mine long ago) and flip it onto the plate. The cooked side of the crepe should be facing up.

Repeat with the remaining batter, piling the crepes on the plate on top of each other, cooked side facing up. You should be able to get 14 crepes in total. Allow the crepes to cool to room temperature. You can wrap them tightly in plastic wrap and refrigerate them for a day or two, or freeze them for up to a month until you are ready to fill them.

To form the blintzes, arrange about ¼ cup of filling in a log shape in the middle of the lower half of the circle. Fold up the bottom to cover the filling, and then fold each side into the center to make a small package. Roll up the crepe to form a compact blintz. Repeat with the remaining crepes and filling. If you haven't already stored the filling or the crepes for any extended length of time, you can store the blintzes in the refrigerator for up to 5 days, or tightly wrapped in the freezer for up to a month.

To serve, preheat the oven to 300°F. Heat 2 or 3 tablespoons of unsalted butter in a large frying pan set over medium-high heat. Place the blintzes in the pan seam side down, and fry until brown and crisp. Turn them over and fry the other side until browned. Using a spatula, gently lift the blintzes out of the pan and place seam side down on a cookie sheet. Set in the oven for at least 10 minutes to finish cooking. If you have to keep them longer, cover with aluminum foil, turn down the heat to 250°F., and hold for up to 1 hour.

Serve with sour cream and applesauce.

cinnamon danish

HOT OUT OF THE OVEN, buttery cinnamon Danish are food from the gods. They take a little bit of time and planning if you want to have them ready for breakfast or brunch. But when your house fills with the aroma of cinnamon and brown sugar, you realize they are worth it. I use the same dough I use for Cheese Danish (page 190).

MAKES **18** DANISH

kosher status MILCHIG

roll the dough out into a giant rectangle approximately 16 by 24 inches. Spread the dough with the softened butter. Sprinkle the brown sugar, cinnamon, and raisins on top of the butter. Drizzle the honey over the whole thing. Roll up the dough like a jelly roll, starting along the longer side of the rectangle. Don't worry if some of the filling falls out. Using a sharp serrated knife, slice the log into 18 rounds, about 1¼ inches thick. Place each round into a muffin tin, gently trying to coax it into the indentation without distorting the shape. Repeat with the remaining half of the ingredients. Let rise for about 1 hour.

Alternatively, you can arrange the Danish in two baking pans that have been well buttered. It usually takes me both a 9 by 13-inch pan and a 9-inch square pan to fit all the Danish without packing them so tightly that they don't have space to rise.

Preheat the oven to 400°F. Bake the Danish for approximately 25 minutes, until they have risen and browned. An instant-read thermometer should read 190°F. when inserted in the center of one of the Danish in the middle of the pan. If the Danish start to darken too much, turn down the heat to 350°F. and continue cooking. Remove from the pans while still warm so they don't adhere, and cool on wire racks completely before eating.

1 batch Cheese Danish dough (page 190)
1½ sticks (6 ounces) unsalted butter, at room temperature
¾ cup light brown sugar
2 teaspoons ground cinnamon
¾ cup golden raisins
⅔ cup honey

SPECIAL EQUIPMENT

Two large muffin tins with indentations for 24 large muffins, or one 9-by-13-inch and one 9-inch square baking pan
Sharp serrated knife

a bissel advice

So much butter? This isn't diet food.

How do I time this right for brunch? You can split it up in two ways. You can make the dough, roll it out, fill it, and cut it the night before. Arrange the Danish in the baking pans, cover them tightly with plastic wrap, and refrigerate them overnight. They will be ready to bake in the morning. Alternatively, you can make just the dough the night before and finish making the cinnamon Danish in the morning.

matzo brei

THERE ARE SOME PASSOVER DISHES I like so much I tell myself I ought to make them throughout the year. Matzo brei is one of them. And given my propensity for procrastination, it goes without saying that I've only ever eaten it at Passover. I grew up on sweet matzo brei, with apples or pineapple chunks cooked right in it and cinnamon sugar on top. I have since come to enjoy savory matzo brei, too, with sautéed onions and sometimes pieces of smoked salmon inside. Either way, I just can't seem to get around to making it until Passover time.

Although some Jewish restaurants around New York like to serve their matzo brei scrambled, I think it ought to remain whole, like a giant pancake. In order to achieve this feat, I use a nonstick pan and I flip it with the aid of a plate. Once you've mastered the technique, you can use it to turn over other large pancakelike dishes.

a bissel advice *Instead of a pancake I made a mess!* **Don't worry; just finish cooking the matzo brei in the pan, no matter what it looks like, and serve it broken up into pieces. This is a tradition, too.**

2½ matzos, broken into 1-inch pieces

1 small apple or pear, peeled, cored, and diced, or ½ cup drained pineapple chunks, cut up into 1-inch pieces

2 large eggs, beaten

Pinch of kosher salt

1 to 2 tablespoons unsalted butter

1 to 2 tablespoons Cinnamon Sugar (page 239)

SPECIAL EQUIPMENT

10-inch nonstick frying pan

Place the broken matzos in a mixing bowl and pour over ¾ cup cold water. Let soak for a minute or two until the matzo absorbs as much water as it can. Drain off any excess water. Add the fruit, eggs, and salt, and stir to combine.

Heat the butter in the nonstick frying pan over medium-high heat. When hot, dump in the matzo mixture. Use the back of a spoon to smooth it out into a even, flat pancake. Let the matzo brei cook for about 5 minutes on the first side, until it has turned an even, dark brown. With a spatula, check to make sure the matzo brei is loose from the bottom of the pan. Invert a clean dinner plate over the top of the pan and flip the whole thing over so that the matzo brei has transferred, cooked side up, onto the plate. Slide the matzo brei off the plate back into the pan and finish cooking the second side for about 3 minutes, or until set and browned. While the second side is cooking, sprinkle the matzo brei with the cinnamon sugar. When done, slide out onto a clean plate and serve hot.

savory matzo brei with onions

THOUGH NOT PART of my childhood, this is nevertheless a delicious breakfast or lunch dish, whether it's Passover or not. Adding the lox makes it a little fancier.

3 tablespoons butter

½ medium onion (3 ounces), thinly sliced

2½ matzos, broken into 1-inch pieces

2 large eggs, beaten

2 ounces smoked salmon, cut into small pieces *(optional)*

½ teaspoon kosher salt

Pinch of freshly ground black pepper

Heat 1½ tablespoons of the fat in a 10-inch nonstick frying pan. Add the onion and sauté until light golden brown, about 7 minutes. Follow the procedure for the sweet Matzo Brei above, adding the sautéed onion and smoked salmon (if using) instead of the fruit and omitting the cinnamon sugar.

challah french toast

IS THERE ANY BETTER USE for stale challah than thick, custardy French toast? No. But there are two pitfalls

to avoid: (1) don't cut the bread too thin—a good ¾- to 1-inch slice produces the best results; (2) don't be afraid to let

the bread soak up the custard mixture—there is nothing more disappointing than cutting into a golden brown piece of

French toast to reveal a bready center. To help avoid this, be sure the bread is stale, make enough of the egg mixture for the bread you have on hand, and let the bread soak for a good couple of minutes before cooking. Of course, bread other than challah can be used to make French toast—I use whatever's lying around. (You can even use leftover Passover Sponge Cake, page 168.) But nothing compares to the rich texture and taste of homemade challah French toast.

A word about condiments. We never put maple syrup on our French toast at home—that was for pancakes and waffles. Instead, my mother sprinkled granulated sugar on top while the second side cooked. The sugar sort of melted and formed a cruncy crust that proved enough

sweetness for us without the added sogginess of syrup. You go ahead and eat your French toast however you'd like.

a bissel advice

So much fat? You can use 2 percent or skim milk if you prefer, but because it is less viscous, you should decrease the amount by a tablespoon or so. Don't try to use buttermilk or sour milk, which will give the French toast an unpleasant, off taste. On my birthday or other special occasions, I confess to using half-and-half or heavy cream instead of whole milk. But that's why I can always stand to lose a few pounds.

Can I make French toast for a crowd? It's easy to make French toast for a crowd. Increase the ingredients in the egg mixture proportionate to how many people you are serving or how much bread you have—1 egg to ¾ cup milk. You will not have to use a proportionate amount of vanilla or cinnamon because I find their strength increases exponentially. Decrease the measurements incrementally; for instance, if you double the recipe, only increase the vanilla and cinnamon by 1½ times. Before you begin frying the French toast, preheat the oven to 300°F. Have a cookie sheet handy. Fry the first pieces of French toast and place them on the cookie sheet when they are done. Cover with aluminum foil and set them in the preheated oven. Repeat with the remaining bread, placing the finished pieces in the oven, until everything is cooked. Between batches, you may want to wipe out the frying pan with a paper towel to prevent any burnt remnants from ruining the flavor of the French toast.

the whole meshpucha

See some tips for bulk cooking in the "advice" section on previous page.

kosher status MILCHIG. Forget the bacon on the side.

2 large eggs

1½ cups whole milk

1½ teaspoons pure vanilla extract

¼ teaspoon ground cinnamon

4 tablespoons (½ stick) unsalted butter

6 to 8 medium slices stale challah (about 10 ounces)

1 tablespoon sugar or Cinnamon Sugar (page 239)

SPECIAL EQUIPMENT

Large, heavy frying pan, such as cast iron

In a wide, shallow bowl, beat the eggs with a fork. Slowly beat in the milk. Add the vanilla and cinnamon and mix until combined.

Heat 1½ tablespoons of the butter in a frying pan over medium-high heat. Place one or two slices of bread, depending on the size of the bowl, in the egg mixture and let sit for a minute while the butter heats up. Flip over the bread and continue to let it soak.

When the butter is bubbling, lift the bread from the egg mixture with a large fork or spatula (truthfully, I use my hands). Shake it a little to drain off any excess egg mixture. Place in the hot pan and repeat with the remaining slices. Cook until dark brown and crisp, 8 or 9 minutes. Flip. Add some of the remaining butter to the pan and continue cooking on the second side until crisp and cooked through, an additional 5 to 7 minutes. Just before the French toast has cooked completely, sprinkle the sugar evenly over the top. Remove from the pan and serve.

cheese danish

THE HARBORD BAKERY IN DOWNTOWN Toronto is just down the street from where my sister Leslie lives. An old Jewish institution now staffed mostly by Philippinos, it still makes the best cheese Danish I've ever had. Since I live in New York and I don't get back to Toronto as often as my family would like, I sometimes have to make my own cheese Danish to satisfy my craving. Here is the recipe I use, which produces light, flaky Danish.

You can put any of the sweet fillings (pages 226–235) inside, or make up your own. You can also experiment with the shape, although the one for which I have given directions—with the four corners of dough folded into the center—is the most traditional shape for cheese danish. The same dough can be used to make superb Cinnamon Danish (see page 185) or Babka (page 192).

a bissel advice

So much rolling out and folding up? **The technique of folding and rolling out the dough for Danish pastry (called "turning") is similar to the way French puff pastry is made. The layers of butter that result give the finished dough a crisp, light texture and buttery flavor. The key is to make sure the dough doesn't get too warm; that's why you have to keep putting it back in the refrigerator, or else the butter will melt and the whole thing will become a sticky mess.**

How do I time this right for brunch? **Make the dough the day or night before and turn it once or twice before you go to bed. Wrap it in plastic wrap and refrigerate it overnight. You can also prepare the cheese filling in advance. The next morning, turn the dough a couple of more times. Roll out, fill, shape, and bake the Danish as directed. If you are feeling really industrious a day or two before, you can roll out, fill, and shape the Danish in advance and refrigerate or freeze them until you are ready to bake.**

Does the Harbord Bakery ship mail-order? **I wish.**

¾ **pound (3 sticks) unsalted butter, chilled**

⅓ **cup unbleached all-purpose flour**

1 **recipe Sweet Yeast Dough (page 256),**
   chilled

1½ **recipes (3 cups) Sweet Cheese Filling**
   (page 229) or other filling

1 **large egg beaten with 1 teaspoon of water**

1 **tablespoon crystallized sugar or Sugar in**
   the Raw

SPECIAL EQUIPMENT

Pastry scraper

Parchment paper

Using a pastry scraper and the palm of your hand, knead the butter and flour together into a smooth, soft mixture. I like to smash the butter into the counter with the heel of my hand and scrape it off with a pastry scraper. Work quickly so the butter doesn't melt. Shape this mixture into a rectangle about 8 by 6 inches.

Roll out the chilled Sweet Yeast Dough to form a large rectangle, about 16 by 8 inches. Place the butter and flour mixture in the center of the dough and fold each side over the dough like a business letter to make a compact rectangle. Roll this out to a large rectangle and fold into thirds again. Cover in plastic wrap and refrigerate for 45 minutes. Roll out and fold twice more, using a little flour to prevent the butter in the dough from sticking. Refrigerate for at least 4 hours.

Remove the dough from the refrigerator and slice it into two equal pieces. Roll out each half into a 12-inch square. Cut the large square into nine 4-inch squares. Place a heaping tablespoon of the cheese filling in the center of each square. Dab the edges with water. Fold the 4 corners to the center, enclosing the cheese. The edges should overlap slightly; pinch them together to seal. Place on a parchment-lined cookie sheet. Let rest for 15 minutes.

Preheat the oven to 400°F. Brush the Danish with the egg wash and sprinkle with the crystallized sugar. Bake for about 25 minutes, until the dough has risen and turned golden brown. If the Danish start to darken too much, turn down the heat to 350°F. Cool completely before eating.

babka

THIS YEAST-RAISED COFFEECAKE IS one of my favorite Jewish snacks. Typically, babka is made from a sweet yeast dough that is rolled with a filling—chocolate, cinnamon and nuts, cheese—and baked in a loaf. At Barney Greengrass on Manhattan's Upper West Side they serve individual babkas baked in muffin tins that are like little Danish muffins. Zingerman's Delicatessen in Ann Arbor, Michigan, ships a regal babka with almond paste, imported chocolate, organic raisins, and a price to match. I prefer babka made with Danish dough because it is at the same time lighter and more buttery. But to save time, you can make a perfectly acceptable babka from a plain sweet yeast dough that hasn't been turned with extra butter.

a bissel advice

Another production you want me to make? These are actually very easy breads to prepare if you play around with the timing. The dough and the filling can be made a day or two in advance. The babkas can be shaped the day before, covered, and left in the refrigerator to rise before they are baked (straight out of the fridge).

Which filling should I choose? As I said, I prefer chocolate. But in doing the research for this book, I came across a lot of different varieties of babka, including streusel, cheese, and poppy seed. Any of the Sweet Fillings on pages 226–235 will produce a delicious babka.

What's vanilla sugar? Just what it sounds like: vanilla-flavored sugar. It is available in small packets imported from Germany, usually under the brand name Dr. Oetker. Be sure you get vanilla sugar made from real vanilla, not the fake vanillin stuff. You can make your own vanilla sugar by keeping a handful of vanilla beans in a canister of sugar.

1 recipe Cheese Danish dough (page 190)

1 recipe Sweet Yeast Dough (page 256)

1 recipe sweet filling (pages 226–235); my preference is for chocolate, but you can use any of them

¼ cup all-purpose flour

¼ cup light brown sugar

½ teaspoon ground cinnamon

1 package (1 teaspoon) vanilla sugar (optional)

3 tablespoons unsalted butter, at room temperature

1 egg beaten with 1 teaspoon cold water

SPECIAL EQUIPMENT

Two 6-cup loaf pans, 8½ by 4½ by 2½ inches

Pastry brush

generously butter two loaf pans. Whether using Danish Dough or Sweet Yeast Dough, divide the dough in half. On a lightly floured surface, roll out the first half of the dough to roughly an 8-by-10-inch rectangle. Spread the dough with half of the filling, leaving a ½-inch border on the two longer sides. Starting at one of the narrower sides, roll up the dough like a jelly roll to form a log. Place the log in the loaf pan, seam side down. Gently press the edges to seal. Cover with a clean dish towel and place in a warm spot to rise until almost doubled in bulk, about 2 hours. Repeat with the remaining half of the dough and filling.

Meanwhile, in a small bowl, combine the flour, brown sugar, cinnamon, and vanilla sugar (if using), and mix to blend. Add the butter, and using your fingertips to rub the ingredients together, work the dough into a crumb.

Preheat the oven to 400°F.

Once the babkas have risen, brush the tops of the loaves with the egg wash. Divide the crumble in half and sprinkle one half on top of each loaf. Place in the preheated oven and bake for about 20 minutes, until the babkas have risen above the sides of the pan and have begun to brown slightly. (Some of the crumble may fall off onto the bottom of the oven. You can put a cookie sheet under the pans to catch it if you'd like.) Babkas made with the Danish Dough will rise higher and less uniformly than those made with the Sweet Yeast Dough. Turn down the heat to 325°F. and bake for another 15 or 20 minutes, until the babkas are deep brown, sound hollow when tapped, and an instant-read thermometer inserted in the center registers at least 185°F. If you are making chocolate babka, you will be able to tell it is done when there is a strong smell of chocolate. If the babkas are getting too brown, turn down the heat to 300°F., and continue baking.

When they are done, remove the babkas from the oven and let cool in the pans for 5 to 10 minutes. Run a knife around the edge of the pan. Invert the babkas onto a clean dish towel, being careful not to knock off the crumble topping, and invert again so they are right side up on a cooling rack. Cool completely before slicing.

oatmeal pancakes

ON THE OFF CHANCE THAT you are kosher and you like meat at breakfast (other than bacon, of course), I thought I would include these delicious pancakes. I made up the recipe first for my mother and some of my friends who have developed an intolerance to lactose. And then one day I realized they might come in handy for a kosher breakfast with meat. The thing is—and I'm almost afraid to admit it—these pancakes are so delicious I make them for myself. And I *hate* soy milk! As an added bonus, unlike most of the other recipes in this book, they are low in fat.

a bissel advice

What if I don't have a problem with milk? Substitute ½ cup buttermilk and ½ cup regular or skim milk for the soy milk and follow the recipe as written.

¾ cup unbleached all-purpose flour

⅓ cup quick-cooking rolled oats

2 teaspoons sugar

Pinch of kosher salt

½ teaspoon baking powder

¼ teaspoon baking soda

1 cup plain or vanilla soy milk or a
    combination of ½ cup buttermilk and
    ½ cup regular milk

1 large egg or 2 egg whites

½ teaspoon pure vanilla extract

Pinch of ground cinnamon *(optional)*

1 or 2 tablespoons peanut oil, for frying

MAKES FIVE TO SIX 4-INCH PANCAKES

kosher status PAREVE, with soy milk
MILCHIG, with real milk

In a mixing bowl, combine the flour, oats, sugar, salt, baking powder, and baking soda, and mix well. In a separate bowl, beat together the soy milk, egg or egg whites, vanilla, and cinnamon (if using). Pour the liquid ingredients into the dry ingredients and mix with a fork just until blended. Let the batter sit at room temperature for about 20 minutes.

Heat a couple of teaspoons of peanut oil in a nonstick skillet, cast-iron frying pan, or on a griddle over medium-high heat. Spoon about a ¼ cup batter into the hot pan to form a pancake. Repeat to fill, but not crowd, the pan. When the surface begins to bubble and the edges have browned, 4 to 5 minutes, flip. Cook the second side for 2 or 3 minutes. Remove from the pan and eat quickly.

charoseth pancakes

FOR WHATEVER REASON, THERE IS always a lot of charoseth leftover after my seders. And with all of those apples and nuts in it, it's a shame to throw it away. That's why I developed this recipe for breakfast the morning after the Seder. Because the apples turn brown very quickly, you can't really keep the charoseth any longer than the

next morning. But that's when you should want to eat these pancakes, anyway. Once cooked, the pancakes can actually be kept for a few days—just reheat them for 40 seconds apiece in the microwave. They have a distinct apple and walnut flavor.

MAKES **8** PANCAKES

kosher status MILCHIG
PESADICH

1 cup Charoseth (see page 216)

¾ cup whole milk

2 large eggs

½ cup matzo meal

1 tablespoon sugar

Pinch of kosher salt

2 tablespoons unsalted butter, for frying

Cinnamon Sugar (page 239)

In a small bowl, mix the charoseth, milk, eggs, matzo meal, sugar, and salt. Heat half the butter in a heavy frying pan set over medium-high heat. Spoon the batter into the pan to form 3-inch pancakes. Fry until the edges are browned and the pancakes have set, about 5 minutes. Carefully flip (the pancakes are delicate) and cook the second side, about 3 minutes. Serve with a dusting of Cinnammon Sugar.

6

Put the Sauce on the Side and Bring Me Another Napkin

condiments

con
dim
ents

What is

gefilte fish without horseradish? A corned beef sandwich *sans moutarde?* Though often relegated to the side—especially by loud, demanding people who think a spoonful of blueberry sauce on three cheese blintzes fried in butter is the thing that is going to make them gain weight—condiments can make or break a dish.

THE CONDIMENT'S ROLE IS MANIFOLD: it adds flavor and spice, contrast, and sometimes even crunch. My mother's pickled cucumbers are always on her dinner table. The acidity in the pickling solution helps cut through the richness of the rest of her food. And dinner just wouldn't be the same without them. Pickles are one of the few vegetables Jews eat with abandon. (Pickles are also probably why in delicatessens Jews always need more water NOW.)

homemade sauerkraut

I KNOW YOU THINK WHAT I'm about to say is ridiculous, but making your own sauerkraut is easy — after all, it just sits there and ferments while you go on with your life — and nothing you can buy compares. This is another thing that I never would have imagined doing until I met my friend Daňo, a chef in upstate New York, whose Mittleuropean upbringing heavily influences his style of cooking. Daňo makes all of his own sauerkraut, and it factors heavily on his Viennese-inspired menu. I come from a family of sauerkraut lovers, and when I make my own and then use it in things like pierogi fillings (page 17), or I just braise it with mushrooms for a side dish (page 135), everyone is in heaven.

You need to figure on about three weeks of fermentation at room temperature to make a good — meaning very sour — sauerkraut. Because the top has to breathe, for the first few days the smell of rotting cabbage can be kind of strong, but after that you won't even notice it. If you have a basement, keep it there. I live in a small New York City apartment, and whenever I start a new sauerkraut, everybody in my building knows it.

a bissel advice

How should I shred the cabbage? Rather than using a box grater or a food processor, I like to slice the cabbage into shreds with either a sharp knife or a mandoline. As when making coleslaw, you don't want the cabbage sliced too finely or it will disintegrate into mush while it ferments.

Why onion and garlic? That's not in the sauerkraut I buy at the store! No, but neither are any other of the flavorings I've suggested. Why make the same thing at home that you can buy? I think the added flavors make the finished sauerkraut much more interesting. But you can easily omit any of the flavorings I've suggested and just make a plain sauerkraut. All you need for the fermentation to take place is the cabbage and the salt.

I don't seem to get any liquid. Depending on what time of year your cabbage was harvested and how it was stored, it will contain more or less liquid than other cabbages. If after 1 day you don't have enough liquid to cover the shredded cabbage, just add salted water as advised.

5 pounds green cabbage (about 1 large,
    densely packed head or 2 smaller ones),
    shredded
1 medium onion (about 6 ounces), thinly
    sliced
1 small garlic clove, thinly sliced
2½ tablespoons (1 ounce) kosher salt
2 teaspoons whole juniper berries
1 teaspoon caraway seeds
2 medium bay leaves

SPECIAL EQUIPMENT
1-gallon nonreactive container or crock,
    made out of glass, ceramic, or stainless
    steel—a tall, deep shape works best
Cheesecloth

In a large bowl or pot, combine the cabbage with the onion, garlic, salt, juniper, caraway, and bay. Let sit for about 30 minutes at room temperature until the cabbage begins to wilt. Using your hands, tightly pack the mixture into the nonreactive 1-gallon container, pressing down on the cabbage until it is firmly jammed in. If any liquid has been drawn out of the cabbage, pour that on top. Invert a clean plate on top of the cabbage and weigh it down with a heavy bottle or something else that won't react with the fermentation liquid (metal cans or weights may rust). Cover the container with a double layer of cheesecloth and secure it over the top with an elastic band or a piece of string.

Allow the sauerkraut to sit at room temperature and ferment for about 3 weeks. After 6 hours or so it will start to give off some serious liquid. The weighted plate is there to ensure that the cabbage remains immersed in that liquid. If the sauerkraut is too dry—meaning some of the cabbage is exposed to air—add salted water (½ teaspoon of kosher salt for every 1 cup of water) to cover. Also check under the plate every other day or so to see if any scum has formed. Remove this scum with a spoon and discard. Replace the weight and the cheesecloth and leave it to ferment.

After about 2 weeks the sauerkraut will taste mildly sour. You can try it at any time, but up until about the 16-day mark it has a slightly off taste. By day 20, it will have turned very pleasantly sour. You can keep it fermenting at room temperature until it has achieved the sourness you want. I find that at room temperature of about 72°F., the sauerkraut is perfect after 20 days. If your place is warmer, it will be done more quickly.

When the sauerkraut has fermented to the point that you like it, you should transfer it to jars. I rinse it very quickly under cold water and pack all of it, including the spices, into 1-quart jars. It will keep in the refrigerator for up to 6 months.

deli-style mustard

WHEN I TOLD MY FRIEND Peggy that I had made mustard one weekend, she looked at me funny and said, "Mustard can be made?" Not only is it possible, it's easy. And the mustard you end up making has a freshness and fire that is hard to find in commercial mustards. What's more, because people like Peggy, who happens to be a great cook, think mustard results from some alchemical hocus-pocus, it makes a great gift.

a bissel advice

Fresh is better. Be sure your mustard seeds and dry mustard are relatively fresh because the pungent oils that give mustard its characteristic flavor have a tendency to dull and turn bitter over time. For sources, see page 273.

⅓ cup (2 ounces) brown or black mustard
    seeds
⅓ cup (2 ounces) yellow mustard seeds
¾ cup apple cider or white wine vinegar
    (5 percent acidity)
¾ cup dry white wine or water
1 small shallot or small piece onion, minced
    (2 tablespoons)
1 teaspoon kosher salt
1 tablespoon white horseradish *(optional)*
2 teaspoons dry mustard *(optional)*

SPECIAL EQUIPMENT
Blender (a food processor just doesn't work)

MAKES **2** CUPS

kosher status PAREVE, and perfect on a corned beef or cheese sandwich

In a small nonreactive (glass, stainless steel, or ceramic) bowl or jar, combine the mustard seeds, vinegar, wine, shallot, salt, and horseradish, if using. Cover and refrigerate for at least 1 day and up to 3, until the mustard seeds have swollen and softened. Place the ingredients in a blender. Pulse to start pureeing the mixture. A froth will form on top. Then let the blender run on high until it reaches the consistency of the mustard you would like. Bear in mind that the mustard will thicken as it sits. Return to the bowl or jar and stir in the dry mustard to thicken, if necessary. The mustard will mellow as it sits and matures at room temperature. Store in a nonreactive container with a tight-fitting lid, indefinitely.

tahini sauce

NO FALAFEL IS COMPLETE WITHOUT a drizzle of tahini sauce. Tahini is a paste made from ground sesame seeds. You can buy it in the Middle Eastern food section of some grocery stores in jars or cans. The problem is tahini sold this way usually separates into oil and a cementlike paste, and I find it difficult (and messy) to make it go back together. I prefer to buy my tahini out of a bulk tub in the health food store because for some reason in that form it doesn't separate. Storing it in the refrigerator prevents it from separating once you get it home.

Tahini is somewhat bitter, but in a pleasant way, I think. In fact, I use it sometimes as a calcium-rich substitute for peanut butter. To take the bitter edge off, I combine it with honey and lemon juice. Adding a little oil or mayonnaise also helps remove some of the bitterness, too, but I don't think it is necessary.

a bissel advice
What could be easier? **You don't even have to dirty a mixing bowl.**

MAKES 1 CUP

kosher status PAREVE

Into the glass jar, place the tahini, ⅔ cup water, the lemon juice, honey, salt, and pepper. Cover the jar tightly and shake vigorously to form a thick, creamy sauce. Taste and adjust the seasoning. If you find the flavor too bitter, add a drop of mayonnaise or vegetable oil and shake again. If it is too thick, add some more water, but not too much because the sauce will thicken as it sits. Tahini sauce will store in the refrigerator almost indefinitely, so you can always have some on hand.

½ cup tahini
Juice of 1 or 2 lemons (3 to 5 tablespoons), to taste
2 teaspoons honey
½ teaspoon kosher salt
Pinch of freshly ground black or white pepper
Mayonnaise or vegetable oil, to taste (optional)

SPECIAL EQUIPMENT
2 to 4 cup glass jar with a wide mouth and a tight-fitting lid

horseradish

IF IT DOESN'T MAKE YOUR nose hurt and your eyes water, it isn't good horseradish. Obviously, you can buy it in a jar and call it a day. But the pungency of freshly made horseradish cannot be beat. (And if you are making your own gefilte fish, why put a commercially made horseradish on it?) It doesn't take much time or effort, but you do need to start a day in advance.

Fresh horseradish looks like some sort of prehistoric root—a cross between a parsnip and driftwood. Don't be put off by it, but do handle it carefully. If you put your face over the food processor when you lift off the lid, you will sorely regret it. The texture is woody and dense, so I find a sharp serrated knife the best way to saw through it.

To make the somewhat milder red horseradish, stir in some fresh beet puree (see page 249). The beets help tone down the heat. I usually make both kinds because I like the way the contrasting colors look when served together.

a bissel advice

So much horseradish? You can easily cut the recipe in half, but I like to have fresh horseradish around. I stir it into mashed potatoes, borscht, sour cream, salad dressings, you name it. It will keep forever, but it loses its pungency rapidly after a couple of days.

2 pounds fresh horseradish root

4 teaspoons kosher salt

2 cups white vinegar

¹/₂ to 1 cup beet puree (see page 249)
   (optional)

SPECIAL EQUIPMENT

Sturdy, sharp vegetable peeler

Food processor

1-quart glass jar

Using a sturdy, sharp vegetable peeler, remove the dark, woody outer layer of the root. Use a sharp paring knife to get at hard-to-reach places and to remove any dark patches in the flesh. With a serrated knife, saw the horseradish into chunks small enough to fit into the feed tube of the food processor.

Using the shredding disk, shred the horseradish into longish strands. Look away while you carefully remove the lid or your eyes will burn for an hour. Transfer the shredded horseradish to a bowl, add the salt, and mix until evenly distributed. (Again, keeping your face away from the bowl.) Pack the salted horseradish into a 1-quart glass jar. Pour in the white vinegar to fill the jar. Cover and refrigerate for at least 1 day and up to 3.

On the day you intend to serve it, transfer about half of the horseradish along with half of the vinegar to the bowl of a food processor fitted with the metal chopping blade. Pulse until the horseradish is as smooth and pureed as you can get it. With your face turned away, remove the lid and transfer to a serving dish or smaller glass container. Repeat with the remaining horseradish. Stir in the beet puree if desired.

MENTAL NOSH

Although folklore would have you believe that horseradish gets its name because the gnarly root resembles a horse's hoof, the truth is that horse *or* hoarse *refers to the coarseness and pungency of the root. It is not related to the more familiar red and white radish.*

kosher dill pickles

THE EXPRESSION OUGHT TO BE "easy as pickles." In late August and September, when local Kirby

cucumbers and fresh dill are available at farmers' markets and road-side produce stands, I like to put up a whole mess

of pickles, just like my mother. In only 10 days they turn from cucumbers into crunchy, garlicky full-sour dills. It's like

magic. Kosher dills are different from regular dill pickles because of their high garlic content and lack of sugar. (My mother uses enough garlic to make Transylvania nervous.) They fall into the category of brined pickles because they ferment in

their own liquid without the aid of heat. Short-brine pickles, such as Bread-and-Butter Pickles (page 206), are ready to eat as soon as they are made.

Select small, firm Kirbys—the smaller the better—without any blemishes or bruises. Don't use the large, watery, overgrown Kirbys they sell in grocery stores throughout the year. They will turn soft and limp once they are pickled. Clean the Kirbys well by soaking them in cold water and scrubbing them with a vegetable brush. The pickles should ferment in a large, nonreactive container. For 5 pounds of cucumbers, I use a 2-gallon ceramic crock or a 2½-gallon glass jar.

a bissel advice

What's pickling spice? It's just a combination of spices that come premixed in the grocery store. Because I always have a ton of spices on hand, I make my own. For this recipe I use the following combination: 1 teaspoon coriander seeds; 1 teaspoon yellow mustard seeds; 2 bay leaves, crushed; ½ teaspoon red pepper flakes; ½ teaspoon dill seed; 1 teaspoon black peppercorns; 2 whole allspice berries; 1 whole clove.

So much garlic? You can use less garlic if you are afraid the pickles will be overpowering. I have made them with about half the number of cloves I call for here. But for a truly garlicky kosher dill like my mother makes, use the amount I suggest.

What if I can't find good Kirbys? Don't make these pickles. With lesser cucumbers you can make Bread-and-Butter Pickles (page 206) or Pickled Cucumbers (page 208).

½ cup kosher salt

2 tablespoons pickling spice

2 tablespoons white vinegar

1 large bunch (4 to 5 ounces or 20 sprigs)
    fresh dill, rinsed

2 heads (4 ounces) garlic (about 14 cloves),
    peeled

5 pounds small, firm Kirby cucumbers (about
    50), soaked and scrubbed with a
    vegetable brush

SPECIAL EQUIPMENT

2-gallon nonreactive ceramic or glass
    container

Six 1-quart glass jars or three half-gallon
    jars

Cheesecloth

In a large pot, combine 3½ quarts (14 cups) water with the salt, pickling
spice, and vinegar, and bring to a boil. Cool

Meanwhile, lay 4 or 5 sprigs of dill on the bottom of a 2-gallon nonreactive ceramic or glass container. Sprinkle with 4 or 5 cloves of garlic. Tightly
pack a layer of cleaned Kirbys on top. Make another layer of dill and garlic,
and top with another tightly packed layer of cucumbers. Finish with a layer
of dill and garlic.

Pour the cooled water and spice mixture over the cucumbers to cover. If
there isn't enough liquid to cover the cucumber entirely, add more saltwater
solution (in the ratio of 2 tablespoons kosher salt to 3½ cups water). Place
a plate just big enough to fit inside the container on top to keep the cucumbers from bobbing above the surface. Cover the container with a double
piece of cheesecloth and secure with a piece of string or an elastic band, but
do not seal — air should be able to circulate in and out of the container.

Allow the pickles to sit at room temperature for up to 10 days, peeking
underneath the cheesecloth once a day and skimming off any scum that
rises to the top. After about 5 or 6 days, you will have what is known in New
York deli parlance as "half sours": slightly green, crunchy pickles somewhere between a cucumber and what I call a pickle. After 10 days you will
have "full sours." When the pickles have reached your desired doneness,
remove the cheesecloth and the plate. With tongs, lift the pickles out of the
brine and pack them into clean quart or half-gallon glass jars. Pass the brine
through a fine strainer into the jars until they are immersed. Cover tightly
and refrigerate. They will keep refrigerated for about two months.

bread-and-butter pickles

AN ALTERNATIVE TO GARLICKY KOSHER DILLS, these flavorful pickles are great on sandwiches, chopped up in salads, such as potato or chicken (see page 25), or eaten plain as a side dish. Make them at the end of the summer when small, firm Kirby cucumbers are in season. They will keep for months in the refrigerator, and can be processed in a water bath (i.e., canned) for longer storage.

a bissel advice

How thin? I like my bread-and-butter pickles as thin as possible. To get them that way, I slice the cucumbers and onion on one of those hand-held plastic Japanese mandolines called a Benriner. You can also use the slicing disk of a food processor.

I relish the idea . . . To make a fresh hamburger relish, finely mince a handful of pickles and some onion and combine with a drop or two of the liquid to make a paste.

5 or 6 small Kirby cucumbers (2 pounds), unpeeled, washed well, and thinly sliced

1 large yellow onion (½ pound), thinly sliced

¼ cup kosher salt

1¾ cups cider vinegar (5 percent acidity)

1¾ cups sugar

1 teaspoon celery seed

1 teaspoon yellow mustard seed

1 teaspoon ground turmeric

SPECIAL EQUIPMENT

1-quart glass jar

MAKES 1 QUART

kosher status PAREVE—unless, of course, you put them on a cheeseburger, and then the whole shebang is traif

In a mixing bowl, layer the sliced cucumbers and onion with the salt. Cover with cold water (about 2 quarts) and let sit at room temperature for 4 to 6 hours to brine. Drain, rinse with cold water, and drain again.

In a saucepan, combine the vinegar, sugar, celery seed, mustard seed, and turmeric, and set over medium-high heat. Bring to a boil. Add the rinsed cucumbers and onion and bring back up to a boil, stirring occasionally. Turn off the heat. While still hot, use a slotted spoon to transfer the pickles to the glass jar. Pour the hot liquid on top to cover the pickles and fill the jar. Cover and let cool to room temperature, then refrigerate.

MENTAL NOSH

These pickles are categorized as "short brine" or "fresh pack" because they sit in the salt solution for only a short period of time. Kosher dills (page 204) are known as brine or long-brine pickles because they stay in the salt solution for days.

pickled beets

YUM IS ALL I CAN SAY. If you hate beets, you won't like homemade pickled beets. But if you like beets, you will love them. Actually, if you hate beets because all you've had are sour, mushy, commercially produced pickled beets, then you might be surprised that you actually like these. There are two traditional flavorings for pickled beets: sweet spices like cinnamon and allspice, or caraway. I prefer caraway, but I'm in the minority among my friends. To make everyone happy, I usually make a jar of each. For directions on how to cook beets, see page 248.

a bissel advice

It is better to give . . . Quarts of pickled beets make lovely gifts (presuming your friends like beets). Use attractive jars. Pickled beets can be canned and stored at room temperature for up to a year. Refer to a dependable canning or preserving book for instructions.

MAKES 1 QUART

kosher status PAREVE

In a large saucepan, combine the vinegar, ½ cup water, sugar, and either the allspice, cinnamon, and cloves or caraway, salt, and bring to a boil. Add the sliced beets, bring back to a boil, and turn off the heat.

Using a slotted spoon, layer the beets in the glass jar with the sliced red onion. Pour in enough of the cooking liquid to cover the beets, and add some of the spices to the jar. Cover and let cool to room temperature. Refrigerate at least 1 day before serving. The pickled beets will keep for several months in the refrigerator.

2 cups white or cider vinegar (5 percent acidity)
½ cup sugar
¼ teaspoon (about 10) whole allspice berries
1 cinnamon stick, about 2 inches long
½ teaspoon (about 14) whole cloves
2 teaspoons caraway seeds (if not using allspice, cinnamon, and cloves) *(optional)*
½ teaspoon kosher salt
2 pounds Boiled Beets (page 249), thinly sliced
1 medium red onion (about 6 ounces), thinly sliced

SPECIAL EQUIPMENT
1-quart glass jar

pickled cucumbers

I'VE ALREADY SAID THAT THERE aren't many vegetables in the Jewish culinary canon. But as long as there is a gathering of Jews at my mother's house, there will always be pickled cucumbers. While traveling through Hungary, I was surprised to learn that the very same pickled cucumbers go by the name *uborkasaláta,* or "cucumber salad," and

that they are de facto Hungary's unofficial national dish. Before you go all William Safire on me and point out that pickles are just pickled cucumbers anyway, let me reiterate that in my family, culinary semantics are very loose.

All the Davises are lovers of sour things, so we never put any sugar in the dressing. But if you find the vinegar solution too strong, you can add a tablespoon or two of granulated sugar to help cut through the acid. You can also play around with peeling or not peeling the cucumbers, a decision

I make based on what color I would like to add to the meal, or my mood, or my degree of laziness at the time of preparation.

a bissel advice

Cucumbers speak a language? **English cucumbers are long, thin seedless cucumbers that are available in pretty good form all year long. They have a delicate skin that is usually not waxed, so you have the option of peeling them or not. In a pinch you can use regular cucumbers, but be sure to peel them and remove the seeds with a teaspoon before you slice them very thin.**

To peel or not to peel? **My mother always peels her cucumbers, but sometimes I want the bright green ring of peel around each slice and so I leave the skin on. With the peel, the cucumbers have a little more texture, too.**

2 English (seedless) cucumbers (about
1¾ pounds) *(peeling optional)*

2 tablespoons kosher salt

1 large yellow or white onion (½ pound),
peeled and very thinly sliced

1 cup white vinegar (5 percent acidity)

1 to 2 tablespoons sugar, to taste *(optional)*

Using a food processor or a handheld mandoline, thinly slice the cucumbers and place them in a large bowl. Sprinkle the cucumber slices with the salt, tossing the slices around to distribute the salt evenly. Place a plate on top of the salted cucumbers to weigh them down, and let sit at room temperature for at least 1 hour but no more than 2, until the cucumbers have given up a lot of their water and wilted.

Drain the cucumbers, rinse under cold water, and drain again. Add the sliced onion to the cucumbers. Combine the vinegar and 1 cup cold water and pour over the cucumbers. If using sugar, it is best to dissolve it in a little hot water and then add that mixture to the cucumbers. Pack into a 1-quart glass jar or other nonreactive container and refrigerate. The cucumbers can be eaten right away, but they are best after they have sat for a day or two. They will keep about 2 weeks in the refrigerator.

pickled grapes

MY FRIEND EVELYNNE BROUGHT ME my first jar of pickled grapes as a gift once when I had invited her to dinner. I love just about any kind of pickle, but the idea of pickling fruit had never occurred to me before. For a while she kept me well stocked—pickled grapes, pickled sour cherries, you name it. She made labels on her computer and stuck them to pretty jars of fruit macerating in sweetened and spiced vinegar. Sometimes she would just bottle the vinegar. Her original technique was based on a recipe from another friend, Rose Levy Berenbaum. The technique is very simple.

Right now I have a jar of pickled sour cherries in my refrigerator. I use them in chicken salad and sauces for seared foie gras or venison. They are delicious in cocktails. Although I've tried different kinds of fruit, grapes, cherries, peaches, and most berries work best as far as I'm concerned. One word of advice is that you shouldn't try to mix fruit; the colors and flavors get all blurry. Oh, and by the way, they make a great gift.

a bissel advice

Pickled fruit salad? Don't mix fruits. You can use the same vinegar mixture on different fruits, but pack them in separate jars. Otherwise the colors have a tendency to blend into a mess, and so do the flavors.

So I've pickled fruits, now what? Experiment with them. The acidity tends to cut through fatty foods, such as pot roast or pâté, the way cranberry sauce works at Thanksgiving. Add some of the fruit and the vinegar solution to sauces or gravies for meat. You can use a few to add zing to a salad or to garnish some new-fangled cocktail. Use the flavored vinegar in salad dressings. If you can't think of anything to do with them, but just like the idea, put them in a pretty jar and give them as a gift.

What's so Jewish about this? Well, not much, I guess. Except I just think pickled anything seems Jewish to me (beets, cucumbers, eggs . . . pig's feet).

gently pack the fruit into the 1-quart nonreactive jar. In a nonreactive saucepan, combine the sugar, vinegar, cinnamon, cloves, star anise, and the all-spice and black pepper (if using), and set over medium heat. Bring to a simmer and cook until the sugar is dissolved and the spices give off a pronounced scent, about 5 minutes. While still hot, pour this mixture into the jar over the fruit. If the liquid doesn't quite cover the fruit, you can add some water until it does. Seal the jar and let sit for about 12 hours or overnight at room temperature. Turn the jar upside down once or twice and let it sit that way to be sure all of the fruit macerates evenly. The pickled fruit will keep refrigerated for several months. I've had my pickled cherries for over a year!

3 cups fresh fruit, such as green or red seedless grapes, pitted sour cherries, or blueberries

1¼ cups sugar

1 cup white vinegar (5 percent acidity)

2 cinnamon sticks, about 3 inches long

2 whole cloves

1 small piece star anise

1 or 2 whole allspice berries (optional)

2 black peppercorns (optional)

SPECIAL EQUIPMENT

1-quart nonreactive glass or ceramic jar with a tight-fitting lid and a pronounced "shoulder" that will keep the fruit tucked under the liquid

chunky applesauce

NO LATKE (OR PIEROG OR BLINTZ, for that matter) is complete without applesauce. Although I think sour cream is essential, too, if you are keeping kosher and are serving the latkes with brisket or some other form of meat, you can be excused from serving sour cream. From applesauce, though, there is no excuse. And before you go out and buy a jar, Mr. Smarty Pants, you should know that all commercial applesauce pales next to the homemade variety. If you start making it just as you are about to make the latkes, both will be ready at the same time. You can also make applesauce up to a week in advance and keep it in the refrigerator until you need it. (A spoonful of applesauce stirred into plain yogurt makes for a delicious breakfast.)

Omit the butter if you are kosher and intend to serve the applesauce with meat, or if you'd rather not have the added calories or fat. You can also omit the sugar if your apples are sweet enough just as they are.

If I have a lot of applesauce to make—I recently made 10 pounds' worth for a latke party—I vary my technique slightly. You don't have to peel or core the apples if you cook them until soft and pass them through a vegetable mill. I give the directions for this technique as a variation after the recipe.

a bissel advice

Which apples? Generally, apples that are good to eat aren't very good to cook. For flavor and texture purposes, I prefer a combination of apples that includes some Northern Spys, some Golden Delicious, Empire, Rome, Reinette, and a few others.

4 or 5 cooking apples (2 pounds), such as
Northern Spy, Gala, Golden Delicious,
Cortland, or any combination, peeled,
cored, and cut into 1/2-inch pieces
(about 6 cups)

1/4 teaspoon ground cinnamon

1 teaspoon pure vanilla extract

Juice of 1/2 lemon (2 tablespoons)

2 tablespoons sugar *(optional)*

1 tablespoon butter *(optional)*

P ut the apples, cinnamon, vanilla, lemon juice, and sugar (if using) in a
medium saucepan. Add 2 tablespoons water, cover, and set over low
heat. Simmer until the apples are soft, 15 to 25 minutes, depending on the
type of apples you are using. Mash with a fork until the mixture is a chunky
puree. Stir in the butter, if using, and cool. Adjust the seasoning with more
cinnamon, sugar, or lemon juice to taste.

applesauce for a crowd

YOU CAN INCREASE the recipe above proportionately and invite your whole temple over for a latke party. But if I
have a lot of applesauce to make—say more than 4 pounds' worth of apples—I use a different technique. It requires a
food or vegetable mill, which is a utensil that looks like a cross between a saucepan and a food processor that has a
blade you turn with a handle. As you turn the blade, it forces whatever is in the mill through a perforated disk, thereby
mashing or pureeing it. This is smooth applesauce, rather than chunky. You will get slightly more applesauce because
you don't lose any flesh by peeling or coring them.

MAKES **6 CUPS**

kosher status same as above

10 cooking apples (4 pounds), such as
Northern Spy, Gala, Golden Delicious,
Cortland, or any combination, *not* peeled
or cored

1/2 teaspoon ground cinnamon

2 teaspoons pure vanilla extract

Juice of 1 lemon (4 tablespoons)

3 tablespoons sugar *(optional)*

2 tablespoons butter *(optional)*

Q uarter the apples and place them in a large pot with 1/4 cup water. Set
over low heat and simmer for 30 to 40 minutes, until the apples are
soft. Set the vegetable or food mill over a mixing bowl. Spoon the cooked
apples into the mill with their juice and turn the handle clockwise to puree. As
the seeds and peels begin to build up under the blade, turn the handle
counterclockwise to loosen and discard. Repeat until all of the apples are
pureed. Add the cinnamon, vanilla, lemon juice, sugar, and butter (if using).
Cool. Adjust the seasoning to taste.

blueberry sauce

SOMEWHERE IN THE TALMUD it must say that you cannot serve blintzes without blueberry sauce. This is a simple sauce that can be made with either fresh or frozen blueberries (actually, I think a combination works best). It's good on vanilla ice cream, Cheesecake (page 170), pareve Oatmeal Pancakes (page 194), and Challah French Toast (page 188), too.

a bissel advice Can I use anything other than blueberries? **Any berry works fine. And I would still advise the combination of frozen and fresh.**

2 tablespoons unsalted butter

1 pint (2 cups) fresh blueberries, or

    1 (10-ounce) package (2 cups) frozen
    blueberries, or a combination

2 tablespoons sugar

1 teaspoon arrowroot or cornstarch, or

    ½ teaspoon potato starch

Juice of ½ lemon (1 or 2 tablespoons)

Pinch of ground cinnamon

MAKES 1¼ CUPS

kosher status MILCHIG, but if you must, you can omit the butter to make it PAREVE

In a medium frying pan set over medium-high heat, heat the butter. Add the blueberries and sugar, and sauté until they plump and give off some liquid, 6 or 7 minutes.

If you are using frozen blueberries they will give off a lot of liquid. This requires an extra step in the preparation. Strain the blueberries in a sieve and return the liquid to the pan. Set over high heat and reduce for 5 minutes or so to thicken. Place the blueberries back in the pan.

In a small bowl, stir the starch into the lemon juice to dissolve and add to the pan along with the cinnamon. Cook another 2 or 3 minutes until the sauce has thickened slightly. Serve warm.

MENTAL NOSH

Food scientists will look at this recipe and think I'm nuts. Acid, such as that contained in lemon juice, drastically reduces the thickening potential of starch, and here I am having you dissolve the starch directly into the lemon juice! But this is the only way I have found to make a sauce that doesn't have an unappealingly starchy texture or taste. This isn't a technique I would ever recommend for other recipes that call for starch thickeners, but in this instance it happens to work pretty well.

fresh plum conserve

ONE SEPTEMBER WHEN MY MOTHER was visiting me in New York, I passed by a farmers' market on my way to meeting her at the airport. Prune plums had just come into season, and knowing how much she likes to eat them, I bought a few pints—well, more like seven. They were just so beautiful. When we got home I had to figure out something to do with them. I made a Crumb Cake with plums (page 166) and a plum compote. With the remaining three pints I made this conserve. It lasted through the year and I used it for everything: Hamentaschen (page 158), Rugelach (page 145), on toast, on ice cream, in cakes—you name it. My roommate was actually catering a very fancy party and used it on a foie gras hors d'oeuvre. Anyway, my point is, don't sit and wonder why you might make this conserve, just do it, and myriad uses will unfold. You can use any plum.

a bissel advice

What if it burns? It's happened to me before, too. You can still use most of the conserve. Carefully ladle it out of the pot without scraping the bottom. To clean the pot (and any other pot that's been burned beyond recognition), fill it with warm water. Add some dish soap and a tablespoon or two of baking soda and bring to a boil. Turn down the heat and simmer for about 10 minutes. Turn off the heat and let cool. Whatever was burnt to the pot should be easy to remove.

MAKES **2** QUARTS

kosher status PAREVE

3 pints (about 3 pounds or 50 plums) fresh
    prune plums or any variety, stems and
    pits removed, cut into medium dice
1 pound (2 cups) raisins
2 oranges, rind and all, cut into very small
    dice, with juice
Juice of 2 lemons (about ½ cup)
1 pound (2 cups) coarsely chopped walnuts
6 cups sugar

SPECIAL EQUIPMENT
8-quart heavy-gauge pot
Instant-read or candy thermometer

Combine the plums, raisins, diced oranges and any juice that runs off from them, lemon juice, walnuts, and sugar in the large pot and stir to combine. Set over medium heat and bring slowly to a boil. Turn down the heat to low and simmer for 65 to 70 minutes, until the mixture has thickened and it reaches 220°F. on an instant-read or candy thermometer. As it boils, a froth will form on top of the mixture. After about 20 minutes this will dissipate and the bubbles will get larger and lazier. Stir the conserve regularly while it is cooking so that the bottom doesn't stick to the pan or burn.

charoseth

CHAROSETH IS SUPPOSED TO REPRESENT the mortar that the Israelite slaves used to build the pharaohs' cities. Considering the texture of some of the charoseths I've tasted, it doesn't take much of a conceptual leap. I have always heard that Sephardic Jews have a whole slew of different types of charoseth to choose from—made

with dried fruits, spices, nuts and other exotic ingredients. I've also heard Ashkenazi Jews say they were jealous at the selection their Mediterranean cousins had to choose from. "The only time I ever liked anything at the Passover seder," a friend told me recently, "was when my mother experimented with a Sephardic charoseth." Well, sue me, but I happen to like the combination of apples, honey, nuts, and sweet wine that my family called charoseth. Maybe it was just because everything else at our seder was so delicious, but for a little sweet symbolic thing you eat on a piece of matzo once a year, I don't see what the big deal is. Anyway, this is an approximation of the charoseth

we always use (you think anybody ever had a recipe?). A seder without it would just not seem right somehow.

a bissel advice

How far in advance can I make this mortar? It can't sit around long because the apples turn brown and the whole thing has a weird color already. Try to do it just as the seder is about to start. (I guess one of the benefits of the Sephardic dried-fruit charoseth is that they can be made far in advance. They get all the food breaks.)

What else can I put in here? Anything—you name it: pears, raisins, other dried fruit, Sauternes. Have a blast. Create your own tradition.

What can I do with the leftovers? Again, the apple turns brown quickly, so you don't have much time. The morning after the Seder, you can put a couple of tablespoons of charoseth in a sweet Matzo Brei (page 186). Otherwise, try my recipe for delicious Charoseth Pancakes (page 195).

3 large, sweet eating apples (1½ pounds),
    such as Golden Delicious, Gala, Cortland,
    Mutsu, Empire, or what have you
1 lemon, cut in half
1 cup walnut pieces, toasted
2 tablespoons honey
¼ cup sweet red wine
¼ teaspoon ground cinnamon
Pinch of kosher salt

Peel the apples and cut into quarters. Remove the core. Squeeze some lemon juice on the apples to prevent them from browning. With a sharp knife, cut the apples into fine dice. Place in a mixing bowl. Add the nuts, honey, red wine, cinnamon, and salt, and mix well. Adjust the seasoning to taste.

It's What's on the Inside That Counts

Like literary tropes, there are many sweet

and savory fillings that recur in the Ashkenazi culinary canon. Wrapped and stuffed and rolled, these fillings pop in and out of our lives in different disguises. The savory fillings include potato, cheese, spinach, kasha, and meat, and they appear regularly in a variety of filled things, such as pierogi, knishes, kreplach, blintzes, and their cousins. The sweet fillings include chocolate, cheese, poppy seed, and prune, and they, too, pop up in myriad forms such as hamentaschen, blintzes, and Danish.

THERE ARE NO HARD-AND-FAST recipes or rules for making fillings. They provide an excellent way to refashion leftovers or little bits of ingredients lying around, so the recipes can be adapted to suit whatever you have on hand. The flavors should be strong. The ingredients should be bound together with something that will hold: I find an egg and some matzo meal, or some leftover mashed potatoes, work best for savory fillings; cheese and some sort of starch, such as flour or bread crumbs, can be used for sweet. I also find it easier to work with fillings when they are well chilled because this makes them stiffen, especially if they contain butter or any other animal fat, which makes them hold their shape better.

potato filling

THIS MAKES DELICIOUS KNISHES. By sautéing some chopped celery and shredded carrot with the onions you have a delicious stuffing for a breast of veal (see page 78). If you have leftover mashed potatoes lying around, substitute 2 cups for the potatoes. Otherwise, choose a starchy potato such as Yukon Gold or Russet.

a bissel advice
The drier the potatoes the better. If you drain the potatoes and they seem really wet or waterlogged, lay them out on a cookie sheet and dry them in a 300°F. oven for 30 to 45 minutes.

1¾ pounds (about 4 medium) starchy potatoes, such as Yukon Gold or Russet
4 tablespoons Chicken Schmaltz (page 236),
unsalted butter, peanut oil, or a
combination
1 large yellow onion (½ pound), finely
chopped
1 celery stalk, finely chopped *(optional)*
1 large carrot, shredded *(optional)*
1 large egg
2 ounces Gribenes (page 237), finely
chopped (¼ cup) *(optional)*
2 teaspoons kosher salt
¼ teaspoon freshly ground black pepper

MAKES 2½ CUPS

kosher status PAREVE, if made with oil and no gribenes
MILCHIG, if made with butter and no gribenes
FLEISHIG, if made with schmaltz and/or gribenes
TRAIF, if made with butter and gribenes

place the potatoes in a pot and cover with cold water. Bring to a boil, turn down the heat, and simmer until the potatoes fall apart when poked with a fork, about 30 minutes. Drain.

Meanwhile, heat the fat in a small frying pan set over medium-high heat. Add the chopped onion and sauté until translucent, 5 or 6 minutes. Add the celery and carrot (if using), and continue sautéing until the onion is golden brown, an additional 5 to 7 minutes.

Mash the drained potatoes with a fork and add the sautéed onion mixture. Add the egg, gribenes (if using), salt, and pepper, and stir to combine. Adjust the seasoning with salt and pepper and chill.

potato and cheese filling

THIS IS ONE OF MY FAVORITE FILLINGS for pierogi or savory blintzes. For something different, use crumbled sheep's-milk feta for the cheese, which has a more pungent flavor than the more traditional pot cheese.

MAKES **3** CUPS

kosher status TRAIF, if you've made the potato filling with schmaltz or gribenes
MILCHIG, if you haven't

1 batch Potato Filling (page 220)
¾ cup farmer cheese, pot cheese, crumbled feta, or large-curd cottage cheese or ricotta, drained

repare the potato filling as indicated in the recipe on page 220. If you want to keep it kosher, be sure you do not use schmaltz or gribenes. Cool the filling completely to room temperature. Stir in the cheese and chill before proceeding with your recipe.

sauerkraut and mushroom filling

THIS FILLING MAKES delicious pierogi and knishes, too.

MAKES **2** CUPS

kosher status PAREVE, if the Braised Sauerkraut is made with oil
FLEISHIG, if it's made with schmaltz
MILCHIG, if it's made with butter

1 batch Braised Sauerkraut with Mushrooms (page 135), altered as indicated at left

repare the Braised Sauerkraut, but omit the wine from the recipe and decrease the cooking time by 10 minutes. Also, cook the filling in a sauté pan instead of a saucepan to encourage the evaporation of any excess moisture. Chill.

beef filling

FOR KREPLACH OR KNISHES, THIS MEATY FILLING is excellent. It's good for savory blintzes, too. Any leftover cooked beef or veal can be used. Chicken would work, too. I think the chicken liver helps the flavor tremendously—and I defy anyone who hates liver to even notice it's been used—but if it grosses you out, omit it. If you have leftover mashed potatoes lying around, you can use them to bind the filling. Otherwise, I find a combination of matzo meal and egg works well. For the Kreplach recipe on page 46 you will need only half of this recipe.

4 tablespoons Chicken or Beef Schmaltz
(pages 236–238), peanut oil, or unsalted
butter, or a combination
1 large onion (½ pound), finely chopped
2 chicken livers (¼ pound), finely chopped
(optional)
1 pound cooked brisket, roast beef, or meat
loaf, finely chopped (about 2½ cups),
plus 2 tablespoons pan juices (with the
onions if you have them)
¾ cup mashed potato or ¼ cup matzo meal
plus 1 large egg
1½ teaspoons kosher salt
½ teaspoon freshly ground black pepper

MAKES 2½ CUPS

kosher status TRAIF, if you use butter
FLEISHIG, if you don't

heat the fat in a medium saucepan over medium-high heat. Add the chopped onion and sauté for 5 or 6 minutes, until translucent. Add the chopped livers and continue cooking until the livers have changed color, 3 or 4 minutes. Add the cooked meat and pan juices, and cook just until heated through. Transfer to a mixing bowl. Add the mashed potato or matzo meal and egg, salt, and black pepper, and mix to combine.

cream cheese–sauerkraut filling

THIS IS A CREAMY, FLAVORFUL FILLING with a pleasantly sour bite that is easy to work with because the cream cheese holds everything together, so you don't have to. It is excellent for pierogi, knishes, and blintzes.

MAKES ABOUT 2 CUPS

kosher status MILCHIG

2½ cups Homemade Sauerkraut (page 198) or commercially produced sauerkraut, tightly packed

6 ounces (2 small packages) cream cheese, at room temperature

place the sauerkraut in a sieve and let drain for a couple of minutes. If you would like a more subtle, less sour filling, rinse the sauerkraut two or three times under cold water. Squeeze handfuls of sauerkraut to remove any excess moisture. Alternatively, you can place it in a clean dish towel and wring it. In a mixing bowl, use a wooden spoon to combine the drained sauerkraut with the cream cheese, mixing until the cream cheese is evenly distributed. Chill.

spinach and cheese filling

USE THIS FILLING IN KNISHES or pierogi. Any cooked green will work, but frozen spinach is easy to find.

For variations, try cooked Swiss chard, beet tops, or mustard greens.

3 tablespoons unsalted butter

½ large yellow onion (¼ pound), minced

1 (10-ounce) package frozen spinach, defrosted, squeezed to remove excess water, and finely chopped

¾ teaspoon kosher salt

½ cup farmer cheese, pot cheese, crumbled feta, or large-curd cottage cheese or ricotta, drained

1 large egg

¼ teaspoon freshly ground black pepper

Small pinch of ground nutmeg

MAKES ABOUT **2** CUPS

kosher status MILCHIG

heat the butter in a medium sauté pan. Add the onion and sauté until translucent, about 5 minutes. Add the chopped spinach and salt and cook for an additional 5 minutes. Remove from the heat, transfer to a small bowl, and cool slightly. Add the remaining ingredients and mix well. Chill.

savory cheese filling

THIS SIMPLE FILLING HAS a clean, fresh taste. It's delicious in pierogi, savory blintzes, or knishes.

1 pound (2 cups) farmer or pot cheese

4 ounces (½ cup) cream cheese, at room temperature

1 large egg

1 teaspoon kosher salt

¼ teaspoon white pepper

MAKES **2** CUPS

kosher status MILCHIG

using a wooden spoon, blend the farmer or pot cheese with the cream cheese until smooth. Mix in the egg, salt, and pepper. Chill. Adjust the seasoning.

kasha filling

THIS FILLING IS CONTROVERSIAL BECAUSE some people hate kasha, but it's worth the effort for those who love it. Kasha knishes are my favorite.

MAKES **2** CUPS

kosher status FLEISHIG, if made with schmaltz
MILCHIG, if made with butter
PAREVE, if made with oil

1 potato (6 ounces), peeled and cut into chunks, or ⅔ cup leftover mashed potatoes

4 tablespoons Chicken Schmaltz (page 236), unsalted butter, peanut oil, or a combination

1 medium yellow onion (6 ounces), finely chopped

¼ pound button mushrooms, finely chopped

1½ cups cooked Kasha (see page 116)

1 large egg

1 teaspoon kosher salt

¼ teaspoon freshly ground black pepper

If using fresh potato, place in a small saucepan, cover with cold water, and set over high heat. Bring to a boil and cook until tender, about 20 minutes. Drain. Mash with a fork or potato masher until smooth. Set aside.

Meanwhile, heat the fat in a large sauté pan over medium-high heat. Add the onion and sauté until translucent, 5 to 7 minutes. Add the chopped mushrooms and continue sautéing until the mushrooms have given off some liquid, about 5 additional minutes. Remove from the heat. In a mixing bowl, combine the mashed potato, sautéed mushroom and onion, kasha, egg, salt, and pepper. Stir until well mixed. Adjust the seasoning. Chill.

chocolate filling

THIS IS A TERRIFIC CHOCOLATE FILLING, with more flavor and texture than just a piece of plain chocolate or a handful of chocolate chips. I love it in Hamentaschen (page 158), Yeast-Raised Rugelach (page 147), and coffee cakes such as Babka (page 192). Whatever you do, don't use flavored bread crumbs or you will end up with a gross mixture tasting of powdered garlic and dried oregano instead of chocolate. You can omit the chocolate chips if you don't have any, but the resulting filling will, of course, be less chocolatey.

¾ cup sugar

½ cup chopped walnuts

⅓ cup unflavored toasted bread crumbs (see page 243)

½ cup cocoa powder

4 tablespoons unsalted butter, melted and cooled

¼ cup milk or soy milk

1 teaspoon pure vanilla extract

½ cup semi-sweet chocolate chips

SPECIAL EQUIPMENT

Food processor

MAKES ABOUT 1¼ CUPS

kosher status MILCHIG. For a PAREVE filling, substitute soy milk for the milk, peanut oil for the butter, and use pareve chocolate chips.

place the sugar, nuts, and bread crumbs in the bowl of a food processor fitted with a metal chopping blade. Pulse 8 to 10 times until the walnuts are ground fine. Transfer to a mixing bowl. Add the cocoa, melted butter, milk, and vanilla, and stir to combine. Stir in the chocolate chips.

streusel filling

THIS IS A CLASSIC rugelach filling. You spread the jam on the dough and sprinkle it with the nut and sugar mixture. It also works well with coffee cakes, such as the Russian Sour Cream Cake (page 172), but for that you leave out the jam. Sometimes I leave out the cinnamon when I'm making rugelach and/or add raisins.

a bissel advice

Why so many options? I think that fillings were invented to use up left-overs, so they present you with a lot of options. I know that streusel isn't streusel without the cinnamon, but sometimes I just don't feel like using cinnamon.

MAKES ABOUT 1¹⁄₄ CUPS

kosher status PAREVE

1 cup (about 4 ounces) chopped walnuts

¹⁄₂ cup light brown sugar

¹⁄₄ cup granulated sugar

1 teaspoon ground cinnamon *(optional)*

¹⁄₂ cup apricot, raspberry, or currant jam, or your preference

¹⁄₄ pound (about ³⁄₄ cup) golden raisins *(optional)*

Preheat the oven to 350°F. Spread out the chopped walnuts on a cookie sheet and set in the preheated oven for 10 to 15 minutes until you can smell a strong, toasted-nut smell, and the color of the nuts has darkened. Rake them once or twice while they bake to be sure they toast evenly. Cool.

Combine the toasted nuts, sugars, and cinnamon until well blended. When it comes time to assemble, spread the dough with some jam and sprinkle generously with the streusel mixture. Sprinkle the mixture with raisins (if using).

lemon and almond filling

LIKE THE STREUSEL FILLING (PAGE 227), this is not a filling per se, but a combination of jam that is spread on dough or batter and the nuts and sugar that are sprinkled on top. My friend Bonnie always has rugelach filled with this combination on hand at her office around holiday time to give to anyone who stops in. For variety I alternate the flavor of jam I use. Get creative with flavors like plum, peach, and pineapple, if you like. The combination also makes a good topping for coffee cake.

1 cup whole almonds (about 6 ounces), with
    skins on
½ cup sugar
Zest of 1 lemon (about 2 teaspoons)
½ cup apricot, raspberry, or currant jam, or
    your preference

SPECIAL EQUIPMENT
Food processor

MAKES ABOUT 2 CUPS

kosher status PAREVE

Preheat the oven to 350°F. Spread out the almonds on a cookie sheet and set in the preheated oven for 10 to 15 minutes until you can smell a strong, toasted nut smell, and the color of the nuts has darkened. Rake the nuts once or twice while they bake to be sure they toast evenly. Cool.

Combine the sugar, almonds, and lemon zest in the bowl of a food processor fitted with a metal chopping blade. Pulse five or six times until the nuts are finely chopped and uniform. When it comes time to assemble, spread the dough with the jam and sprinkle generously with the nut mixture.

sweet cheese filling

THIS FILLING IS EQUALLY DELICIOUS in Danish (page 185), Blintzes (page 182), Hamentaschen (page 158), or as the filling for Babka (page 192). I like to flavor it either with citrus zest or cinnamon, but not both because I think that together the flavors compete with the mild cheese. Some of my friends prefer it plain, with neither. I like raisins in everything, but since I know some people can't stand them, I've made them optional, too.

a bissel advice

What if I don't know a farmer? **Although in some recipes you can substitute ricotta or cottage cheese for farmer or pot cheese, I find that in this one the resulting filling is runny and difficult to work with. Farmer cheese, which is really just a pressed cottage cheese that is dry and crumbly, or pot cheese, which is like a very large-curd cottage cheese drained from its whey, is usually unsalted. If you find one that is salted, I would omit the salt in the recipe. Oddly, the farmer cheese at my local grocery store comes in 7.5-ounce packages. This means that two packages fall an ounce short of a pound, but the recipe works fine, anyway.**

MAKES ABOUT **2** CUPS

kosher status MILCHIG. Use tofu cheese and I'll find you and kill you.

1 pound (1½ cups) farmer or pot cheese

4 ounces (½ cup) cream cheese, at room temperature

1 large egg

⅓ cup sugar

1 teaspoon pure vanilla extract

1 teaspoon grated lemon or orange zest or ¼ teaspoon ground cinnamon *(optional)*

½ teaspoon kosher salt

½ cup golden raisins *(optional)*

Using a wooden spoon, blend the farmer or pot cheese with the cream cheese until smooth. Mix in the egg, sugar, vanilla, zest or cinnamon (if using), and salt. Stir in the raisins (if using). Chill.

poppy seed filling

MOHN OR *MON* IS YIDDISH FOR "POPPY SEEDS," and if it is possible to make a gross generalization (why not? I've made several in this book already), the use of mohn as a principal ingredient distinguishes Eastern European baking from other types of baking. Despite popular North American belief, poppy seeds need not be relegated to the tops of bagels. Ground, sweetened, and delicately flavored, they have a distinct taste and maybe even a hallucinogenic quality. I myself know that a good poppy seed Danish sends me into a dream state. I also know that the slightly bitter flavor makes some people gag. Suit yourself.

I have tried several ways to make a poppy seed filling without first grinding the seeds, a step I fear may prevent a timid cook from tackling this recipe. But none was as good as the real thing. When you don't grind the seeds, the filling has an unappealing graininess and chewy texture. The truth is, it doesn't take much effort to grind them if you have a handheld electric coffee grinder. Don't try to use a blender or food processor; the seeds are too small for either to be effective. Whether or not you have a separate coffee grinder for spices, you should clean out your grinder before and after grinding the poppy seeds by running some fresh white bread through it.

Poppy seed filling is traditional for Hamentaschen (page 158), but it's also well suited to Yeast-Raised Rugelach (page 147), coffee cakes, and Danish (page 185). I've even made poppy seed blintzes (page 182). Be sure to use extremely fresh poppy seeds. The seeds have a high oil content that makes them turn rancid quickly, resulting in an unpleasant bitter aftertaste. For an excellent mail-order source, see page 273.

a bissel advice

Grind my own poppy seeds? What is this, the 19th century? **If you live in an area with a heavy Eastern European population, you can sometimes find poppy seeds already ground for baking. But be extra sure that they are freshly ground, because grinding exposes the seed oils to oxygen, which makes them turn rancid very quickly.**

½ cup chopped walnuts *(optional)*

2 slices fresh bread, for cleaning the coffee
    grinder

1½ cups (½ pound) whole poppy seeds or
    1¼ cups ground poppy seeds

1¼ cups half-and-half

½ cup sugar or honey, or a combination

2 tablespoons butter

Grated zest of 1 lemon (about 2 teaspoons)

Juice of ½ lemon (about 2 tablespoons)

Pinch of kosher salt

½ teaspoon vanilla extract

⅓ cup dried currants *(optional)*

SPECIAL EQUIPMENT
Coffee grinder

If using walnuts, preheat the oven to 350°F. Spread out the chopped walnuts on a cookie sheet and set in the preheated oven for 10 to 15 minutes until you can smell a strong, toasted-nut smell, and the color of the nuts has darkened. Rake them once or twice while they bake to be sure they toast evenly. Cool.

If using whole poppy seeds, you will have to grind them in a coffee grinder. Tear a slice of bread into pieces and put them in the coffee grinder. Grind by pulsing three or four times. The bread will remove any oily residue of coffee or other spices. Dump out the bread crumbs and wipe out the grinder with a piece of paper towel.

Grind the poppy seeds about ¼ cup at a time to a coarse flour by pulsing the grinder several times. As they grind, the poppy seeds will clump on the bottom of the grinder around the blade. Dump the ground seeds into a medium saucepan and continue until all of the poppy seeds are ground.

Add the half-and-half, sugar, and butter to the pot and set over medium-low heat. Bring to a simmer while stirring constantly. Cook until the mixture thickens to a paste, 10 to 15 minutes. Add the lemon zest, juice, salt, and vanilla, and the currants and toasted walnuts (if using). Continue cooking for an additional minute or two. Remove from the heat and cool. Chill before using. This filling can be stored in the refrigerator for up to 1 week.

prune filling

ACCORDING TO THE CALIFORNIA PRUNE Board, the official name of prunes is now "dried plums." As far as I know, *lekvar* is still Hungarian for "prune spread." A lot of people just use commercially prepared lekvar as prune filling for Hamentaschen (page 158) and call it a day. But my sister Carrie makes her prune filling from scratch, and the texture and flavor don't compare. Though perhaps not traditional, Carrie adds walnuts and raisins to her prune filling. For a variation, substitute orange juice and zest for the lemon.

½ pound (1¼ cups) pitted prunes, roughly
    chopped
¼ pound (¾ cup) seedless golden raisins,
    roughly chopped
¼ cup chopped walnuts, toasted
Juice of ½ lemon (about 2 tablespoons)
Finely grated zest of 1 lemon (about
    2 teaspoons)

MAKES ABOUT **2** CUPS, ENOUGH FOR **1** CAKE OR
1 BATCH HAMENTASCHEN

kosher status PAREVE

place the prunes and raisins in a small nonreactive saucepan with 1¼ cups water and set over medium heat. Bring to a simmer and cook, stirring with a wooden spoon, until the prunes fall apart and the raisins plump, 15 to 20 minutes. If the mixture gets very dry, add some more water in tablespoon increments, and pay attention so the mixture doesn't burn. The finished filling should be like paste. Remove from the heat and stir in the walnuts, lemon juice, and zest.

apple filling

LIKE A CHUNKY APPLESAUCE THAT still has some bite, this filling is delicious in blintzes or on the side.

Use a wide sauté pan to encourage the evaporation of any liquid that cooks out of the apples.

MAKES 2¼ CUPS

kosher status MILCHIG. You can make this filling pareve by omitting the butter.

2 tablespoons unsalted butter

4 or 5 cooking apples (2 pounds), such as Northern Spy, Cortland, Gala, Golden Delicious, or a combination, peeled, cored, and cut into large dice

Juice of ½ lemon (2 tablespoons)

¼ cup sugar

1 teaspoon pure vanilla extract

¼ teaspoon kosher salt

¼ teaspoon ground cinnamon

heat the butter in a large, wide sauté pan set over medium-high heat. Add the apples, lemon juice, and sugar and cook, stirring often, until the apples have begun to soften, about 5 minutes. Add the vanilla, salt, and cinnamon and continue cooking until the apples are tender but not falling apart, about 7 additional minutes. Periodically I like to push the apples all the way to one side of the pan to allow the juice to evaporate. Remove from the heat, cool to room temperature, and chill.

Learning the basics

is like learning scales on the piano: if you don't practice them, someone is going to rap your knuckles with a ruler until they bleed. Any self-respecting Jewish cook should know how to make a challah, how to boil a beet, how to render schmaltz. This section has recipes and techniques that are called for throughout the book and throughout life. There are a couple of frivolous things in here, too—such as a recipe for making your own matzo—but I think you will find them all useful.

chicken schmaltz

AAH, SCHMALTZ. THE BACKBONE (or artery clogger?) of Jewish cuisine. As a rule, my mother cooked with only two fats: butter and schmaltz. It wasn't a question of keeping kosher, it was a question of taste. And when it comes to taste, nothing compares. Schmaltz is essential in some dishes, such as Chopped Liver (page 6) and Matzo Balls (page 41). And it enhances just about anything that is sautéed or fried. Although you can buy rendered chicken schmaltz in areas where there is a high concentration of Jews (it's usually in the freezer section of the local butcher shop), you are better off making it at home. This enables you to flavor the schmaltz and to control the amount it is cooked. Rendering the fat yourself also gives you a delicious by-product—Gribenes.

To gather the fat to render, you can save the trimmings from fresh chickens or chicken breasts in a bag in the freezer, and render it off when you have enough. Otherwise, you can ask your butcher for raw chicken fat. I usually ask for a couple of pounds at a time, and keep the rendered fat on hand in the freezer.

I have made two discoveries concerning schmaltz in doing the research and recipe testing for this book. The first is that if you render the schmaltz with a vanilla bean instead of onion, you can use it in sweet baked goods. The idea for this first came to me while I was reading *In Memory's Kitchen,* a cookbook of recipe memories by Holo-caust victims in Terezin, a staged Jewish ghetto outside Prague that was supposed to demonstrate how well the Jews were being treated (it was a lie—they were starving and being killed). Many of the pastry recipes they remembered were made with (goose) schmaltz. I've never been satisfied with the flavor or texture of pie crust and other pastries that don't use butter or lard. But adding a little schmaltz to the mixture greatly improves the finished product. Even people who were grossed-out by the idea became convinced once they tasted these treats.

The second discovery concerns gribenes. Traditionally, chicken fat is rendered to the point that the bits and pieces of skin in it turn dark brown and crisp. To my taste, this gives the schmaltz an unappetizing dark color and an unpleasant bitter flavor. Instead, I've been rendering the schmaltz until it's a light golden color. Then I take out the skin, lay it on a baking sheet, and roast it until dark brown and crisp. Tossed in kosher salt, these tasty snacks—akin, ironically, to *chicharrónes,* or fried pork rinds—are impossible to keep around.

kosher status FLEISHIG

Note that although I sometimes refer to sweets made with schmaltz as pareve (i.e., Pareve Rugelach on page 148), what I mean is that they can be eaten with meat. The nomenclature is inexact, but Fleishig Rugelach just sounds too weird.

2 pounds chicken fat, skin, and scraps, roughly cut up

1 large onion (about 8 ounces), cut into eighths

lace the chicken fat and skin in a small, heavy saucepan, and set over very low heat. After about 10 minutes, when about ½ inch of fat has rendered on the bottom of the pan, add the onion and stir. Continue cooking over low heat for another 45 minutes to 1 hour, until all of the fat has rendered from the skin. Do not allow the onion or the chicken skin to color—the liquid fat should be golden yellow in color, no darker. Strain through a fine sieve into a container with a tight-fitting lid. Cool, cover, and refrigerate or freeze until needed. There may be some dark liquid on the bottom of the container. This is the juice from the onion and chicken scraps, not fat, and should be ignored.

sweet chicken schmaltz for pastries

Follow the preceding recipe, but omit the onion and add instead 1 vanilla bean split in half.

gribenes

THESE ARE the crunchy pieces of skin that are the delicious by-product of making your own schmaltz. Instead of cooking them until crisp in the rendered schmaltz, which gives the schmaltz an unappetizing color and bitter flavor, I finish them in the oven until dark brown and crisp. Gribenes make a delicious bar snack. Chopped fine, they are a welcome ingredient in everything from potato knish filling to cholent.

MAKES 4 TO 6 OUNCES

kosher status FLEISHIG

Strained chicken skin left over after rendering schmaltz (above)

1 teaspoon kosher salt

reheat the oven to 350°F. Using tongs, remove any pieces of onion mixed in with the skin. Lay the skin on a baking sheet; make sure the pieces aren't touching. Set in the middle of the oven for 30 to 45 minutes, until skin is dark brown and crisp. Turn two or three times. If pieces begin to burn, remove them from the oven. Remove the browned gribenes from the oven, lay on a paper bag or paper towel to drain, and toss with the salt.

beef schmaltz

I KNOW IT ISN'T AS HEALTHY as other types of fat, but schmaltz made from beef sure is delicious. Because of its strong flavor, you have to use beef schmaltz a little more discriminatingly than you would chicken or duck fat. But a drop added to a mushroom and onion sauté or to the base of a soup is a welcome addition, indeed. My great-grandmother Eva used to save all the fat she trimmed from brisket and other beef in the freezer until she had enough to render. Now I do, too.

a bissel advice

Isn't this a heart attack waiting to happen? I didn't say you had to eat it all the time. Rendered beef fat will keep sealed in the refrigerator for about a year. Use it sparingly, but use it well.

6 to 7 ounces clean, white beef fat

MAKES ½ CUP

kosher status FLEISHIG

trim away any evidence of blue USDA stamps or other imperfections in the fat before rendering. Leave any pieces of meat. Cut the fat into small pieces, place in a small saucepan, and set over low heat. The fat will begin to sizzle and smell like roast beef almost immediately. Once all of the fat has rendered, 20 to 30 minutes later, strain it into a container and keep it refrigerated until ready to use.

cinnamon sugar

THIS WAS A STAPLE IN OUR HOUSE while I was growing up. I believe it to be an Ashkenazi tradition, but I can't find much evidence for that besides the fact that it is sprinkled on almost every sweet thing you can make. I like cinnamon sugar on Matzo Brei (page 186), Challah French Toast (page 188), and Cheese Latkes (page 106), and it's my favorite topping for Doughnuts (page 160). Sometimes when we weren't feeling well, my mother just made cinnamon toast, by sprinkling cinnamon sugar on toasted and buttered challah. I ask you: how much better does food get than that? Just be sure your cinnamon is fresh and the best quality.

a bissel advice

How do I use it? Keep it in an old spice jar with a shaker top. If it settles, just shake it up before you sprinkle it on top of everything.

MAKES 1 CUP

kosher status PAREVE

1 cup sugar

2 teaspoons ground cinnamon

In a small bowl, mix the sugar with the cinnamon to combine. Store in an airtight container or jar and shake away.

egg noodles (lokshen)

YOU CAN BUY PERFECTLY GOOD egg noodles, or lokshen (pronounced LUCK-shuhn or LUCKSHN), in the grocery store—whether Dutch, Italian, or Jewish. But making your own egg noodles, especially if you are serving them in soup or will use them in a kugel, as my great-grandmother used to do, is a rewarding endeavor. The texture is more tender, the flavor is finer, and the message you are giving your guests—that they are the most important people in the world and that you should want to break your back for them, *but don't feel guilty*—is unmatched. If you have a hand-cranked Italian pasta machine, it takes only about 30 minutes (plus drying time) to make about a pound of noodles. Because some kugel recipes call for $3/4$ pound (12 ounces) noodles, and others call for 1 pound (16 ounces) of noodles, I've given proportions for both. For authenticity's sake you can prepare the noodles right on the counter by making a well with the flour and beating the eggs in the center, or you can just mix everything together in a bowl.

a bissel advice

Which pasta machine? Don't use a pasta extruder—one of the machines they advertise on late-night television into which you simply dump all of your ingredients and out comes pasta like Play-Doh—because the result is a gummy mess. The one I'm talking about is metal and clamps to the countertop. It has a hand crank and two rollers that you can adjust. Imperia is a popular manufacturer.

And if I don't have a machine? You can roll out the pasta by hand, but it will take some time and it won't be as thin and delicate (although it will be more like my great-grandmother made it) as it would be made with a machine. Let the dough sit for an hour before you roll it out. Divide it in quarters. Using a long, thin rolling pin (a *mattarello* in Italian), roll it out as thin as possible. If your rolling pin has handles, don't use them. Instead roll the pin with your palms on the wood, applying all the pressure you can muster. Once the dough is rolled out, roll it up like a jelly roll to produce a log. Slice the log into $1/4$-inch strips, and unroll them into noodles. Drape the noodles over the broom handles to dry as directed.

FOR 3/4 POUND OF NOODLES

2 cups unbleached all-purpose flour

3 large eggs

FOR 1 POUND OF NOODLES

3 cups unbleached all-purpose flour

4 large eggs

1 tablespoon water

SPECIAL EQUIPMENT

1 hand-crank pasta machine

2 clean broom handles

to use the well technique, pile the flour in a mound on a clean work surface and make an indentation or well in the center about 3 or 4 inches in diameter. Crack the eggs into the well (and add the water, if using), being careful to shore up any obvious weaknesses in the flour walls. Using a large dinner fork, gently beat the eggs in the well. Once the eggs look scrambled, start incorporating some of the flour from the sides of the well into the egg mixture. As you continue to beat and incorporate more and more flour, use your other hand to support and reinforce the flour walls. Continue stirring with the fork until most of the flour has been moistened and a soft dough has formed. Use your hands to knead the dough and incorporate as much flour as possible. Discard any excess flour that will not mix into the dough. Continue kneading by hand until smooth, but firm.

Alternatively, you can just combine everything in a mixing bowl and stir with a fork or the paddle attachment of an electric mixer to form a stiff dough. All of the flour may not be incorporated into the dough, but don't force it. Transfer the dough to a work surface and knead by hand until the dough is smooth, but firm.

Lay out two broom handles horizontally across two supports that are at equal heights—such as a counter and a tabletop. The noodles will dry by hanging over these handles. Lay a clean towel on the floor beneath to catch any noodles that fall. If you are making the larger batch (1 pound) of noodles, you should cut the dough in half. With your pasta machine firmly attached to the counter, begin cranking the dough through the rollers on the widest setting (which usually corresponds to the number 1). Crank it through, fold the dough in thirds, and crank it through again until the dough becomes smooth and elastic, 8 to 10 times in all. Run the dough through the machine on the same setting one final time. Now begin to increase the setting, one notch at a time, as you roll the dough pro-

MENTAL NOSH

Do we have Marco Polo to thank for lokshen kugel? Probably not. Although most people think the Italian explorer introduced noodles to Europe when he returned from his travels in China in the 13th century, many historians believe Europeans, particularly the Italians, were eating them long before. (Besides, Polo's travel account, which he dictated while imprisoned in Genoa in 1298, wasn't well known until it was printed at the end of the 16th century.) The true origins of lokshen may never be known. Chinese, Koreans, Arabs, and Italians all lay claim to having made the first noodle. And since Jews mingled with the Arabs and Italians (and probably ate in ancient Chinese restaurants on Sundays), they've probably been eating noodles for a long time, too.

recipe continues →

egg noodles (lokshen)

(continued)

(

gressively thinner. By the time you get up to 3 or 4, you will probably have to cut the dough in half (again) in order to be able to manage it. Place one half of the dough under a clean dish towel to prevent drying while you continue to work the other up to the highest setting. You may have to divide the dough in half again to keep it manageable. When the dough is rolled through the thinnest setting, hang it over the broom handles to dry slightly while you finish rolling out the rest. This short drying time will keep the noodles from sticking together when you cut them.

For very wide noodles, you can cut the dough by hand into strips. I generally use the fettuccine attachment on my pasta machine, which makes egg noodles equivalent to the commercial designation "medium." Once cut, hang the noodles over the broom handles and allow to dry for 10 hours or overnight. The noodles will curl and some will fall off onto the towel below. For old-fashioned Kasha Varnishkes (page 118), cut the noodles into 1½-inch squares, toss with flour, and let dry on a cookie sheet. Once dried, gather your noodles and proceed with your recipe. You can store the fully dried noodles for several weeks in brown paper bags in a cool, dry place. When you go to cook them, remember to use plenty of boiling, salted water (at least 4 quarts with 1 tablespoon kosher salt) and pay attention because they will take only a minute or two to reach al dente.

bread crumbs

ALTHOUGH THEY ARE NOT EXACT equivalents, I use matzo meal and bread crumbs pretty much interchangeably. And because I don't like to have to buy them, I make my own bread crumbs from leftover pieces of bread or challah—whatever I have lying around. In fact, I freeze leftover bread in a resealable plastic bag until I have enough to bother with. Leftover challah makes particularly tender bread crumbs. The secret is to use stale bread and then to dry it out completely in a low oven before you grind it in a food processor. This gives the crumbs a slightly toasted flavor. If you don't have a food processor, you can use a plastic bag and a rolling pin.

MAKES 2½ CUPS

kosher status PAREVE, depending on the bread you are using

1 pound stale bread, with some of the crusts removed

SPECIAL EQUIPMENT
Food processor or rolling pin
Sieve

preheat the oven to 250°F.
If the stale bread is in large pieces, slice it. Lay the pieces of bread out on a cookie sheet in a single layer. Set in the preheated oven until completely dry and toasted, 2 to 2½ hours. Remove from the oven and cool to room temperature.

Depending on the size of your work bowl, transfer about half of the dried bread to a food processor fitted with a metal chopping blade. Pulse until the bread is ground to fine crumbs. Don't be scared by the loud noise; your food processor won't break. Pass the crumbs through a coarse sieve to remove any lumps.

If you don't have a food processor, you can make the crumbs by hand. Place the dried bread in double or triple plastic bag. Seal tightly, removing as much air from the bag as possible. Using a rolling pin, roll over and bang the bread to pulverize it to crumbs. Periodically pass the whole mess (minus the bag!) through a sieve to remove the crumbs. Then you can continue to pulverize the lumps to crumbs. Freeze until needed.

a bissel advice

Any bread? I actually use all breads except those with any strong flavors, such as caraway or herbs, because I don't know what I will eventually use the crumbs for.

mushrooms and onions

WE NEVER NEEDED AN AIR FRESHENER in our house because the smell of mushrooms and onions simmering in butter almost always emanated from the kitchen. My mother believes that anything is better with a generous helping of mushrooms and onions in it or on it. (If a perfume were made with the scent, she would probably give up her beloved Opium.) My mother even serves mushrooms and onions on plain pieces of toast as an appetizer for company. She smothers barbecued steak with mushrooms and onions. She stirs them into farfel and kasha and noodles and rice and mashed potatoes and anything she can get her hands on.

The secrets to her mushrooms and onions are enough butter to impress a French chef and a lot of salt and pepper. In fact, my sisters and I determined she doesn't really sauté her mushrooms and onions, she boils them in butter. Instead of using a sauté pan she uses a saucepot, which also keeps the mixture wetter than most. This makes for a rich, juicy, flavorful concoction that adds not just flavor but also fat and moisture to whatever it is stirred into. What could be bad?

You can make mushrooms and onions with a combination of different mushrooms (I often add portobellos), but my mother always used only button mushrooms. Although at first you will think you have too many mushrooms, remember they cook down to less than half their volume. If you are going to make mushrooms and onions as a topping for Broiled Skirt Steak (page 73) or to stir into Kasha Varnishkes (page 118) or Farfel with Mushrooms and Onions (page 114), then do them in a pot and make them wet. If you are going to be using them for a filling in hors d'oeuvre puffs, or Knishes (page 22), then cook them in a large frying pan so the moisture evaporates.

a bissel advice

Mushroom and onions all the time. You can make the mushrooms and onions in advance and keep them in the freezer in small containers. That way whenever you want to make something like Farfel (page 110) or Kasha Varnishkes (page 118), you just have to defrost a container and you're ready to go.

kosher status MILCHIG with butter
FLEISHIG with schmaltz
PAREVE but not very good if made only with peanut oil

4 ounces (1 sticks or ¹/2 cup) unsalted butter, or a combination of peanut oil and chicken schmaltz to equal same

2 large (1 pound) yellow onions, chopped (about 2 cups)

12 ounces (³/4 pound) mushrooms, button, portobello, romano, or a combination, sliced or chopped

2 teaspoons kosher salt

³/4 teaspoon freshly ground black pepper

heat the fat in a large saucepan or frying pan. Add the onions and sauté until translucent, 7 to 8 minutes. Add the mushrooms, salt, and pepper, and continue cooking, stirring often, until the mushrooms have given off most of their water and the mushrooms and onions are soft, about 30 minutes. If you desire a drier mixture, use a frying pan to allow the moisture to evaporate while the mushrooms and onions cook. Adjust the seasoning with additional salt and pepper if necessary.

homemade matzos

YEARS AGO I SAW A RECIPE in the *New York Times* for homemade matzos based on a testimonial from medieval Spain. I may have been the only person crazy enough to have tried to make them, and I'm almost sorry I did: since my family took their first bites, these matzos have become a tradition at our Passover seders. They bake into

beautiful beige and brown disks with a sweet, peppery flavor. These matzos are best the day they are made. They take a little time to roll out, but I usually get into a rhythm, using three cookie sheets and rolling out some matzos while others are baking and cooling. The only problem is, of course, that the matzos are not kosher for Passover (details, details). This doesn't bother my family. But should it bother yours, you can also make them using matzo cake meal as I have explained in the recipe.

a bissel advice

Be forewarned. These delicious matzos may just become a tradition in your house and you will have to make them every year hence.

4 cups plus ½ cup unbleached all-purpose
flour

1 tablespoon freshly ground black pepper

1 teaspoon kosher salt

4 large eggs, beaten

5 tablespoons mild honey, such as acacia or
wildflower

4 teaspoons olive oil

preheat the oven to 400°F.

In a large mixing bowl, combine 4 cups of the flour with the pepper and salt, and mix well. Make a well in the center. Into the well pour the eggs, honey, olive oil, and 7 tablespoons of water. Using a fork, mix to form a stiff dough. If a lot of flour remains unincorporated, add another tablespoon or so of water. Knead once or twice by hand until smooth, then let rest, covered, for 30 minutes.

Divide the dough into 12 equal portions and shape each portion into a ball. Use the remaining ½ cup flour to lightly flour your work surface. With a long, thin rolling pin (I prefer an Italian *mattarello* intended for making pasta), roll each ball out into an 8-inch disk. Using a fork with the tines dipped in flour, pierce the entire surface of the dough with little holes. Repeat with another piece of dough. Bake the matzos in the preheated oven two at a time on cookie sheets for 10 minutes, or until they are slightly puffed and browned around the edges. Turn them over once while they are baking so they brown evenly. Remove from the oven and let cool on a wire rack. Brush off any excess flour.

While they are baking, continue rolling out the next couple of matzos. Keep working in this way until all 12 matzos are baked. On the day they are made, store them in the open air. Wrap airtight to keep longer.

pesadich spanish matzos

Though still not suitable for ceremonial purposes, these Spanish matzos can be made Pesadich by substituting matzo cake meal for flour. Increase the water to ¾ cup. The dough will be more difficult to roll out and the resulting matzos will be smaller. But they do have an excellent flavor.

beets

THERE ARE BASICALLY TWO WAYS to cook beets: boiling and roasting. The results are slightly different, but virtually interchangeable in recipes that call for cooked beets. Roasted beets have a more concentrated flavor, darker color, and slightly drier texture than boiled beets. The method I choose depends on whether I want to clean a pot or a cookie sheet, and just how intense a beet flavor I am looking for.

Unless you are planning to cook a borscht or some other beet soup, you needn't worry about peeling the beets before cooking. In fact, once they are cooked (either way) the peels just slip off. If the beets are going to be kept whole, sliced for pickling, or cut into chunks for a salad, they should be cooked until a fork or the point of a knife is easily poked into the center of the beet. If they are going to be pureed, they should be cooked longer, until very tender.

I like to buy beets from a farmer's market with the tops intact. The tops make fabulous greens if they are cleaned, blanched, and sautéed. They can be used like spinach, or in dishes such as Savory Noodle Kugel (page 130). Choose beets that are the same size to ensure even cooking.

boiled beets

MAKES ABOUT 3½ CUPS DICED BEETS OR 2¼ CUPS PUREED BEETS

2 pounds fresh beets (without tops), about 6 to 8 depending on size, unpeeled

To prepare the beets for cooking, cut off the stems, leaving about an inch attached to the beet (this helps prevent the color from leaching out while they cook). Trim the root end, too. Wash well under cold, running water, using a vegetable brush if necessary to remove dirt.

Place the trimmed beets in a medium saucepan and cover with cold water, at least an inch above the top of the beets. Set over high heat and bring to a boil. Lower the heat to a simmer and cook until fork-tender, 45 minutes to an hour depending on the size of the beets. If you are going to puree the beets, cook them 15 to 20 minutes longer. Turn off the heat and let the beets cool in the water until you can handle them. Remove from the water and rinse. Using a paring knife, cut off the stem at the top and remove the peel. Slice or dice the beets as called for in the recipe.

To puree, cut the cooked beets into chunks and place in the bowl of a food processor fitted with the metal chopping blade. Using pulses, puree the beets until smooth, scraping down the sides periodically.

roasted beets

MAKES ABOUT 3 CUPS DICED BEETS OR 2 CUPS PUREED BEETS

2 pounds fresh beets (without tops), about 6 to 8 depending on size, unpeeled, and trimmed as explained above

Preheat the oven to 350°F. Place the beets on a greased cookie sheet and set in the middle of the preheated oven. (You can also just put them right on your oven rack, but they may make a mess on the bottom of the oven.) Roast for an hour or so until fork-tender. Remove from the oven and cool to room temperature, about 1 hour. Using a paring knife, trim off the stem and remove the peel. Cut up or puree as explained above.

challah

I'M GOING TO GO OUT on a gastronomic limb here and declare challah the most delicious and versatile of all breads. It's not that I don't love other breads, but they all seem more limited in scope. Challah is great fresh out of the oven, toasted and dripping with butter, slathered with peanut butter and jelly, in bread pudding, as French Toast (page 188), and in Stuffing (page 122). It can even be doctored up to produce a sweet dough for coffee cakes and Danish. When I lived in Paris, I described challah as a sort of light brioche. It is the bread of my youth.

It's also easy to make, in part because the dough is so agreeable. It is supple and soft without being sticky or hard to knead. It can be made in a food processor or electric mixer. But I find it just as easy to do a loaf or two by hand, and then when you are done, all you have to clean is a bowl and a baking sheet. You can make the dough a day in advance and refrigerate it until you are ready to bake it.

Depending on what you intend to use the challah for, you can make it with either oil or melted butter. I prefer butter, but you can use peanut oil or Crisco soybean oil to produce an equally delicious bread. If I am going to be using the dough for coffee cake, babka, or Danish, I will be sure to make it with butter because I like my sweets to have a buttery flavor (also because I add sour cream to the dough, so it's already milchig). The amount of sugar can be varied, too. Generally, sweeter challahs are made around Rosh Hashanah, the Jewish New Year,

a bissel advice

But I've never made bread before! This recipe is a good introduction to yeast baking because challah is made with a simple, almost foolproof dough. The biggest problem is usually the yeast, which is dead more often than you would think. That's why proofing (a fancy term for letting yeast do its stuff—that is, rise) is important. If your yeast doesn't react, I'm afraid you can't make bread.

Yeast is really alive? Yes. In its dried state, it is dormant because of lack of moisture. But when it comes into contact with water, it comes alive. Be careful, though, because two things can kill it: direct exposure to salt or sugar, or too much heat. That's why I have you dissolve the sugar in the water (which is lukewarm to provide a good environment for the yeast to grow) and I don't have you add the salt until later in the recipe.

Where should I let the dough rise? A damp, warm place is ideal. I usually leave my dough near a steam pipe in my kitchen. An oven with a pilot light (be sure the oven is off) is also a good place. The warmer the area, the more quickly the yeast will rise. If it is too hot, however, the yeast will die. To be safe, keep the temperature below 110°F.

What if I let the dough rest as long as you say and it doesn't double in bulk? If you proofed the yeast before you made the dough and it bubbled and frothed, give your dough some more time. So many factors affect the speed at which dough rises that it may just need some more time.

to augur a sweet year. These challahs are also usually studded with raisins for the same reason, and rolled into turban shapes to indicate the ongoing cycle of life. Challah dough can also be braided, baked in loaf pans, or knotted into buns called bulkas. Topping plain buns with chopped onions and poppy seeds makes delicious onion rolls for sandwiches or burgers. Shape the dough into long cigars and you have hot dog buns to die for.

Freshly baked challah stays fresh for only a day or two. By the end of the second day it must be toasted or reheated in the oven. But freezing it preserves freshness for 3 to 4 weeks. Slice it before you freeze it in an airtight plastic bag so you can pop slices into the toaster right from the freezer.

This is a simple but delicious dough that you can use as a base for a variety of baked goods, from festive braided loaves to sticky buns.

MAKES 2¼ POUNDS OF DOUGH, ENOUGH FOR 1 LARGE, FESTIVE LOAF, 2 SMALLER LOAVES, OR 1 DOZEN ROLLS

the whole meshpucha

You can easily double this dough to make two large, braided challahs. Actually, what I usually do is make one large challah and a dozen rolls.

kosher status PAREVE, if made with oil
MILCHIG, if made with butter

*P*reparing the dough by hand: In a large mixing bowl, combine the water and the honey or sugar and stir to dissolve. Sprinkle the yeast over the liquid and set aside to proof about 5 minutes. The yeast should dissolve and froth if it is active. If it does not react this way, discard and purchase new yeast. Unfortunately, you'll have to wait to make challah.

Using a sturdy wire whisk, beat in the eggs and the ¼ cup oil or melted butter until frothy and well blended. Add 2 cups of the flour and the salt and continue beating to form a smooth batter. Switch to a sturdy wooden spoon and stir in 2¼ more cups of the flour to form a stiff dough.

Dust a work surface with some of the remaining ¼ cup flour and turn out the shaggy dough from the bowl onto the floured surface. Using a dough scraper and your hands, knead the dough until it is smooth and holds its shape, anywhere between 5 and 10 minutes depending on how strong you

FOR THE DOUGH

1 cup lukewarm water (around 120°F., or warm to the touch)

¼ cup mild honey, such as acacia or wildflower, or sugar

1 package (2¼ teaspoons) active dry yeast

2 large eggs

¼ cup plus 1 teaspoon peanut or Crisco (100% soybean oil), or unsalted butter, melted and cooled

4½ cups unbleached all-purpose flour

1 tablespoon kosher salt

FOR THE GARNISH

1 large egg beaten with 1 teaspoon water

2 teaspoons poppy seeds, sesame seeds, or a combination

SPECIAL EQUIPMENT

2 large mixing bowls

Dough scraper

Baking sheet or loaf pans

Pastry brush

Electric mixer with dough hook *(optional)*

recipe continues →

challah

(continued)

are and how rigorously you are kneading. If the dough is too sticky to handle, add some of the remaining flour in small doses, trying to keep it on the soft side. To knead properly, keep folding the dough in half on top of itself and pushing it down on the counter away from you to reform a sort of blob. Scrape it off the surface with the dough scraper and fold again. When you are finished, the dough should be smooth, not sticky; soft but elastic enough to hold its shape; and pale yellow in color without any evidence of unincorporated flour.

Preparing the dough in an electric mixer: In the bowl of an electric mixer, combine the water with the honey or sugar and stir to dissolve. Sprinkle the yeast over the liquid and set aside for about 5 minutes to proof. The yeast should dissolve and froth if it is active. Using the paddle attachment, beat in the eggs and the ¼ cup oil or melted butter until frothy and well blended. Add 2 cups of the flour and the salt and continue beating to form a smooth batter. Switch to the dough hook. Add 2¼ cups flour and knead with the dough hook for 4 to 5 minutes, until a smooth, elastic dough forms. Dust the work surface with some of the remaining ¼ cup flour and turn out the dough. Knead five or six times until soft.

Proofing the dough: Once kneaded, shape the dough into a ball by folding the edges underneath and stretching the surface. Place the remaining tablespoon of oil or melted butter in a clean bowl (here's where the second bowl comes in handy) and distribute it over the surface with your hands. Place the ball of dough upside down in the bowl to coat the surface with grease and invert to right side up. Cover the bowl with plastic wrap and allow the dough to rise in a warm place (near a preheating oven, for example) until doubled in bulk, about 1 hour 45 minutes.

Remove the plastic wrap and punch down the dough with your fist to compress it to its original size. Recover and let sit for 15 minutes. If the challah is to be used in another recipe, proceed with that recipe at this point. Otherwise, very lightly flour the work surface and shape as desired.

challah shaping

THREE-STRAND BRAID

This is a standard, attractive challah. Turn the dough out onto the lightly floured surface. Divide the dough into three equal portions, each weighing about ¾ pound. One at a time, roll the pieces out on the work surface using the palms of your hands, forming ropes roughly 14 inches long and 1¼ inches in diameter. Lay one rope or strand of dough down the center of a cookie sheet. Place the other two ropes on either side of the first. Pinch one end of all three ropes of dough together and fold the pinched end underneath to secure. Braid the challah as you would hair, weaving all three strands of dough together to produce a long, evenly braided loaf. (Do not pull the braid too tightly or the bread will be constricted when it rises. Too loose a braid, on the other hand, won't hold its shape.) Pinch the opposite ends together and fold underneath to secure. The finished loaf should be about 14 inches long with a thick center that tapers toward each end. Cover with a clean dish towel and let rise in a warm place until doubled in bulk, about 1 hour.

FOUR-STRAND BRAID

This is a more traditional shaping technique that produces a taller, more festive challah. It is more difficult to describe than it is to actually do. Divide the dough into four equal portions, each about ½ pound. One at a time, roll the pieces out on the work surface using the palms of your hands, forming ropes roughly 12 inches long and 1 inch in diameter. Lay the four strands side by side on a cookie sheet. Pinch them together at one end and tuck the end underneath to secure. Take the strand farthest on the right and lift it over the two strands immediately to the left of it. Now take that same strand and twist it under the strand to the right of it. In essence, you've gone over two strands and back under one. Repeat this movement in reverse with the strand on the far left, lifting it over the two strands immediately to the right of it and pulling it back under the one strand to the left. Each time you do this, you change the position and order of the strands, and the overall effect is to produce a high, tight braid. With a little practice it becomes easier than it sounds. Pinch the opposite ends together and fold underneath to secure. The finished loaf should be about 14 inches long with a thick center that tapers toward each end. Cover with a clean dish towel and let rise in a warm place until doubled in bulk, about 1 hour.

recipe continues →

ROUND CHALLAH

This shape is sometimes called a turban and it is traditional for Rosh Hashanah. Turn the dough out onto the lightly floured surface. Sprinkle ½ cup golden raisins on the dough and knead slightly to incorporate. Pat the dough on the work surface with the palms of your hands to form a large rectangle, about 16 inches by 12 inches. Poke any stray raisins into the dough. Roll up the dough like a jelly roll along the longer edge to form a log about 18 inches long and 2½ inches in diameter. Starting at one end, roll the log into itself to form a turban or snailshell shape and transfer to a cookie sheet or pizza pan. Tuck the outer end underneath to secure it. Cover with a clean dish towel and let rise in a warm place until doubled in bulk, about 1 hour.

SANDWICH LOAVES

Grease two 6-cup loaf pans (I prefer metal to glass), 8½ by 4½ by 2½ inches. Turn the dough out onto the lightly floured surface. Divide the dough in half. Pat or roll each half out into a rectangle, roughly 8 by 10 inches. Roll the dough up like a jelly roll, starting at one of the 8-inch edges, and place in the pan, tucking the ends underneath to seal. Cover with a clean dish towel and let rise in a warm place until doubled in bulk, about 45 minutes to 1 hour.

BULKAS

These are classic challah rolls shaped like knots.

Turn the dough out onto the lightly floured surface. Divide the dough into 12 equal portions, each weighing about 3 ounces. Roll each piece out on the work surface with the palms of your hands, to a rope about 6 inches long and 1 inch in diameter. Tie a knot in the center of each rope, tuck under the ends to form a round shape, and place on a cookie sheet, leaving a good inch or two between the rolls so they have room to rise. Cover with a clean dish towel and let rise in a warm place until doubled in bulk, about 45 minutes to an hour.

ONION ROLLS

My friends just can't get enough of these delicious rolls.

Finely mince a small onion (about 6 ounces) and combine with 1½ teaspoons poppy seeds and ½ teaspoon kosher salt. Set aside. Turn the dough out onto a lightly floured surface. Divide the dough into 12 equal portions, each weighing about 3 ounces. Gently fold the edges underneath the ball of dough two or three times to stretch the surface and increase the surface tension. Roll each portion into a ball between the palm of your cupped hand and the work surface until smooth.

Place the dough pinched side down on a cookie sheet, leaving a good inch or two between the rolls so they have room to rise. Cover with a clean dish towel and let rise in a warm place until doubled in bulk, about 45 minutes to 1 hour.

challah baking

Preheat the oven to 400°F. When the dough has finished rising, no matter what shape you are making, brush the entire surface with the egg wash. Sprinkle the challahs or bulkas with poppy or sesame seeds. For the onion rolls, spread a scant teaspoonful of the onion-poppy seed mixture on the top of each roll.

Place in the middle of the preheated oven and let bake for 20 minutes until the surface begins to brown. The bulkas and onion rolls may be baked through at this point. Test by tapping them, they should sound hollow. Or insert an instant-read thermometer in the center, which should reach at least 190°F. For the challahs, lower the temperature to 350°F. and continue baking for an additional 15 to 20 minutes, until the surface has turned a deep brown and the loaf sounds hollow when you tap it. An instant-read thermometer inserted in the center of the bread should read at least 190°F. when done. Remove from the oven, transfer immediately to a cooling rack, and allow to cool completely before serving.

sweet yeast dough

THIS IS A VARIATION OF THE BASIC CHALLAH RECIPE that uses butter for the fat and a combination of heavy cream, sour cream, and water for the liquid. The technique is pretty much the same as for making challah, although the dough is usually a little softer. I use this dough for Yeast-Raised Rugelach (page 147), Cheese Danish (page 190), Babka (page 192), and Doughnuts (page 160).

a bissel advice

Oh, dough is me. Because of the added fat in this recipe, the yeast has to work harder to make it rise—it's just plain heavier. It also makes the dough a little more difficult to handle than a basic challah dough. I prefer to make this dough the night before I intend to use it and let it rise in the refrigerator overnight until I need it the next day. When it is chilled, the gluten relaxes, the butter firms up, and the dough can be rolled or shaped easily.

½ cup lukewarm (between 110°F. and 120°F.) water
⅔ cup sugar
1 package (2½ teaspoons) active dry yeast
½ cup heavy cream
½ cup sour cream
4 tablespoons (½ stick) unsalted butter
2 large eggs
4½ to 5 cups unbleached all-purpose flour
2 teaspoons kosher salt
½ teaspoon peanut oil

SPECIAL EQUIPMENT
Dough scraper
Electric mixer with a paddle and a dough hook *(optional)*

In a small bowl or measuring cup, combine the water with 1 teaspoon of the sugar and the yeast. Set aside to proof for about 5 minutes. If the yeast is active, it should bubble and froth up. If it doesn't, discard it. You will need new yeast. Meanwhile, combine the heavy cream, sour cream, and butter in a small saucepan and heat until it is just about to boil and the butter has melted. Cool until just warm, about 110°F. on an instant-read thermometer.

Preparing the dough in an electric mixer: Transfer the yeast mixture to the bowl of an electric mixer fitted with a paddle attachment. Add the eggs, the cream mixture, and the remaining sugar and beat for a minute or two to blend. Add 2 cups of the flour and the salt and beat with the paddle for 2 or 3 minutes to develop the gluten. Switch to the dough hook. Add 2½ cups more flour and knead with the dough hook until the dough is smooth and shiny, about 5 minutes on low speed. If the dough remains sticky, add a tablespoon or two more of flour and continue kneading. Turn out onto a work surface and knead five or six times to form a ball. Place the peanut oil in a clean mixing bowl or other container and place the dough inside. Move the dough around to coat with oil and let rise until double in bulk, about 2 hours, or overnight in the refrigerator.

Preparing the dough by hand: Transfer the yeast mixture to a mixing bowl. Using a sturdy wire whisk, beat in the eggs, cream mixture, and the remaining sugar. Add 2 cups of the flour and the salt and beat with the whisk until the mixture forms a stiff batter. Switch to a wooden spoon and stir in 2½ cups more flour to form a stiff, shaggy dough. Turn this dough out onto a work surface. Knead the dough vigorously for about 10 minutes, until it is smooth and elastic. The dough will start out very sticky and eventually pull itself together. If after 10 minutes of scraping and kneading it is still sticky, add more flour a tablespoon or two at a time until it is smooth. Shape the dough into a ball. Place the peanut oil in a clean mixing bowl or other container and place the dough inside. Move the dough around to coat with oil and let rise until doubled in bulk, about 2 hours, or overnight in the refrigerator. Proceed with your recipe.

cream puff paste

GIANT CREAM PUFFS FILLED WITH vanilla ice cream and topped with hot chocolate sauce were a staple at my great-aunt May's house. My mother followed her lead, filling light airy puffs with whipped cream and custard for dessert or sautéed mushrooms and onions for an appetizer or hors d'oeuvre. This is a simple, versatile dough—a classic of French cooking, where it is known as *pâte à choux*—that can be used in a variety of ways: tiny puffs that are dried out in the oven are called *mandlen* ("almonds") and are served as a garnish for soup (I use schmaltz to make the dough for these); larger puffs that are dusted with crystallized sugar and dried in the oven are called *kichel* (I'm not sure, but I think it's Yiddish for "sawdust"); drops of dough that are fried in oil and dusted with sugar are called *sufganyot* (Chanukah doughnuts). Then again, there is nothing wrong with the ice cream and chocolate sauce version (known in French as *profiteroles*). My sister Carrie has even perfected a Passover variation of cream puff paste that uses matzo cake meal instead of flour with surprisingly light and delicious results. If you want savory puffs, and you keep kosher, chicken schmaltz makes a perfect substitute for butter. Puffs made with oil are heavy and greasy, and they don't puff as much.

a bissel advice

It's breaking my arm! You can use an electric mixer with a paddle attachment to beat the eggs into the flour mixture. Be sure the mixture is cool enough so that the eggs won't cook. Add them one at a time, beating with the paddle after each addition as explained above.

Can I spice things up? Depending on how you intend to use your puffs, you can put whatever you want in them. Stir in strong cheese, herbs, or other spices that you think will go well with your filling.

the whole meshpucha

You can double or triple this recipe. But just because the paste doesn't look like much in the saucepan doesn't mean you won't get as many puffs as I said. It's deceiving. When increasing the recipe, you can add the eggs two or three at a time.

kosher status MILCHIG, with butter
FLEISHIG, with schmaltz
PESADICH, with cake meal

½ cup (1 stick) unsalted butter or schmaltz

1 cup unbleached all-purpose flour or matzo cake meal

Pinch of kosher salt

4 to 5 large eggs

preheat the oven to 425°F.

In a small saucepan set over medium-high heat, heat the butter or schmaltz with 1 cup water and the salt until vigorously boiling. Add the flour or cake meal all at once. Using a wooden spoon, stir until the mixture forms a ball. Continue stirring for another 2 minutes or so, until you begin to smell the aroma of cooked flour. Remove from the heat and let cool for about 5 minutes, stirring occasionally, until the mixture is cool enough to touch.

Crack 1 egg into the flour mixture and stir with the wooden spoon. The dough will break up into slimy blobs while you stir and then eventually come back together into a paste. Add the next egg and repeat this process, adding 1 egg at a time and beating until the mixture comes together, until you have incorporated 4 eggs total. If after beating in the fourth egg the paste won't come back together again, add some more egg, but probably not a whole one: Crack the fifth egg into a small bowl and beat with a fork. Dribble some droplets of egg into the cream puff paste and mix them in with the wooden spoon. Keep adding the fifth egg by droplets in this way until the mixture comes back together into a smooth, shiny paste. Now you are ready to shape and bake the puffs as you wish.

CREAM PUFFS OR PROFITEROLES

Using two tablespoons, drop a heaping tablespoon of the batter into 1½-inch blobs on an ungreased cookie sheet. Leave about 2 inches between each puff in order for them to be able to expand to double their size. Place in the preheated 425°F. oven for 15 minutes, or until they have noticeably puffed. Then turn down the oven to 350°F. and continue baking for 20 to 25 minutes, until the puffs have turned golden brown and are firm to the touch. Cut one open to be sure the inside is cooked. Remove the puffs from the oven and poke each one on the side with a sharp knife to let out the steam. Cool and stuff with pastry cream, whipped cream, ice cream, or whatever you desire.

HORS D'OEUVRES PUFFS

Follow the procedure for Cream Puffs, using teaspoons instead of tablespoons to drop the dough onto the ungreased cookie sheet. Reduce the cooking time by 10 or 15 minutes, depending on the size of the puffs. Stuff them with a variety of fillings, such as Mushrooms and Onions (page 244), or any of the savory fillings in chapter 7.

SOUP MANDLEN

Follow the procedure for Cream Puffs (schmaltz gives the best flavor), but use teaspoons to drop the tiniest amount of paste, less than ½ teaspoon, on the ungreased cookie sheet. After the initial 15 minutes at 425°F., turn down the oven to 250°F. and let the puffs dry out completely, 45 minutes to 1 hour. If the puffs start to get too browned before they are completely dried out, lower the oven even more or let them sit in the oven overnight with just the pilot light on. Serve in chicken soup. Sometimes I like to make the paste for soup mandlen with chicken schmaltz and add a tablespoon or so of chopped dill to the mix so they add some extra flavor to the soup.

SWEET KICHEL

Follow the procedure for the Cream Puffs, but before they are baked brush each puff lightly with egg wash and sprinkle on crystallized sugar. Once the puffs have finished baking at 350°F., lower the heat to 250°F. and let them dry out completely, 1¼ to 1½ hours. If the puffs start to get too browned before they are completely dried out, lower the oven even more or let them sit overnight in the oven with just the pilot light on.

SUFGANYOT

See Doughnuts on page 160 for directions.

compote

COMPOTE, A SWEET STEW OR cooked salad of fresh and dried fruit, is one of those dishes that pops up in just about every cuisine. Not only is the dish virtually the same from culture to culture, so is the name. Whether speaking French, Yiddish, or English, say "compote" or something else and people will know what you mean. Compote is like tzimmes without the savory parts, or like chutney without the spicy parts. The variations are endless, but for

some reason—maybe constipation brought on by overconsumption of heavy food—Jews seem to always include prunes. What follows is more of a guideline than a recipe, but you'll get the idea. Then you can go off and create your own combination. Serve compote warm or cold at breakfast (yogurt makes a great topping), as a side dish to a main meal (like cranberry sauce), or with dessert (over ice cream or a piece of pound cake).

a bissel advice

But this isn't Hawaii and I don't have pineapple? **Stop whining and use whatever fruit you can get your hands on. Compote is more a technique than a recipe.**

MAKES 1½ QUARTS, ABOUT 16 SERVINGS

kosher status MILCHIG, with the butter
PAREVE, without

In a medium saucepan set over medium heat, melt the butter (if using). Add the sugar or honey, orange juice, cinnamon stick, bay leaf (if using), and vanilla, and bring to a boil. Cook until the sugar is dissolved, then turn down the heat to a slow simmer. Add the prunes and cook for about 8 minutes until soft. Add the pineapple or fruit chunks, and apples or pears, cover, and continue cooking just until the fruit is tender but not falling apart, about 10 minutes. Add the fresh berries (if using), and cook just until soft. The compote should have a loose consistency, somewhere between a jam and a sauce; add more orange juice if the mixture thickens to much. Store covered in the refrigerator for up to 1 month.

2 tablespoons unsalted butter *(optional)*
½ cup sugar or honey
½ cup orange juice or fresh apple cider
2½-inch cinnamon stick
½ bay leaf *(optional)*
½ vanilla bean
2 cups (1 pound) pitted prunes
2 cups fresh pineapple chunks (core removed) or other fresh fruit
2 large apples or pears (¾ pound), peeled, cored, and cut into chunks
½ cup fresh berries *(optional)*

Yiddish for Cooks

A Selective, Annotated, and Thoroughly Un-Kosher Glossary of Jewish Culinary Terms

BEFORE YOU LEAP into this lexicon of Jewish food and food-related terms, here are a few things to consider. Because Yiddish and Hebrew words are transliterated from different alphabets, the English spellings are as good as anybody's guess. Truth be told, an international organization called YIVO promulgates rules of standard spelling, both for Yiddish itself and transliteration—most of which I flaunt. I've also taken some liberties based on how my family pronounces certain words, but you should feel free to write them differently if you say them with a different accent or emphasis. A prime example is *lox* (smoked salmon), which is pronounced "lux" where I grew up in Toronto. (Note that because my family was from the New York area, we fought the pressure of our environment and stuck with "lox.") I am sure that many of the words have standard denotative meanings, but I have emphasized their connotative, culturally constructed, and humorous meanings here, in part because I don't really speak Yiddish. Further understanding can be gleaned from the headnotes to specific recipes.

AS FOR PRONUNCIATION, I have given phonetic approximations [in brackets] for difficult-to-pronounce terms. The one sound that is almost impossible to write phonetically is the ubiquitous "ch" sound, which falls somewhere between the sound made when clearing the throat and a retch. In YIVO transcription, it looks like [kh], but the "k" is soft. As a sound, "ch" conveys a lot of emotion. If you didn't know my mother, you would think when she listens to a beautiful aria and says "Uch" that she didn't like it. But what she really means is that it is so beautiful she can't think of a word to express it. But don't confuse it with "Ich," which means gross. "Ach" is more like an expression of disbelief or frustration. Hang out with a lot of Jews and you'll get the picture.

Appetizing

In Jewish food-shopping parlance, a noun that refers to the dairy deli counter at places like Zabar's and Russ & Daughters, where they display and sell smoked fish, cream cheese, herring, and other stuff that, ironically, some people consider *un*-appetizing.

Bagel

My grandfather called New York bagels, which are known for their heft, "doughnuts dipped in cement." Despite what some national chains will try to tell you, a bagel isn't a bagel unless it is boiled before it is baked. Although I understand that bagels have changed over the years, I am a traditionalist when it comes to flavors: poppy seed, sesame, salt, onion or garlic, pumpernickel, and everything. An occasional cinnamon-raisin bagel is acceptable, but blueberry, chocolate chip, seven-grain, sourdough, and other blasphemous concoctions are to be avoided. I should state for the record here that although I appreciate the traditional manner in which they are made, in my opinion Montreal bagels are nothing to write home about. This is not just because I grew up in Toronto, but because the dough is overly yeasty, sweet, and in desperate need of salt. Where I grew up in Toronto, the bakeries used to sell oxymoronic "matzo bagels" at Passover time.

Balboste [BALL-a-bos-tah]

Jewish housewife, often a good cook, with a knack for inflicting guilt and contributing to eating disorders. Balbostes are also usually a source of unconditional love—after all, "It's for your own good, not mine, that I think you should lose a couple of pounds."

Bialy

Though often grouped with bagels, really its own roll. Like a Jewish foccacia, a bialy is a flat, chewy round with puffy edges. Baked in the indentation in the center is a mixture of poppy seeds and onions. Although they originated in Bialystok, Poland (a recent book by Mimi Sheraton called *The Bialy Eaters* tries to trace their history and evolution), today the best—some would say only—bialys come from Kossars Bialystoker Kuchen Bakery on Manhattan's Lower East Side.

Bissel or Bissl [BIS-ul]

A little bit; a pinch. For the proper broken English construction, omit the preposition—e.g., say "a bissel salt," not "a bissel *of* salt." Also a vacuum manufacturer, but that's another story.

Blintz [BLIN-tse]

The Yiddish word for both the crepe or pancake and the wrapped package it is used to form (see page 182). Blintzes can be filled with anything from cheese or fruit to poppy seed, potatoes, or meat. At a day spa recently I was coated in mud and herbs, covered in Mylar sheets, and wrapped in a heavy body-sized heating pad, which enlightened me about what it must be like to be a blintz. Sweet blintzes should be served with applesauce and sour cream.

Borscht [BORSHT]

Russian for beet soup, but English for any kind of Mittleuropean soup made from Eastern European ingredients like cabbage, beets, pickles—you name it. Borscht is served hot or cold, although we only ever had it hot at my house, and we only ever had beet-free cabbage borscht, at that. The Borscht Belt refers to the area in the Catskill Mountains that used to be home to many Jewish resorts—my parents actually met there—known for funny but bad Jewish comedians. It is to the Borscht Belt that I am obviously headed if my career in cookbook writing doesn't take off.

Bubbe [BUH-bee]

Grandmother. There is a common belief that one's grandmother was the best cook anyone ever knew. I don't buy it. My grandmother was a decent cook, but her mother was supposed to have been the best. We seem to think that the older someone is the better someone cooks. In the consumer-taste-assessment industry, we refer to this misallocation of quality due to outside forces as the "halo effect," meaning that just because we love our grandmother very much doesn't necessarily mean she was a good cook.

Bubbeleh [BUB-uh-leh]

Term of endearment that also sometimes refers to an egg-rich pancake-cum-omelet made with matzo meal. Often said while pinching cheeks—for example, "How's my little *bubbeleh?*" After breading fish or veal (page 95), my mother would mix the egg and seasoned matzo meal together, fry it, and call it a bubbeleh.

Bubbe Meisse [BUB-ah MY-suh]

An old wives' tail. Anything in the kitchen that you think you have to do but has been proven scientifically or otherwise to be wrong, such as searing in the juices of a roast or never salting your beans while they cook, is called a *bubbe meisse*.

Cake, a Piece of

That which plays the same role in Jewish daily life as a drink plays in Gentile life. In a famous Jackie Mason joke he notes that after his show the WASPs are all going for drinks while the Jews are all going for *a piece of cake.*

Cake Meal

Finely ground matzo used at Passover time as a sometimes-less-than-desirable substitute for flour, except it is actually good in a limited number of dishes such as Cream Puff Paste (page 258) and Passover Sponge Cake (page 168).

Challah [KHAH-lah]

The king of breads. Whether braided or shaped like a turban, challah is used both for ceremonial purposes—Sabbath, bar mitzvahs, weddings, Rosh Hashanah—and for really good peanut butter and jelly sandwiches. Similar in concept to the French brioche, especially when made with butter, challah also makes excellent French Toast (page 188).

Charoseth [khah-ROH-set]

Hebrew for the symbolic mortar eaten as part of the Passover Seder. Although Ashkenazi Jews are limited to apple, honey, nuts, and bad sweet kosher wine in their charoseth recipe, Sephardic Jews open up the possibilities by adding any number of dried fruits and spices; see page 216.

Chazzerei [KHAH-zer-eye]

Junk food; bad or rotten food; literally, "pig's stuff." Chazzerei is often *nosherei* (page 271) that is *traif* (see page 272).

Cholent [CHUH-lnt]

Sabbath stew. Because observant Jews cannot cook on the Sabbath, they place a bunch of things in a pot and put the pot in the oven overnight, then eat the dish after temple on Saturday. In small villages, people used to bring their cholent pots to the baker to cook in his oven. Because cholent is made throughout the year, it should actually reflect the season. In fact, my friend Harold, a former rabbi, wants to write a book with recipes for a year of different cholents. The 24-hour cooking time may be the root of the Jewish tendency to overcook meat and vegetables.

Compote or Kompot [Kom-PUT]

A stewed mixture of prunes and other fruit with many uses: breakfast, side dish, dessert topping, and laxative.

Erev [EH-rehv]

Literally, "night"; colloquially, "the night before." For some reason that has to do with time zones, circadian rhythms, a little passage in the Bible, and a plot by calendar manufacturers to confuse Jews and non-Jews alike, Jewish holidays are celebrated the night before they actually begin. Therefore, if your calendar says the first day of Passover is April 11, the first seder actually falls the night before, *erev* Passover, on the 10th.

Farfel [FAR-fl]

Tiny toasted nuggets of egg pasta often served mixed with sautéed mushrooms and onions. It is sometimes called "egg barley" in English. Farfel is sold commercially either toasted or not. For the full, characteristic nutty flavor of farfel, it should be toasted before using. Farfel is also the name of my mother's Siamese cat. (For the name of another cat she once had, see *kasha*, page 267.)

Fleishig [FLAY-shik]

A word used to describe foods that contain meat or meat products to distinguish them from those that contain milk or milk products (see *milchig*, page 270). Fleishig things cannot be eaten with milchig things. Although butter is very much considered milchig by most rabbinical societies, in my house it fell into the pareve category, and my mother prepared many so-called fleishig dishes with butter. A piece of meat, however, would never be served with a glass of milk. There are some things you just don't do.

Ganif [GAH-nif]

Crook, often the butcher. I ought to know; I worked for a "kosher-style" butcher in high school. Take my advice, don't order anything delivered (you'll pay more per pound), and ask to see the rabbinical certification if there is any question in your mind about the kosher status of your meat.

Gedempte [guh-DEMT]

Overcooked, or more politely, potted and/or braised. Although this might seem like a negative quality, it is in fact the way most of the best Jewish meat entrees are prepared. When a piece of meat is cooked beyond recognition, it is sometimes referred to as *gedempte fleysh* or "mystery meat."

Gefilte [gu-FIL-tah]

Literally, "stuffed," but these days more like chopped up with egg and onion and boiled. See *gefilte fish*.

Gefilte Fish

Chopped-up fish—usually a freshwater variety, such as pike, perch, whitefish, or carp—that is seasoned, shaped, and boiled in fish broth (see recipe on page

4). Although it is traditional to stuff the fish back into the skin and cook it whole, this technique is rarely employed in North America today. For reasons that are purely aesthetic, some *goys* (see below) confuse gefilte fish with *knaidlach* (see page 267).

Gelt

Literally, "money," but in the culinary realm, "chocolate coins," usually associated with Chanukah. Almost every time I see my mother, whether it is Chanukah or not, she has a little nylon mesh bag of chocolate gelt for me. Interestingly, the great (German!) Brooklyn steakhouse Peter Luger's gives out chocolate coins, too.

Glatt Kosher

Really kosher. They're not kidding.

Glatt Traif

Really traif (i.e., ham and cheese on matzo). You're really going straight to hell. See you there.

Goy

Gentile. There are the (in)famous Shabbas Goys—non-Jews who are paid to come in and turn on and off the lights of observant Jews on the Sabbath. In the culinary realm, "goyish" is more common. It refers to things that just would not pass for Jewish, such as fruitcake, or anything with a lot of spices (cloves, allspice, ginger) usually consumed around Christmas.

Gribenes [GRI-beh-nes]

The Jewish version of pork rinds, actually made from the skin left over from rendering chicken schmaltz. Toss them in salt and eat them like bar snacks or chop them up and put them into everything from mashed potatoes to chopped liver.

Haimish [HAY-mish]

Homey, friendly, warm. A person who is welcoming, generous, and down-to-earth is said to be *haimishe*. When applied to food, haimishe sort of means "comfort food."

Hamentaschen [HAH-men-tahsh]

Triangular stuffed cookies made for Purim and traditionally filled with *mohn,* prunes, or other good things. They are said to be made in the shape of Hamen's hat, which must have been a tricorn, but there is no historic proof. In some Jewish traditions the cookies are supposed to be shaped like Hamen's ears. Note that hamentaschen is plural, one cookie is called a *hamentash.*

Holishkes [HAW-lish-kus]

Yiddish for stuffed cabbage or cabbage rolls (page 14). Also *praakes.* Sometimes elicits the response, "*Oy vey, what a production.*" For a similar taste without all the work, some *balbostes* (see page 263) rather make cabbage *borscht* (see page 52).

Jewish Spaghetti

Though unknown outside the Davis family, this is a dish that nevertheless ought to be a milchig Ashkenazi classic. Jewish spaghetti, at least as interpreted by my mother, Sondra Davis, is noodles—rarely spaghetti—in a sweet butter-tomato sauce that has to sit all day and be picked at before it can be eaten for real; see page 100.

Jewish Spice Mix

Akin to the French *quatres épices,* this blend of salt, black pepper, garlic powder, and paprika is used to flavor just about everything in an Ashkenazi Jewish household.

Kasha [KAH-shuh]

Toasted buckwheat groats. This Russian peasant food has become synonymous with Jewish cooking. Many Jews and Gentiles hate it. I love it, especially in the form of *kasha varnishkes* (see below). Kasha is available in different granulations: fine, medium, coarse, and whole. Although they all have the same flavor, the textures vary considerably. Kasha was also the name of one of my mother's Siamese cats (for another, see *farfel,* page 265).

Kasha Varnishkes [KAH-shuh VAR-nish-kus]

Toasted buckwheat groats mixed with bow-tie noodles and sautéed mushrooms and onions. Manna.

Kashrut [KAH-shroot]

The talmudic laws that govern what observant, kosher-keeping Jews can and cannot eat. Although they are commonly believed to be based in matters of cleanliness and health, most social historians and cultural anthropologists believe they have evolved for many different reasons, and they are evolving still. They have also been interpreted very differently throughout history. Commercially prepared foods and meats are produced under strict rabbinical supervision, but as not all rabbis are created equal, some observant Jews prefer some indications of kosher over others. Me, I eat mostly *traif* (see page 272).

Kichel [KIKHL]

Not unlike cream puffs made from sawdust, kichel is actually a snack food made from dried-out *Cream Puff Paste* (page 258). Where I grew up it was available in most Jewish bakeries and eaten by many as a form of diet food. I don't know if it works for this purpose, but I thought that it would be funny to try to recreate it.

Believe me, it grows on you. Kichel is not unlike soup mandlen, only larger.

Kishka [KISH-kuh]

Stuffed derma. A fatty, flavored bread stuffing is forced into cow intestines *(kishkes)* and either roasted or braised to simulate a sausage. A piece of kishka is often placed in a *cholent* (page 265), or else it's roasted and served with gravy. Today most kishka is made with a synthetic casing.

Kitchen Judaisism

The religion as practiced by my family and other foodie Jews so far to the left of the reform movement that we aren't welcome at most temples. Just because my family moved all of the Jewish holidays to the weekend, so we could all be together, doesn't mean they held any less spiritual significance for us. There was plenty to celebrate: the miracle of my sister Carrie's moist Passover sponge cake, the sanctity of my mother's one-onion-to-two-potatoes latke formula. The term was actually coined by a professor (and friend) of mine at New York University, Dr. Barbara Kirshenblatt-Gimblet.

Knaidlach [KNAYD-luhkh]

Although technically any dumpling, knaidlach has come to be Yiddish only for matzo balls, whether they are floaters or sinkers. *Knaidlach* sometimes translates to "cannon balls," depending on who's cooking. One matzo ball is called a *knaidel*. My sister Carrie's Hebrew name is Kala Sheyndele, which means "pretty bride"; instead we used to call her Knaidlach Sheyndele, which loosely translates to "Beautiful Matzo Ball."

Knish [ki-NISH or KNISH]

A little baked pocket of dough filled with any number of things, including potato, kasha, meat, spinach, or cheese. At delicatessens and on street carts in New York City, they are made very large. There is a famous Knish bakery on the Lower East Side of Manhattan called Yonah Schimmel's Knish Bakery (or Knishery). Although the knishes are pretty good, I never thought they were great. And then one day I read in the paper that Yonah Schimmel's was accused of money laundering. I knew his mind wasn't on his knishes. The bakery is still there, and they ship mail-order.

Kosher-style

This is a euphemism that is used to sell ordinary meat and other products at elevated prices. I worked in a "kosher-style" butcher shop in Toronto during high school. Our meat was not kosher. But we sold only kosher *cuts* of meat (i.e., from the front half of the cow) — that is, except for the New York strip steaks, which to this day I bet Jewish housewives in northern Toronto think of as a kosher cut. Anyway, we charged prices as though our meat was kosher. But that didn't really stop anybody who cared. And we never lied about it, so all was probably well in the eyes of God. The person (usually a rabbi) who oversees the process to determine whether or not it is kosher is called a *mazhgiekh,* and it is the *mazhgiekh*'s salary and the ritualized way the animals are killed and the meat is treated that account for the inflated price. The food in this book would be considered by most observant Jews to be "kosher-style," if not downright traif.

Kreplach [KREH-plahkh]

Jewish wontons. Leftover brisket and chicken liver are often turned into filling for these little stuffed squares of dough that are exactly like wontons. In fact, if you don't want to make your own dough, you can use wonton wrappers.

Kugel [KOO-guhl]

Pudding, usually of noodles (lokshen) or potatoes. Akin to bread pudding. We always had sweet kugels that were served with the meal or as dessert, but savory kugels are also common. Bread pudding could actually be called "bread kugel."

Kvell [KVELL]

This is what you do when you are beaming with pride about something. Jewish mothers' kvell over their children's accomplishments. It is also what you should do when you have prepared a perfect dinner and everyone is happy and sated.

Kvetch [KVETCH]

Complain, usually while whining. Kvetching is what you do after you spent all day cooking dinner — for example, "Oy, mine back, it's killing me after peeling all of the potatoes for the latkes. Don't you want another one?"

–lach [-lahkh]

Means plural when stuck on the end of a word (see *knaidlach* and *kreplach* above, *rugelach,* below). Note: avoid the tendency to pronounce it "latch" (as in "latch-key kids").

Latke [LAHT-kuh]

Pancake. These days thought to be made of potato, but also traditionally made from cheese. Latkes are also made from other vegetables, farfel — anything that can be turned into a batter and shaped into a pancake. Latkes are traditional for Chanukah because they are fried in oil—symbolic of the drop of oil found in the destroyed temple that was supposed to last for one day but burned miraculously for eight. "Baked latkes" is an oxymoron, not to mention a gastronomic blasphemy.

Lokshen [LUCK-shuhn or LUCKSHN]
Yiddish for "egg noodle" and often served in soup or turned into *kugel* (see opposite). Similar in composition and technique to tagliatelle.

Lox [LAWKS or LUHKS]
Salty smoked salmon, sometimes made with sugar in the brine, and often enjoyed on Sunday mornings with a bagel, a coffee, and a weekend paper. Nova (short for Nova Scotia) is used in the Northeast to denote less salty smoked Atlantic salmon that is more similar to generic Scottish or Irish smoked salmon. Slicing lox is a dying art and several years ago there was a big brouhaha at the smoked-fish counter at Zabar's because a woman was told she was not cut out (as a woman) to be a good lox slicer. I believe a favorable settlement reinstated her.

Mandel [MAWN-duhl or MAWNDL]
Almond. Also anything roughly shaped like an almond, such as soup *mandel,* little *kichel* (see page 267), or "nuts" that float in chicken soup. Not to be confused with the "nuts" who are eating the soup (see *mashuge,* below).

Mandelbrot [MAWN-duhl-brawt or -broyt]
Literally, "almond bread," but more like Jewish biscotti. Although you will see recipes for mandelbrot that don't have almonds in them, they should really be called something else.

Manischewitz [man-ih-SHEH-vits]
Ground zero for Jewish products, especially those made with matzo and the enigmatic TamTam, a hexagonal cracker used in everything from mock *kishka* (see below) to pie crust. Manischewitz also makes an alcoholic grape juice they call wine.

Mashuge [mah-SHUG-ah]
"Crazy," "out of one's mind," "nuts." Used to describe a person, an act, or an idea, as in, "So, all of a sudden you're a vegetarian? Where'd you get that mashugene idea?" Or, "What are you? Mashuge?"

Matzo [MAH-tsah]
The only recipe given in the Bible, as a Judaica scholar, professor, and friend of mine (see *kitchen Judaism,* above) is fond of saying. Matzos are made from flour and water, and at Passover time, the ingredients and the baking technique are carefully observed to be sure no leavening has occurred. In the making of *shmura* or "guarded" matzo, no more than 18 minutes can pass from the time the flour meets the water, and the wheat must have been guarded from the time it is grown until the time the matzo is made to be sure no chance of leavening arises. Throughout the rest of the year, matzos come in all kinds of flavors—onion, chive, garlic, you name it. Egg matzos are popular with some, but I prefer the crunch of plain matzos. When using matzo in a recipe, pay attention to the size of the box; at Passover the boxes contain 1 pound, but the rest of the year many of them have only 10 ounces. After eating matzo for eight days at Passover, many Jews become constipated (see *compote,* page 265) and cranky.

Matzo Brei [MAH-tsah BRY]

A big pancake made from soaked matzo pieces and eggs that is difficult to flip and usually eaten only at Passover. Although I grew up on sweet matzo brei, filled with fruit and dusted with cinnamon sugar, I have learned that savory matzo brei, with onions and sometimes lox, is also considered traditional.

Matzo Farfel [MAH-tsah FAR-fuhl]

Tiny bits of matzo made to simulate *farfel* (see page 265) and used during Passover.

Matzo Meal

Jewish bread crumbs. Matzo are ground into meal that is used to bread food for frying and to bind food (such as meatballs, gefilte fish, latkes) to keep it held together while cooking.

Maven [MAY-vin or MAYVN]

A connoisseur; by extrapolation, a gourmet—what you will be when you finish digesting, so to speak, the recipes in this book. Unfortunately, you will also be *zaftig* (see page 272).

Mazel Tov [MAH-zul tuv]

"Congratulations!" Your friends should utter this expression when you pull the Passover sponge cake out of the oven and it isn't a pancake. Or your mother should say it to you when you finally clean out your refrigerator from all of the rotten food left from the last Jewish holiday.

Mensch or Mentsh [MENCH]

A nice guy, a generous soul, me. Someone who makes a nice meal and gives you leftovers to take home.

Meshpucha or Mishpokhe [mish-PUHKH-ah]

Family. "The whole meshpucha" means something like "everybody and his brother."

Milchig [MIL-khik]

The opposite of *fleishig* (see above), referring to foods that contain milk or milk products and therefore cannot be consumed with meat. In many households, mine included, butter is considered pareve, and milk and cream in dessert is fair game. In observant households, though, strict attention is paid to milchig and fleishig designations, and there must be separate dishes, cooking utensils, and (by the letter of the law) refrigerators to hold them.

Mit

No, not as in "baseball mitt." *Mit* is Yiddish for "with," and it is often used in broken English constructions— e.g., "chicken soup mit knaidlach."

Mitzvah [MITS-vah]

In general, a good deed. In the kitchen, it is usually applied to the nice person who offers and then follows through with doing the dishes.

Mohn [MOO-en or MON]

Poppy seed. One of my favorite fillings for Danish and hamentaschen. Unfortunately, the poppy seeds really have to be ground before making the filling. To grind them, use a coffee grinder, but clean it out first. Some people, like my friend Peggy, have a phobia of getting poppy seeds stuck in their teeth. Though in some way justified, poppy seed Danish are just too good to pass over, so to speak.

Nosherei [nawsh-er-EYE]

Snacks, or things you have around that you eat (nosh) a lot of before you notice they are gone. See Fava Bean Chips (page 13).

Ongepatshket [UHN-guh-potch-kut]

"Overwrought," "overdone." A lot of the fancy-schmantzy food served in restaurants these days with curlicues and sugar domes would be known in Yiddish as ongepatshket.

Oy, vey! [OY VAY]

Exclamation usually uttered in the kitchen when somebody realizes just how much fat and salt is required to make something taste good.

Pareve [PAR-ev]

Neutral, not like the beige carpeting in the living room, but neutral in terms of neither fleishig nor milchig (see above), and therefore able to be eaten with both. Interestingly, vegetables and chemicals are pareve.

Pesadich [PAY-sah-dickh]

Kosher for Pesach, which is stronger than just plain kosher. Every year there are things that have to be done to prepare for Passover in order to make things kosher. Therefore, you have to buy new Passover foods each year. Matzo may be kosher throughout the year, but if your box doesn't expressly say Kosher for Passover, you shouldn't eat it on Passover.

Pierogi [PEER-oh-ghee]

Little doughy dumplings filled with everything from potatoes and meat to cheese. They are usually boiled and then fried in onions. Contrary to my general principle that anything deep-fried — even paper — is delicious, deep-fried pierogi are yucky. Silly though it sounds, one dumpling is called a pierog. In Yiddish, pierogi are called varenikehs (see page 272).

Plotz [PLAWTS]

Literally "burst" as in to explode because of frustration or loss of patience. Plotz is what you do when the Passover Sponge Cake doesn't rise or the pierogi fall apart or your family is late for dinner and everything is overcooked (see gedempte, page 265).

Rokeach [ROH-kay-ukh]

The maker of the canned gefilte fish (and other Jewish products) that was at times served in my house. These days my mother only makes her own from scratch.

Rugelach [RUG-ah-lukh]

Literally, "little rolled things," rugelach are usually made with cream cheese dough. Although some people consider them traditional at Chanukah, they are now available year-round at coffee shops around the country. Rugelach are filled with many different things, such as nuts, cinnamon, chocolate, prunes, mohn (see opposite). Ironically, they have become popular Christmas gifts.

Schmaltz [SHMAHLTS]

The raison-d'être of Jewish cooking (or this book, anyway). Schmaltz most often refers to rendered chicken fat, but it really just means fat. Duck fat, goose fat, and beef fat are also fair game. Nothing replicates the flavor and texture (not to mention the artery-clogging potential) of food cooked with schmaltz. When music or a movie or some other form of entertainment is so sickeningly sweet and wholesome it makes you want to puke, it is said to be "schmaltzy."

Schmear or Shmir [SHMEER]

As a verb, the act of spreading something, usually cream cheese, on something else, usually a bagel. As a noun, the finished thing you get after such spreading has taken place. In bagel-shop parlance, "Give me a bagel mit a schmear." Also used to mean a bribe, as in "I schmeared the palm of the maître d', but that *ganif* still won't give us a table."

Seder [SAY-dur]

Literally, "order," Seder refers to the ritual meal that starts on the night before *(erev)* Passover. There is also a Seder on the second night that some people believe was invented to placate the in-laws. A Haggadah is used to guide the meal and to tell the story of the expulsion of the Jews from Egypt by the Pharaoh. Many symbolic foods are eaten (see *charoseth,* above), prayers are said, and songs are sung. A full-on Seder can take up to four hours and require guests to drink four cups of wine while they recline on pillows (a recipe for napping if ever there was one). In our house, we rarely got to the true end of the seder. We called it quits right about the time my father started making up his own story.

Sufganyot [SOOF-guhn-yawt]

Hebrew for "Chanukah doughnuts," and we don't mean Krispy-Kreme. With the goal of getting as much symbolic oil into the system as possible, Chanukah celebrations are filled with fried foods. This way, while the kids are jumping around playing dreidel games, lighting candles, and opening presents, the adults can unbutton their pants, lie back, and *kvetch,* "How could you let me eat all of those doughnuts after such a big meal of latkes?"

Traif or Treyf [TRAYF]

The sacrilegious combination of milk and meat, or anything that is not kosher, namely, pork. Most of the *kosher-style* (see page 268) food served in my house was traif, but that's one of the reasons it tasted so good. Although why my mother could never fathom making a roast of pork, bacon, Italian sausages, and sliced ham is another story. In fact, one of my mother's favorite ways to eat matzo is as a ham and cheese sandwich (see *glatt traif,* page 266). In some sort-of observant households, the traifness of foods is overcome by the use of disposable paper plates. Interestingly, many traif foods—again, namely pork products—seem to switch to the more favorable fleishig designation when served in Chinese restaurants.

Tzimmes [TSI-mis]

Perhaps the first fusion cuisine. Tzimmes is a concoction of meat and vegetable and fruit that is cooked for a long period of time. Also known as "a bissel this, a bissel that." The word is also used to refer to any confusing mess of anything.

Varenikehs [vah-REN-i-kuz]

Yiddish for *pierogi* (see page 271).

Zaftig [ZAWF-tik]

Literally, "juicy," figuratively, "large and voluptuous." A euphemism for "fat," but in the sense of body size, not schmaltz. Zaftig is what you become after you eat too much food from the Mensch Chef.

I Can Get It for You Wholesale

Sources

OKAY, SO YOU ARE FINALLY GETTING ready to have your first Seder or you are making Rosh Hashanah dinner for your visiting parents or you've invited your Jewish friends over for Friday night dinner, but you don't know where to find the ingredients. If you live in a major metropolitan area or in a place with a concentration of Jews, shopping should be easy. But if you don't, you can still get most of what you need, whether through the Internet, mail order, or just some creative snooping.

THE "ETHNIC" SECTION OF MOST GROCERY stores usually has a bare minimum of Jewish staples, such as matzo meal, matzo, some soup mixes, and probably matzo ball mix. Buy only the matzo meal and the matzo if you need it, and skip over all of the prepared foods and mixes. Just because they are kosher doesn't mean they are any better than other mixes, and in fact many of them are worse. Sometimes Jewish foods fall under the umbrella of "Middle Eastern" products. Look there. Some crossover ingredients, such as lokshen (egg noodles) and kasha (buckwheat groats), can be found in other parts of the store. Use Italian pasta. If it's not in the Jewish section, the kasha is probably somewhere not too far from the couscous or the falafel mix, which is usually near the rice or the Goya section.

IF YOUR LOCAL STORES STILL LET you down, here are some mail-order sources for many of the products I call for in some of my recipes. Because of the tenuous nature of online retailing these days, forgive me in advance if one of my recommendations is no longer in business.

GROCERIES

ethnicgrocer.com

This website is a little hard to navigate because it is organized by country, but if you pop into Poland, for instance, you can find things like kasha and a few other limited Jewish items.

Hudson Valley Foie Gras

80 Brook Road
Ferndale, NY 12734
Phone: (845) 292-2500
Fax: (845) 292-3009
Toll-free: (877) BUY-FOIE (289-3643)
www.hudsonvalleyfoiegras.com

If you want to take me up on my challenge of making old-fashioned chopped liver (i.e., foie gras), give this company a call. They will ship fresh foie gras, duck breasts, duck fat, duck confit, and other related products overnight anywhere in the United States. You can also order on the website.

Kalustyan's

123 Lexington Avenue
New York, NY 10016
Phone: (212) 685-3451
Fax: (212) 683-8458
www.kalustyans.com

How they fit so much into this tiny store, even with the recent expansion, escapes me. Though the owners are Indian, Kalustyan's stocks ingredients for just about every ethnic cuisine under the sun. They have spices, grains, beans, dried fruit, nuts, and myriad other products, all of which can be ordered either online or over the phone.

koshersupermarket.com

This is a one-click stop for just about every kosher product you could want. A recent search for farfel brought up eight different products. The website also ships kosher meat and some religious items (simple stuff like Shabbat candles). Although some of the prices are high, don't forget that these are specialty products.

The B. Manischewitz Company

One Manischewitz Plaza
Jersey City, NJ 07302
Phone: (201) 333-3700
www.manischewitz.com

Perhaps the name most associated with commercially prepared Jewish foods (and that purple stuff they call wine), Manischewitz is also maker of some of the best. Although you cannot purchase products off their website, you can discover where to find them near you. And the website has good recipes and information about how to use everything they sell.

Penzeys Spices

P.O. Box 933
Muskego, WI 53150
Toll-free: (800) 741-7787
Fax: (262) 679-7878
www.penzeys.com

A purveyor of the finest spices in the world, Penzeys is one of my favorite sources for any kind of cooking. In addition to the freshest spices you've ever bought (they are ground to order), Penzeys has poppy seeds and sesame seeds, vanilla extract and vanilla sugar, salad dressing mixes, and related products. You can order online, but ask for a catalog; it's more like a textbook of spices complete with recipes. If you think that paprika is just a tasteless red dust your mother sprinkled on deviled eggs, give Penzeys a try. You can also visit one of their stores if you live anywhere near Brookfield or Madison, WI; Minneapolis or St. Paul, MN; Norwalk, CT; Oak Park, IL; or Houston, TX.

Rokeach Food Distributors Inc.
80 Avenue K
Newark, NJ 07105
www.rokeach.com

When we were little, Rokeach Old Vienna gefilte fish was the only mass-produced brand we could stomach (luckily, my mother started making it from scratch and she hasn't stopped). Rokeach (pronounced roh-KAY-uckh) is actually a distributor of many familiar Jewish product lines, including Mother's, Goodman's, Croyden House, and many more. You cannot purchase their products online, but they have recipes and other information on their website, including a handy calendar of Jewish holidays.

Russ & Daughters
179 East Houston Street
New York, NY 10002
Toll-free: (800) 787-7229
www.russanddaughters.com

This is the epitome of appetizing shops, complete with open barrels of pickles, long display cases filled with smoked fish, baked goods, groceries, and many other Jewish specialties. What's more, you can order it all over the phone to be shipped anywhere in the United States. For a complete list of products, visit the website.

Zabar's
2245 Broadway
New York, NY 10024
Phone: (212) 495-1234
Fax: (212) 580-4477
Toll-free: (800) 697-6301
www.zabars.com

The quintessential Upper West Side Jewish grocery store, Zabar's is impressive for its baked goods, appetizing counter (there are more than 10 kinds of lox), coffees, cheeses, housewares, and more. Shopping there feels like being in a *Seinfeld* episode. The website allows you to order much of their inventory online, including smoked fish, baked goods, cheese, and caviar. You can get most of the rest over the phone. In a lawsuit in 1994 about a smoked-salmon slicer (see *lox* in the Glossary on page 269), Zabar's owner Murray Klein told the judge, "There is one God and one Zabar's."

Zingerman's Delicatessen and Bakeshop
422 Detroit Street
Ann Arbor, MI 48104
Phone: (734) 663-DELI (3354)

Zingerman's Mail Order
620 Phoenix Drive
Ann Arbor, MI 48108
Toll-free: (888) 636-8162
www.zingermans.com

More a gourmet store than a delicatessen, Zingerman's nevertheless has a fine selection of Jewish groceries and baked goods. Though it costs a fortune, the extravagant babka they ship is worth every penny. You can order most of their products online, and anything that isn't there you can get over the phone.

CRAVINGS

Here are some sources of specialty prepared foods for those times when you just don't want to cook them yourself (or you can't find them within 200 miles of where you live).

Barney Greengrass
541 Amsterdam Avenue
New York, NY 10024
Phone: (212) 724-4707

9570 Wilshire Boulevard
(in the Barney's New York store)
Beverly Hills, CA 90212
Phone: (310) 777-5877

The original New York location of this combination deli, appetizing, and grocery store looks like it hasn't changed in 60 years. Barney is the self-proclaimed "Sturgeon King," and one taste of the scrambled eggs with onions and smoked sturgeon and you'll understand why. Although it's rundown, cramped, and expensive, my friend Lonni loves it so much she wants to have her wedding there. The L.A. outpost, in the tony Barney's department store, has a different vibe, but the smoked fish is just as good. You can order it over the phone.

Carnegie Deli
854 Seventh Avenue
New York, NY 10019
Phone: (212) 757-2245
Toll-free: (800) 334-5606
or (877) 898-3354 (for cheesecake)
www.carnegiedeli.com

You can order cheesecake online, but for a sandwich you have to call. They also ship salamis and other delicatessen staples that have made this late-night deli in Midtown a favorite with locals and tourists alike.

foodlocker.com

This specialty food product website can satisfy cravings for Kossar's bialys (shipped in quantities of 2 dozen), H&H Bagels (not my favorite, but who am I to judge?), and Dr. Brown's soda, among others.

Guss' Lower East Side Pickles
35 Essex Street
New York, NY 10002
Phone: (212) 254-4477
Fax: (212) 475-3799
Toll-free: (800) 252-GUSS (4877)
www.gusspickles.com

Here's a source for delicious pickles (half or full sours), sold from open barrels and shipped anywhere you want them.

Harbord Bakery
115 Harbord Street
Toronto, Ontario M5S 1G7
Phone: (416) 922-5767

Although most of the staff is no longer Jewish and they once sold sushi (!), this is still home to some of the best challah and cheese Danish in the world. The prune and poppy danish and the hamentaschen are pretty good, too.

Junior's
386 Flatbush Avenue Extension
Brooklyn, NY 11201
Phone: (718) 852-5257
Toll-free: (800) 9-JUNIOR (958-6467)
Fax: (718) 260-9849
www.juniorscheesecake.com

There's more than cheesecake to eat at this large restaurant, an institution in Brooklyn since the 1930s. But if you have a craving, they will ship one of their dense cream-cheese creations anywhere overnight.

Katz's Delicatessen
205 East Houston Street
New York, NY 10002
Phone: (212) 254-2246

The neighborhood around it has changed, but Katz's looks a lot like it did when my grandfather used to go there as a young man. They still slice their corned beef by hand, and they still give you a taste of it while you are waiting. A sign in the dining room reads "Send a salami to your boy in the army." (Salami and army rhyme, apparently.) Why not send one to yourself?

Kossar's Bialystoker Kuchen Bakery
367 Grand Street
New York, NY 10002
Phone: (212) 473-4810
Toll-free: (877) 4-BIALYS (242597)
www.kossarbialys.com

This small 24-hour bakery makes the best bialys in the world—a claim tested and proven recently by Mimi Sheraton in her book *The Bialy Eaters*. There's nothing like getting them hot out of the oven. But to have them shipped, visit the website or call toll-free.

newyorkfirst.com
This website for homesick New Yorkers and wannabes ships a number of regional specialties including Katz's pastrami, Yonah Schimmel's knishes, and H&H bagels. By the way, you can also order Ray's pizza.

nycfood.com
Another website that ships products from classic New York City restaurants and food purveyors, this one includes Barney Greengrass and Murray's Sturgeon Shop in the mix.

Schwartz's Delicatessen
3895 St. Laurent Boulevard
Montreal, Québec H2W 1X9
Phone: (514) 842-4813

They don't ship to the United States—some Canada addresses can get delivery—but if you are ever in or near Montreal, don't miss the hand-cut Montreal smoked meat sandwiches at this tiny deli. The fries are really good, too.

2nd Ave. Deli
156 Second Avenue
New York, NY 10003
Phone: (212) 677-0606
Toll-free: (800) NYC-DELI (692-3354)
Fax: (800) 2AV-DELI (283354)
www.2ndavedeli.com

Besides my own home, my favorite place to eat Jewish food is the 2nd Ave. Deli. They must put some sort of drug in the pastrami that makes it addictive. If you can't get there yourself or you don't want to wait on line, you can order many of their glatt kosher deli specialties over the phone and have them shipped overnight anywhere in the United States.

Snowdon Deli
5265 Décarie Boulevard
Montreal, Québec H3W 3C2
Phone: (514) 488-9129

Vying for Schwartz's as home of the best Montreal smoked meat (they don't ship to the United States, either), this nondescript deli in a residential neighborhood also has excellent Danish and other baked goods.

Yonah Schimmel's Knish Bakery
137 East Houston Street
New York, NY 10002
Phone/Fax: (212) 477-2858
www.yonahschimmel.com

When you just don't want to make them or you just have to have a genuine New York knish, fax an order to Yonah Schimmel's "knishery." You can make a selection and fill out an order online, but you'll have to print it and fax it in. They ship knishes by the dozen anywhere in the continental United States.

INFORMATION AND RECIPES

epicurious.com
The website for Condé Nast's food publications (*Gourmet, Bon Appétit,* and others) has a limited number of very good Jewish recipes organized by holiday.

jewish-food.org
This website includes the appropriately named "Classic Jewish Recipe Archives," a collection that isn't as vast as it sounds, but that provides a good overview of Jewish food.

kitchenlink.com
This vast website has a good number of Jewish recipes culled from various sources, such as books, magazines, and other websites.

Kosher Today
IMC—225 West 34th Street, Suite 1317
New York, NY 10122
Phone: (212) 643-1623
Fax: (212) 643-9164
www.koshertoday.com

Billing itself as "the official monthly trade publication of the kosher food industry," this broadsheet and its corresponding website have a lot of information about new products, industry scandals, and a lot of boring stuff. Don't kid yourself, kosher foods is big business. The publication also hosts a giant annual kosher food trade show called Kosherfest.

LINKS TO JEWISH RECIPES
www.chebucto.ns.ca/~ab522/jewishfood.html
This inelegant web address is updated regularly and has hundreds of recipes and a number of links to Jewish recipe sites on the World Wide Web.

Open Directory Project
**www.dmoz.org/Shopping/Food/
Ethnic_and_Regional/Kosher/**
Visit this portion of the vast public website directory project to find links to websites on which you can purchase kosher food.

Orthodox Union
11 Broadway
New York, NY 10004
Phone: (212) 563-4000
Fax: (212) 564-9058
www.ou.org

The Union of Orthodox Jewish Congregations of America has a website with plenty of information about kosher foods and what to do with them. This is the organization that certifies kosher foods with a little "u" inside an "o." More than 250,000 brand names currently meet with their approval (check your can of Coke). This sophisticated website also has information about a host of other Jewish topics.

Study and You'll Become Somebody Someday

Further Reading

I BET YOU DIDN'T THINK I was going to give you homework. Well, I hope this book has piqued your interest in Jewish cooking. And since, as I said in the beginning, my scope here is limited, if you want more information, more recipes, or a different perspective, you should do what Jews have been doing for centuries, and turn to books. (Whenever you asked my father a yes or no question, he would hand you five books and tell you the answer was inside.) I have a full library of Jewish cookbooks — some new, some old, some good, some bad. Here are few of my favorites. New ones are coming out all the time, so consider this just a partial list.

GENERAL JEWISH COOKBOOKS

Sephardic Flavors: Jewish Cooking of the Mediterranean *by Joyce Goldstein (Chronicle, 2000)*
    This beautiful book explores the Middle Eastern and Mediterranean Jewish food traditions. Goldstein was the chef/owner of Square One in San Francisco, and her approach to Sephardic cooking is both personal and informative.

The New Jewish Holiday Cookbook: An International Collection of Recipes and Customs *by Gloria Kaufer Greene (Times Books, 1999)*
    This is a large book that divides all the recipes into holidays. Each chapter includes a lengthy explanation of the holiday and the significance of specific foods to that holiday. Every time I open it I learn something new.

1,000 Jewish Recipes *by Faye Levy (IDG Books, 2000)*
    Faye and I recently judged the James Beard Foundation Annual Latke Cookoff together, and I was happy to have the opportunity to tell her how impressively I think she handled the daunting task before her. More recipes than history or anecdotes, this book is nevertheless an asset to any library of Jewish cookbooks.

The World of Jewish Cooking: More than 500 Traditional Recipes from Alsace to Yemen *by Gil Marks (Fireside, 1996)*
    This is a friendly, easy-to-use book with a lot of interesting historic information about food and food customs. Marks is both a rabbi and historian, so unlike many cookbook writers he has the sources to back up his points.

Jewish Cooking in America by Joan Nathan (Knopf, 1994)

> This is the modern-day classic book of American Jewish cooking (Nathan has even spun off a successful television series). It's filled with recipes and anecdotes about Jewish cooks and cooking around the country.

The Book of Jewish Food: An Odyssey from Samarkand to New York by Claudia Roden (Knopf, 1996)

> Raised in Egypt and a resident of England, Roden has an interesting perspective on Jewish cooking that avoids New York centrism and includes a lot of information about Sephardic cooking. The book also happens to be beautiful.

From My Mother's Kitchen . . . Recipes and Reminiscences by Mimi Sheraton (HarperCollins, 1991)

> Of all the Jewish cookbooks I own, this one has a food sensibility closest to my family's own. Mimi has become a colleague of mine over the years and I look to her book first when I want to experiment with a new recipe.

DELI COOKING

The 2nd Ave. Deli Cookbook: Recipes and Memories from Abe Lebewohl's Legendary Kitchen by Sharon Lebewohl and Rena Bulkin (Villard, 1999)

> If the 2nd Ave. Deli is a shrine, then this must be a bible. In fact, it is filled with great recipes for most of your Jewish favorites. The book is also rich with stories about the deli and all the goings-on there since it opened in 1954.

Welcome to Junior's! Remembering Brooklyn with Recipes and Memories from Its Favorite Restaurant by Marvin and Walter Rosen with Beth Allen (Morrow, 1999)

> Junior's is so tied to Brooklyn that this book reads more like a history of Brooklyn with recipes than an ordinary cookbook. I actually went to college with Alan Rosen, one of the sons who now manages the business. As if to foreshadow our future careers, for a class project once we actually transformed a university cafeteria into a Jewish delicatessen.

BAKING

How to Bake: The Complete Guide to Perfect Cakes, Cookies, Pies, Tarts, Breads, Pizzas, Muffins, Sweet and Savory by Nick Malgieri (HarperCollins, 1995)

> Though by no means limited to Jewish cooking, Nick's book still has a lot of recipes that would be of interest to Jewish bakers—namely, coffee cakes, Danishes, and other familiar baked goods.

The World of Jewish Desserts: More than 400 Delectable Recipes from Jewish Communities from Alsace to India by Gil Marks (Simon & Schuster, 2000)

> Another impressive book by Marks, this one deals only with the sweet part of the meal. It, too, is full of interesting historical and cultural information about the recipes and certain foods.

Classic Home Desserts: A Treasure of Heirloom and Contemporary Recipes from Around the World by Richard Sax (Chapters, 1994)

> An instant classic by a late friend of mine, this book is another one that isn't exclusively about Jewish baking but is filled with great recipes for cakes, cookies, puddings, and all sorts of baked goods that would be familiar to a Jewish household.

Acknowledgments

AS IN THE PROCESS OF WRITING ANY BOOK, there are a million people who had their hands in this one. Since Jewish food is the food of my soul, I drew up an offbeat proposal that my agent, Lydia Wills, knew was a winner. In the end it was Chris Pavone who recognized the potential of what I had proposed, and his help massaging the idea and the manuscript, along with the support of the whole Clarkson Potter team, was invaluable. Without Chris's faith in the decidedly *traif* nature of the project it would still just be another unrealized (blasphemous) idea.

There would be no Jewish cookbook, of course, without my mother, Sondra, whose unconditional love often takes the form of food. I grew up on stories about her grandmother's cooking, and having an excuse to actually record them—and re-create some of the dishes I had always heard about—was one of the reasons I wanted to do a Jewish cookbook in the first place. Somehow at holiday time the cooking often fell on me and my sister Carrie, and it is still over food and cooking that we have our most enthusiastic conversations and happiest memories. It was her detail-oriented eyes that signed off on the final version of the manuscript. For all our talk, my sister Leslie, who isn't really a foodie but who loves to eat well nonetheless, actually cooks more on a daily basis than I do. Her motivation to come to New York periodically is divided equally between seeing me and eating a corned beef sandwich. During our frequent late-night telephone conversations, she often comments that she will be impressed by technology only when I can fax her a piece of cheesecake. My brother, Sheldon, doesn't cook Jewish food very much, but sitting around my mother's dining room table with him and my niece, Helen, and the rest of the family, listening to and telling the same stories for the hundredth time, laughing, and critiquing the food is, I think, inextricably wrapped up in my fondness for this type of cooking.

I work with a great group of people at the James Beard Foundation—friends, really—who not only gave me time to write this book and were eager to eat and comment on the results of the recipe testing, but also didn't mind arguing for hours about the best way to make a latke or the merits of one bagel over another. They also picked up the slack when I was up late, knee-deep in Yiddish dictionaries and manuscript pages. Mildred Amico, Jane Miller, Peggy Grodinsky, Emily Hoffman, Scott Meola, Len, Yvon, Diane, Arlyn, and everyone else at the Eighteenth Street and Twelfth Street offices were, thankfully, hungry and accommodating.

As for friends and family who were at the ready to help think of titles, talk about techniques, sample dishes, tell me when something sucked, help me stay motivated, convince me I could get the work done, do the dishes, play when I needed to escape, or just sit around a table and eat, there are almost too many to name: Anthony Bagliani, Alan Brake, Andrew Carmellini, Michael Frank, Michael and Laurie Ginor, Marko Gnann, Dorita Hannah, Phyllis Hoberman, Gwen Hyman, Marjorie and Lenny Kagan, Maria and Jack Kelly, Harvey and Polly Knaster, Edward Kuo, Josephine Leo, Oliver Ludwig, Lauren McGrath, Joe Meizel, Felice Ramella, Suzanne Rannie, Adam Rapoport, Suzanne Rostler, Steven Shaw, Bonnie Stern, Lonni Tanner, Karla Vermeulen, and my former roommate of many years, and Polish advisor, Izabela Wojcik.

Several family members, friends, and colleagues I haven't already mentioned contributed recipes and advice and stories about Jewish cooking. Some but not all of them ended up in the final draft of the book, and regardless I am grateful for their support. Among them, Jennifer Berg, Mrs. (Edna) Cooper, the Davis family in Westchester, Phyllis Isaacson, Nick Malgieri, Harold Rabinowitz, Maxine Rapoport, and Barbara Ann Rosenberg. I spent several days cooking with Daňo Hutnik and his wife, Karen Gilman, at their restaurant in Ithaca, New York. For technical information about Judaism, Yiddish, and other related topics, I am indebted to my NYU professors Barbara Kirshenblatt-Gimblett and Hasia Diner, and Paul (Hershl) Glasser of the YIVO Institute for Jewish Research.

Coming up with a title was a huge challenge, and just about everyone I know (and a few complete strangers) gave me their two cents. In the end, it was my friend Peggy's sister and brother-in-law (Ray and Leslie Kimmelman) who picked the winner. The title debate sparked a few anthropologist friends of mine (Julie Chu, Matt Harris, and Ramona Perez) to make a documentary about the making of the cookbook in general, and the choosing of an ethnically provocative title, in specific. In the end, their documentary will survive as a testimony to my original title idea.

For all those I have forgotten to mention—and I'm sure there are many—I have only this to say, "So what do you want, a medal or something?" No, really, I'm sorry. I hope there will be more books to come, so I'll have a chance to acknowledge you later.

Index